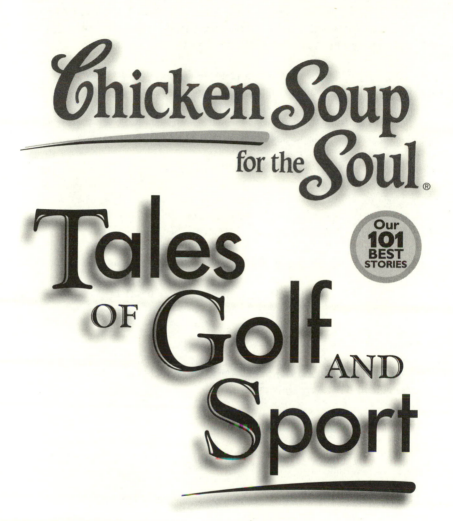

Chicken Soup for the Soul®

Tales OF Golf AND Sport

Our **101** BEST STORIES

Chicken Soup for the Soul® Our 101 Best Stories:
Tales of Golf and Sport; The Joy, Frustration, and Humor of Golf and Sport
by Jack Canfield, Mark Victor Hansen & Amy Newmark

Published by Chicken Soup for the Soul Publishing, LLC   www.chickensoup.com

The publisher gratefully acknowledges the many publishers and individuals who
granted Chicken Soup for the Soul permission to reprint the cited material.

Cover photo courtesy of PunchStock/Valueline. Back cover photo and interior photo courtesy of
JupiterImages/Photos.com.

Cover and Interior Design & Layout by Pneuma Books, LLC
For more info on Pneuma Books, visit www.pneumabooks.com

Distributed to the booktrade by Simon & Schuster. SAN: 200-2442

Publisher's Cataloging-in-Publication Data
(Prepared by The Donohue Group)

Chicken soup for the soul. Selections.
   Chicken soup for the soul : tales of golf and sport : the joy, frustration,
and humor of golf and sport / [compiled by] Jack Canfield [and] Mark Victor
Hansen ; [edited by] Amy Newmark.

   p. ; cm. — (Our 101 best stories)

   ISBN-13: 978-1-935096-11-5
   ISBN-10: 1-935096-11-7

1. Golf--Literary collections. 2. Golf--Anecdotes. 3. Sports--Literary collections. 4.
Sports--Anecdotes. 5. Sportsmanship. 6. Athletes--Conduct of life. 7. Child athletes-
-Literary collections. I. Canfield, Jack, 1944- II. Hansen, Mark Victor. III. Newmark,
Amy. IV. Title. V. Title: Tales of golf and sport

PN6071.G63 C48 2008
810.8/02/0357   2008934914

PRINTED IN THE UNITED STATES OF AMERICA
on acid∞free paper
16 15 14 13 12 10 09 08   01 02 03 04 05 06 07 08

Chicken Soup for the Soul

Tales of Golf and Sport

Our 101 BEST STORIES

The Joy, Frustration, and Humor of Golf and Sport

Jack Canfield
Mark Victor Hansen
Amy Newmark

CSS

Chicken Soup for the Soul Publishing, LLC
Cos Cob, CT

Chicken Soup for the Soul

Contents

❶
~Love of the Sport~

❷
~The Sporting Family~

❸
~Wisdom of the Game~

❹
~The Roar of the Crowd~

❼

~The "Little" League~

❽

~Defining Moments~

❾

~From the Heart~

Chicken Soup for the Soul

A Special Foreword

by Jack and Mark

For us, 101 has always been a magical number. It was the number of stories in the first *Chicken Soup for the Soul* book, and it is the number of stories and poems we have always aimed for in our books. We love the number 101 because it signifies a beginning, not an end. After 100, we start anew with 101.

We hope that when you finish reading one of our books, it is only a beginning for you too—a new outlook on life, a renewed sense of purpose, a strengthened resolve to deal with an issue that has been bothering you. Perhaps you will pick up the phone and share one of the stories with a friend or a loved one. Perhaps you will turn to your keyboard and express yourself by writing a Chicken Soup story of your own, to share with other readers who are just like you.

This volume contains our 101 best stories for golfers and sports fans. We share this with you at a very special time for us, the fifteenth anniversary of our *Chicken Soup for the Soul* series. When we published our first book in 1993, we never dreamed that we had started what became a publishing phenomenon, one of the best-selling series of books in history.

We did not set out to sell more than one hundred million books, or to publish more than 150 titles. We set out to touch the heart of one person at a time, hoping that person would in turn touch another person, and so on down the line. Fifteen years later, we know that it has worked. Your letters and stories have poured in by the hundreds of thousands, affirming our life's work, and inspiring us to continue to serve you.

On our fifteenth anniversary, we have new energy, new resolve, and new dreams. We have recommitted to our goal of 101 stories or poems per book, we have refreshed our cover designs and our interior layout, and we have grown the Chicken Soup for the Soul team, with new friends and partners across the country in New England.

Golfers are a special breed. They endure bad weather, early wake up calls, great expense, and "interesting" clothing to engage in their favorite sport. They are also great sportsmen. In this new volume, we have selected our 101 best stories about golfers and golfing, and we have also included a generous number of anecdotes we thought you would appreciate about other sports and athletes, including stories about the admirable principles of team play and sportsmanship that transcend any particular sport. The stories that we have chosen will inspire you, teach you, and make you laugh.

We hope you will enjoy these stories on an occasional rainy day. We enjoyed selecting them for you, and hope you will share them with your families and friends, on and off the greens. We have identified the sixteen *Chicken Soup for the Soul* books in which the stories originally appeared, in case you would like to read more stories about golf and sports. We hope you will also enjoy the additional books about families, pets, faith, and life in general in "Our 101 Best Stories" series.

With our love, our thanks, and our respect,
~*Jack Canfield and Mark Victor Hansen*

Tales OF Golf AND Sport

Love of the Sport

Sports do not build character;
they reveal it.
~Heywood Broun

A Thoughtful Gift

My husband, Richard, is an avid golfer and likes to practice his golf swing on our lawn. Often, during the summer, he breaks a window or two. "Oh, well," we always say, "at least it was our own window." And we have the glass replaced.

One year when he had trouble with his slice, he broke a grand total of four windows. The following spring, a parcel arrived, addressed to him. It was a box of a dozen golf balls, and the enclosed note read, "Have a good season. From Mike, your Window Guy."

~Kay B. Tucker
Chicken Soup for the Golfer's Soul, The 2nd Round

I Hate Golf — I Love Golf!

I'm not saying my golf game went bad,
but if I grew tomatoes, they'd come up sliced.
~Attributed to both Miller Barber and Lee Trevino

I used to be an 11-handicap golfer. That was before "slope indices," before "soft spikes," before golf carts even.

Today, fully equipped with the latest technology, I am a 22-handicapper going south.

Yes, way back then my woods, crazy though it may seem, had wooden heads. The shafts were of shiny metal. No titanium, no matched graphite, no range of flexes.

The golf balls would smile back when you mishit a wedge shot or topped a 6-iron. Slice a 4-iron and you could see the seemingly endless rubber band that wrapped around the ball's rubber core.

I could hit the ball a ton back then. I could get out of sand traps and two-putt greens, too. I have happy memories.

In 1947 I even defeated Chad Brown, a friend at the post office. In the tournament I beat Chad 8 and 7, finishing him off with a fearless, curling fifteen-foot birdie putt. I admit I caught bon vivant Chad on an Excedrin day.

Back then I played in the high 70s.

Today, though I try to play a fair amount, things are different. Chad Brown would kill me. Everyone else does.

I slice off the tee, losing distance in the process. My long irons sting my hands. The ball is seldom airborne. Nor can I chip. Putting? Forget it.

It's not the equipment, for I have the latest in technology. I have four Tight Lies, but mine go straight up. I have great Titleist DCI irons — Black Cats, too. I have Cobras given to me by Hale Irwin himself. I have a big 975 Titanium Titleist driver, also a Taylor Made bubble driver and the biggest Bertha ever made. My high-performance wedges run the gamut — fifty-six degrees, fifty-eight degrees, sixty degrees. I have 'em all. I even have an "Alien."

My golf balls are high-tech. Zylin Covered XLs, Tour Distance-Wound 90s, the Slazenger 420s. You name the kind of ball you like, I've got it.

Sometimes I play with a guy worse than me. He's into all this high-tech stuff. He goes, "I sure like the feel of these new balatas," or "This new baffled 3-wood really works for me." Or "The only putter that makes any sense at all is the Scotty Cameron — that Tel3 is so true. Talk about center cut. I have three of them Scottys — I love the Microstep and the Teryilium insert."

The poor son-of-a-gun hasn't gotten a wedge off the ground in the last three outings and his baffled 3-wood emerges from the fairway carrying a divot the size of an adult toupee. The last time he two-putted a green was when I gave him a four-footer.

He goes, "This new Maxfli Multi-layered Revolution lands quiet. I can just feel the difference on my wedge shots — on my putting, too." Sure, right!

High tech is great. Don't get me wrong. Look at Davis, Tiger and Freddie; but let's face it — high tech hasn't solved my web of problems.

Practice is my main problem. I hate it. I am allergic. I break out in a rash if I go out and hit practice balls. I can't help it.

Putting is the worst part of my game, followed closely by sand play and chipping. A good friend, a guy who supported me as president and was respectful back then, put it rather succinctly last week when he said, "George, you stink."

Anyway, a couple of weeks ago out at Muirfield—a course on which a guy like me should be forbidden to play—I invoked the "no-laughing rule."

My playing partners agreed—"Okay, no laughing."

I put them to the test. In one sand trap I flailed away four times, before going in the pocket. I found brooks and eddies that Jack Nicklaus didn't even know existed when he laid out this monster.

Things were dragging for me. I was thinking, "Why do I need this? I am seventy-four. I have a boat and a nice wife—why this torture?"

But then on the sixteenth I hit a perfect 9-iron—long and straight with a lot of spin on it. It stopped but six feet from the hole. My partners were ecstatic. "You're back!" "What an effort!" "You pureed that one."

But then came my turn to putt. I admit my attitude was negative as I lined up for my downhill putt. I pushed it off to the left. It gathered speed as it ripped past the cup, stopping about six feet away. But I had another six-footer to make coming back.

I jabbed my second putt. It took off like a cruise missile. The direction was great. The speed was wrong. It lipped the cup and was whiplashed violently off course. Four and a half feet still to go for putt number three.

I froze over the ball, my long putter wagging like a vaulter's pole. I came back slowly, and then literally shanked the putt. As it careened off to the right, the "no-laughing rule" was broken. They didn't mean to hurt my feelings—for fifteen dreadful holes they had been careful not to. My partner knocked away my remaining four-footer. "A gimme!" he says.

As I have done several times before, I decided right then and there to give up golf. I hate it.

But after a two-week moratorium I was back.

Playing with our Cape Arundel pro, Ken Raynor, I felt inspired.

The first nine was bad—the chipping and putting betraying me.

Then came the magic. On the par-4 eleventh, my drive was fine.

I then topped my 5-wood shot—a scorching grounder that stopped sixty yards short of the green.

I pulled out my fifty-six-degree Cleveland Classic-588. My swing was surprisingly smooth. The "True Temper" shaft gave me that velvet feeling. I felt the grooves gently spin the ball. I felt the "touch" of my Tour Distance-90. It feathered on to the green—landing like a butterfly. Breaking gently to the right, it meandered sixteen feet, right into the hole.

Golf? I hate it, sure, but I really love it.

I'll be on the first tee tomorrow at 6:50 A.M.

~George Bush
Chicken Soup for the Golfer's Soul

The Accidental Purist: Diary of a Beginning Golf Junkie

I am a public school girl from Pittsburgh. I played varsity basketball and tennis, and I had always maintained that golf was an elitist sport. A borderline sport at that. People can play it wearing a belt, for crying out loud.

I was a reverse snob. And then I got a job as a senior editor at a golf magazine. I never seriously considered that I would take up the game. I dropped the elitist riff, though, and just told people that I was a working mom with two young children and they immediately seemed to get why I didn't actually play.

This began to nag at me, though. Because, one, I AM an editor for a golf magazine, and it's a little embarrassing explaining how I can do what I do and not play golf. Since the day I took the job, I had read every golf publication I could get my hands on. I've become familiar with Herbert Warren Wind and Arnold Haultain and, of course, Dan Jenkins. I can't seem to get through *Golf in the Kingdom*, but I think you get the picture. I know golf manufacturers and golf professionals. I know women who knit golf head covers for a living. I have Sign Boy's home phone number, for Pete's sake. I have ridden around Clint Eastwood's golf course in Carmel with the man himself. I have witnessed John Daly playing guitar with Lisa Loeb and Dweezil

Zappa. I have interviewed David Duval and Tom Lehman. I've talked to the likes of Ray Leonard, Terry Bradshaw, Joe Mantegna, Branford Marsalis and Mario Lemieux about golf. I notice how much guys LOVE talking about golf. It is not lost on me that most men cannot remember where the butter is in the refrigerator, but they can tell you precisely what clubs they used and give you play-by-play action of a shot they hit ten years ago on some course in East Podunk, Ohio.

I am doing everything with golf that a person can possibly do. But I am beginning to tire of explaining — with a smile, for the thousandth time — how I can do what I do without actually playing the game. The idea taunts me like low-hanging fruit until I just can't take it anymore: It's a sunny day in Colorado, and I call this golf school near my house. I have a noon appointment. I am Eve and I am about to be damned. Bring on the golf lessons.

Lesson one:

Mike Schlager, my instructor, walks me to the range, hands me a 9-iron and watches me swing. He knows I'm a skier and explains that like skiing, balance is important in golf. He tells me that the set-up in golf, what goes on before the motion, is more important than the actual swing. He teaches me about where my hands should be — in the center of my body, on a straight path from my sternum — and where they should hang. He gives me two drills to practice with my eyes closed. One's about finding the center of my body that involves holding a golf club over my head and doing a kind of deep knee bend. Then he tells me to swing the club back and forth as fast as I can and only come off of my feet at the end. It feels like a samurai golf swing. We chip a bit and he gives me a chipping drill. We also putt. He says to practice making short one- to two-foot putts. The more it goes in, the more confidence I'll have. I take this all home with me.

Cost (gulp), one hundred dollars. This is a lot of green for a mother of two looking at college tuition for 2013. This is a lot of green for someone whose favorite store is Target. But somehow, I don't think twice.

I have one club at home, some kind of wedge, and I start doing my drills. I've taken to putting with the wedge even while I'm on the phone. Every time I lean my neck in to hold the phone so I can make a stroke, I end up hanging up on someone. I hung up on my boss three times in one conversation. I hung up on Phil Mickelson's agent (don't tell my boss). I take my mystery wedge with me on a ski vacation to Steamboat and do my exercises religiously. I putt at the coffee table.

Lesson two:

I arrive early, and Mike sends me out to the practice area. I putt and putt and putt. I am a two-foot wonder, which I know is good because Mike told me in my first lesson that someday I'm going to play in a scramble and everybody loves a woman who can make a putt.

Mike says, "Let's go up to the range." I tell him that's what I'm scared of — going up to the range. But I press on. I find my balance and swing. It feels pretty good. Mike says it is pretty good. I hit several decent shots, and at one point he laughs and says, "You don't know how good these are." I decide I like Mike a lot. He helps me adjust my grip. He notices my small hands and suggests more of a baseball hold. I practice with the new grip, and the ball starts going a fair amount farther. "Over the pin," he says with a degree of satisfaction like Master Po used to use with the Grasshopper on the old Kung Fu TV show.

We go to pitch around the green with a sand wedge. At first, I am smooth, I get the motion, but then I lose it completely. Some piece gets mixed up in my head. Mike makes me stay until I hit a decent closer, and I'm down another C-note.

Lesson three:

We head out to a driving area on a part of the course where I've never been. I get out of the cart and face the wrong way, which cracks me up. I am a blind person on a golf course. Correction: I am a blind person who has never played golf.

We work on my set-up. Mike makes me talk about my mistakes. He wants me to be able to figure them out. There is one other person on the range, a young woman who Mike says is the hardest worker on the University of Colorado golf team. He asks me to look at her swing and explain what's wrong. To my surprise, I know. She hesitates so much in her backswing that she's losing all her momentum. Like life, in golf, it's much easier to look at somebody else and know what's wrong.

I, however, am having problems of my own. Mike gives me a practice drill. He holds two clubs, one to my left side and one to my right, waist-high. Both are parallel to the ground. Then he tells me to swing. I am thinking that Mike is a pretty brave guy because I have no qualms about taking the club back hard, though I can't for the life of me figure out how I'm going to actually swing. I somehow make contact and hit the ball right into Mike's foot.

Eventually, I start whacking the hell out of the ball. Mike then introduces me to a 5-wood. I make minimal contact, and the ball skids a bit forward. So I step back and just take some swings. After I get the feel for a solid swing, I set up and whack the ball. It's practically out of the ballpark. "Jesus," is what I say because I am so stunned by the flight of that little monster. And then I apologize for my language. "How's that feel?" Mike asks. But he already knows the answer.

I am one happy girl. I am so excited that I'm just aching for my clubs. I've ordered a set from my friend Stephanie at Cleveland Golf. When I get home there's a message from her asking if I have received them. When I call to tell her that no clubs have arrived, she calls UPS to discover that someone named Hubert at West Dillon Road signed for them. I live at 902 Sycamore Lane. I tell my husband I'm going to put the kids in the car and go find Hubert. He puts the kibosh on the idea and says I should let UPS do its job. Of course, I'm thinking that I did let them do their job, and they gave my clubs to Hubert.

The next day the UPS guy is heading down my street and I flag him down. "Hey," I say. "Whaddya do with my golf clubs?" "Cleveland?" he asks. "Yeah, that's right," I say. He says he dropped them at the La Quinta on Dillon Road. So I call the La Quinta and tell them I'm on my way—no more waiting for UPS. And there they are, behind the counter. MY CLUBS. My first clubs. I grab that beautiful brown Cleveland box, and it's Christmas morning.

I'm itching to desert my family for the range, but my father-in-law is visiting from New York, so I can't exactly just jump in the car and zoom off. But at four o'clock, when he's on the sofa with the girls watching the *Wild Thornberrys* on Nickelodeon, I head into the yard with my 9-iron and my 5-wood. I am swinging away with my very own clubs in the Colorado sunshine, and it feels, well, divine. My husband opens the glass sliding door and says, "I can't believe this." And the funny thing is, I can't believe it either. In the course of three lessons, I have become a golf addict. Somewhere my friends are going to start wondering what happened to the old Kate. Somewhere, my late father is going to be rooting me on and telling me not to lose my patience. Somewhere the golf gods are smiling. They've converted another heathen.

~Kate Meyers
Chicken Soup for the Golfer's Soul, The 2nd Round

The Collection Basket

Golf is not just an exercise;
it's an adventure, a romance...
a Shakespeare play in which disaster and comedy are intertwined.
~Harold Segall

My mother was my dad's grand passion in life. One of my fondest childhood memories was watching my father flip on the radio each morning before he left for work, then whirl my mother around the kitchen floor in a joyous dance.

But second only to my mother in the love department was my father's adoration of golf. My dad, a Michigan dentist named Cy Collins, cherished the game. He was a deft player, regularly shooting in the low seventies for eighteen holes. He played whenever he could, at home and on vacation in Hawaii, Scotland, and other locales. Golf was truly his nectar of the gods.

In the early 1980s, we began noticing the early signs of the Alzheimer's disease that eventually took his life. Dad became confused and forgetful. Though he had paid the family bills for decades, numbers now mystified him. Once he took the family car out for a drive and became lost, stopping only when he ran out of gas many miles from home. But Dad's love of golf lived on. He couldn't remember many things, but he remembered perfectly how to play the game. His drives and his putts were as good as ever.

And this is the part of the story where Dad's love of golf and generosity of spirit converged in the most touching way. A few years before he died in the small northern Michigan town where they had a summer home, Mom and Dad went to Sunday Mass as usual. Dad smiled and shook hands with friends and neighbors, then listened attentively to the priest's sermon. And when the collection basket was passed down his pew, Dad very deliberately reached into his pocket and placed in the basket the most precious gift he could imagine: three golf balls.

~Jan K. Collins
Chicken Soup for the Golfer's Soul

Ladies, Is Golf for You?

I took up the game of golf eight years ago when I was at the age of... never mind. I became so addicted to the game, I didn't have time to do the laundry anymore. Soon after, my husband had a plaque made for me that says "Martha Stewart Used to Live Here." Sometimes I'd have to stop on my way home after a round of golf to buy him a pair of underwear for work the next day. He has two drawers full of BVDs. God forbid, but if he's ever in an accident, not only will he be wearing clean underwear, most likely it'll be brand-new.

Golf is great, but I can still remember what a frustrating experience it can be for the beginner. For the first three months, I wondered if golf was my punishment for the time I sneaked into Sister Mary Margaret's bedroom to see if she really had a poster of Bob Dylan hanging over her bed. That was the rumor around school. I cried so much as a beginning golfer, my husband suggested I have my hormone level checked. He couldn't believe it was just golf doing it. But I persevered and things became better, and so now I would like to share some tips and ideas that can make a woman's initial foray into golf a little smoother.

Whatever your reasons for taking up the game, whether it's to avoid listening to your son practice the French horn or to get away from your mother-in-law, ask yourself a few questions to see if this game is really your bag. You may be athletic, but there's more than skill involved here.

Temperament, for instance. If you have a hair-trigger kind of temper, occasionally coupled with a bad case of anxiety, a club in your hands that particular day can be dangerous. I once saw a woman do quite a number on the 150-yard marker, a pretty shrub in bloom, with her 7-iron just because her favorite pink ball went into the lake.

Vanity. Particularly in the summer. If you worry about your hair flopping on humid days, your foundation running until your face looks like it's melting, or your mascara making black tracks down your cheeks, stay at home and make pot holders.

Prudery. If you're the kind of person easily offended by less-than-ladylike words, forget it.

But before you spend a fortune on clubs and figure out six months later that what you really want to do is skydive, I suggest you borrow most, if not all, of the essentials first. You'll need clubs (up to fourteen, eight of which look exactly alike, but in a few years you'll be able to tell the difference), a bag, shoes (the ones with plastic spikes for traction), balls, tees, a towel and a ball marker (a quarter will do, but don't forget to pick it up when you leave the green).

If your friends don't have a spare set of clubs to loan out, you can find used clubs at garage sales or pawn shops at reasonable prices. Buy something cheap for now. At this point, equipment doesn't matter much since you have no idea what you're doing.

Eventually, if you stick with the game, you'll find yourself buying a new driver all the time. Every time you hear about another that can help you hit the ball ten more yards, you'll go and buy it. I've noticed that no matter who the manufacturer is or what the club material, it's always "an extra ten yards." You'd think, out of all the clubmakers, one company would have an engineer smart enough to come up with a club that'll give us fifty extra yards and get it over with for a while.

I love drivers. They're all so different. They come in persimmon, graphite, titanium, with bubbles, without bubbles, large heads, extra-large heads, stiff and extra-stiff shafts—you name it.

Now once you have your equipment, you need an instructor. But ladies: Do not let your husband teach you. When was the last time you listened to him anyway? What makes you think you're going to start now? Sooner or later even his voice will start grating on your nerves. Trust me, it won't work. Find yourself a real pro. My guess is that the person who said sex is one of the main sources of disagreements between couples didn't teach his wife the game of golf.

One more piece of advice: While you're still a beginner, don't play in events for couples if the format is that of alternate shot. Heaven help you if your shot lands directly behind a tree, on top of a root or in a bunker in a "fried egg" lie and now he has to play it. That's an argument waiting to happen. And it will happen.

Another thought to keep in mind for the sake of keeping peace at home: If you ever hit a hole-in-one, never mention it again after the day it happens. I've had two, and he hasn't even had one. I love my husband too much to upset him, so I don't talk about them in his presence. But my plaques hang in the den, one on each side of the television, where he can see them every night. I also have a vanity license plate, 2-HOLS-N-1 — and he washes my car every Saturday.

Golf's like fishing: There's always the one that got away. In golf there's always the putt that didn't fall. But there's more to golf than making good shots. Fun moments that don't have anything to do with the game can happen on the course. There was the time when my husband uncharacteristically threw his sand wedge after shanking a short chip. The grip hit the cart path first, propelling the club into a 360-degree rotation and directly into the golf bag. Eventually, you'll have your own stories to tell, and you'll remember them years from now.

Above all else, have fun, even on those days when you feel you should have stayed home making those pot holders instead of going to the course, accomplishing nothing more than achieving that dreaded tan line that makes your feet look like you're wearing bobby socks with high heels in your finest evening gown.

Golf can be played long after you start collecting your first Social Security check. When you reach that age, you can start making cute ball markers and tee holders to give your friends at Christmas. By the way, did you know the Senior Tour has players in their seventies? Ladies don't have a Senior Tour. They won't admit when they turn fifty. It's a woman thing.

~Deisy Flood
Chicken Soup for the Golfer's Soul, The 2nd Round

My Life in Pro Ball

The phone rings. I roll over in bed and grab the receiver. The motel operator says, "Wake-up call. It's 9 A.M. Your bus leaves at ten." We are in Cleveland, where last night we—the New York Knicks—lost to the Cleveland Cavaliers. Outside, a cold drizzle soaks the city. I draw a hot bath and sit in it for five minutes to loosen my body's stiffness. My socks, shoes and Knicks uniform hang drying over the chairs, the room heater and the floor lamp. My mouth is dry and burning. My legs ache. I've slept poorly.

Next day, Tuesday, we play at home. Before the game, at Madison Square Garden, an avid fan tells me the Knicks give him something to look forward to after a day at work in the post office. I am his favorite player. He is similar to other fans who have identified with the team and me. They suffer with us when we lose and they are ecstatic when we win. They are the bedrock of our experience as professional players.

That night we win by twenty points. After the game I take a long shower. Then I stuff my wet socks, shoes and jock into the traveling bag with my road uniform for the bus ride to the airport.

We land in Atlanta at 1 A.M. It is twenty-one degrees outside and the frost makes the runway sparkle as if it were sprinkled with bits of glass. We wait forty minutes for our bags, which delays our arrival at the hotel until 3 A.M.

There is an overpowering loneliness on the road. A local acquaintance may show up during the day. There is chitchat with him of times past and of his job and my activities outside of basketball. After that exchange, there is nothing more to say, little common interest. Sometimes I take in an art exhibit or visit an unusual section of town. Or I sit in a hotel room reading books, listening to the radio.

Someday, I say to myself, I won't be spending one hundred days a year on the road. Someday I'll wake up in the same place every morning. I miss that sense of sharing that comes from people living together in one place, over time. I miss permanence.

From Atlanta we fly to Chicago. I go to a luncheon put on by Chicago Bulls' boosters, where I am the principal speaker. About 200 men attend. Part of being a professional basketball player is speaking at shopping-center openings, charity fundraisers, sports banquets, bar mitzvahs and annual company dinners. The audience laughs at my jokes. Even unfunny stories told by athletes make audiences roll in the aisles.

We lose to the Bulls by sixteen points. Our plane touches down in New York at 3:45 A.M. The doorman of my apartment building tells me he is sorry about the loss in Chicago, but he made $100 betting against us. I get into bed around 5:30 A.M. Just one more game this week, then we have two days off. We will have played five games in seven days in four different cities.

Saturday does not begin for me until 1 P.M. Whenever we return from a road trip late, the next day is always a jumble. At 3 P.M., I have my usual pregame steak-and-salad meal (I will not eat again until midnight supper after the game). I sleep for an hour. The alarm goes off at six. I arrive at the Garden just one hour before the game.

The locker room has become a kind of home for me. I often enter tense and uneasy, disturbed by some event of the day. Slowly my worries fade as I see their importance to my male peers. I relax, my concerns lost among the constants of an athlete's life. Athletes may be crude and immature, but they are genuine when it comes to loyalty, responsibility and honesty. The members of my team have seen me, and I them, in more moods and predicaments than I care to remember. Our lives intertwine far beyond the court. It is a good life with congenial people. If victory and unity fuse on one team, life becomes a joy. It is a life that truly makes sense only while you're living it.

I tape my ankles and put on my uniform. Then I turn to the mail that has just been delivered. I usually get forty letters a week, almost none of them from people I know. There are a few autograph requests.

The last letter I open is from Kentucky. It is from the father of a boy whom I had met when he was a sophomore at the University of Kentucky. He came all the way from Kentucky to ask me to show him how to shoot a basketball. He just appeared at my apartment one day. We went up to Riverside Park, talked and shot baskets for about an hour. He thanked me for the help and boarded a bus back home. I saw him later that year in Cincinnati. He had been cut from the Kentucky team. He was down, and convinced that his sprained ankle had something to do with it.

I wrote him a letter two years later, after his sister had written that he had cancer. The boy's father thanks me for the letter but says that his son has died. I put the letter down. Coach Red Holzman begins his pregame conversation. I can't concentrate. I should have written sooner. I feel numbed with anger and sorrow.

From the middle of September until May, there is usually no longer than one day at a time without basketball. There are no long weekends or national holidays for players. It is impossible to take a trip to the mountains or fly to Florida even for two days. We are a part of show business, providing public entertainment. We work on Christmas night and New Year's Eve.

We arrive in Los Angeles for the first stop of a five-game western trip. My normal routine the day before a game in another town is to find a facility where I can get a steaming bath, whirlpool and massage. Games and practices bring injuries, and travel brings fatigue. Hot whirlpool baths, diathermy, ultrasound, ice packs, elastic wraps, aspirin, cold pills, vitamins and sleeping pills are all part of the life.

A professional basketball player must be able to run six miles in a game, one hundred times a year, jumping and pivoting under continuous physical contact. The body is constantly battered and ground away. During this year alone I have had a jammed finger, inflamed fascia of the arch, a smashed nose cartilage, five split lips, an elbow in the throat that eliminated my voice for a week, a bruised right hip, a sprained ankle, a left hip joint out of socket and a contusion of the left wrist.

Every workout brings the fear of re-injury and every night brings the hope for tomorrow's improvement. I wake up in the middle of the night and flex my knee to see if there is pain, or knead my thigh to see if the charley horse has begun to heal.

I often ask myself why I continue to play. In 1967, when I first signed, I was convinced that I would play no more than four years, the length of my initial contract. I'm still playing in 1976. One reason is the money. The average salary in the National Basketball Association (NBA) at this time is close to $100,000. Many players make more than $150,000. There is no question that it gives me a sense of security, and a greater feeling of freedom, mobility and accomplishment. But money is not the sole reason I play. The answer lies much deeper in the workings of the game and in me.

I recall, for about the fiftieth time this season, how it was in 1970, the first time we won the NBA championship. I stood at midcourt in Madison Square Garden, two fists raised, chills coursing up and down my spine. Since I was nine years old, I had played basketball to become the best. Individual honors were nice but insufficient. An Olympic gold medal gave satisfaction, but it was not top-flight basketball. The NBA was clearly the highest caliber in the world, and there I was: a part of the best team.

All those statements of team solidarity expressed since high school; all the hours of loneliness, dribbling and shooting a basketball in a gym somewhere in the world; all the near misses in the smaller championships—high school and college—of America's sports hierarchy; all the missed opportunities in other fields; all the denied personal enjoyment; all the conflicts suppressed and angers swallowed—everything seemed worth it for the feeling at center court on May 8, 1970.

I remember those few moments after victory, in the locker room with the team, when there was a total oneness with the world. Owners and politicians celebrate in the locker room of a champion. But only the players, the coach and perhaps the trainer can feel the special satisfaction of the achievement. They start nine months earlier in training camp. They play the games and endure the travel. They receive the public criticism and overcome their own personal ambitions. The high of the championship is unequaled. The possibility that it could happen again is a sufficient lure to continue. The money is important, but the chance to relive that moment outweighs dollars.

But how fast it is gone! On a flight to Phoenix, I open a magazine to a story about Mickey Mantle at his home in Dallas, Texas, after several years out of baseball.

"I loved it," the author quotes Mantle as saying, his voice throbbing with intensity. "Nobody could have loved playing ball as much as me, when I wasn't hurt. I must have fifty scrapbooks. Sometimes after breakfast, I sit by myself and take a scrapbook and just turn the pages. The hair comes up on the back of my neck. I get goose bumps. And I remember how it was and how I used to think that it would always be that way."

The words seem to jump off the page at me. There is terror behind the dream of being a professional ballplayer. It comes as a slow realization of finality and of the frightening unknowns which the end brings.

When the playing is over, one can sense that one's youth has been spent playing a game, and now both the game and youth are gone.

By age thirty-five, any potential for developing skills outside of basketball is slim. The "good guy" syndrome ceases. What is left is the other side of the Faustian bargain: to live all one's days never able to recapture the feeling of those few years of intensified youth. The athlete approaches the end of his playing days the way old people approach death. He puts his finances in order. He reminisces easily. He offers advice to the young. But the athlete differs from an old person in that he must continue living. Behind all the years of practice and all the hours of glory waits that inexorable terror of living without the game.

~Bill Bradley
Chicken Soup for the Sports Fan's Soul

The Thrill of the Hunt

If there is any larceny in a man,
golf will bring it out.
~Paul Gallico

Finding golf balls is like an adult Easter egg hunt. I relish that juvenile "Hey, cool!" moment of excitement even as I race toward eligibility as a senior golfer. Besides, no one can have too many golf balls. Honestly, the richest I've ever felt was the time I bought a gross of balls. It was heaven. Just grab a couple of sleeves of those glaringly white jewels and head for the links. Once, I poured them all on the carpet and batted them around like a cat with a toy mouse. I would grab them by the handful just to feel the heavy, sensuous pleasure of them tumbling through my fingers like overgrown drops of water. Sadly, they vanished all too quickly.

Hey, look, it was my own fault. If I had spent more time practicing with the range rocks, the pretty ones would have lasted longer. Sure, the feeling of a new sleeve is nice, but nothing approached the joy of having a whole gross. A dozen dozen! It was wealth of truly biblical proportion: "Thou shalt have pristine alabaster orbs of the finest balata and their number shall be without end" (Book of Arnold, Chapter 4, Verse 72).

It's always a treat to find balls. You're out on the course and not having the best day. You carve another high one that clears the right-hand tree line and drops precariously close to OB. You trudge into the woods hoping it's not lost and that by some miracle you'll have a shot. Hmm, let's see, if I can just punch-slap a little knee-high fade around that pine. Well, you know what I mean. Suddenly, you stumble across a stray ball and feel a little better. It's sort of like the golf gods have taken pity and are offering up some compensation.

Yeah, like they really care. These are the same golf gods that have left your match-clinching putts hanging on the lip against your loud-mouth brother-in-law. "Nice lag, Tarzan." Or remember the time they let him snap-hook a 4-iron over water, off a rock and on the green for a tap-in deuce while you pure a 6-iron long into the back bunker? Sympathy is not their strong suit. Besides, if you didn't like abuse, you wouldn't play this game. I'm surprised it is not mentioned more often in the personals column of those freebie classifieds. "Wanted: Submissive male in need of discipline and swing advice. Please call Mistress Flog."

So like any good supplicant, you shamelessly pick the ball up and stuff it in your bag. Trying to save face, you say, "Here's one for the shag bag." Shag bag, right. Like anyone is going to believe that you: a) practice, or b) pick them up yourself. Still no one calls you on it because they've told the same lie. You're like conspiratorial winos in an alley patiently listening to one another swear they're going to quit drinking and straighten up. The truth is, this little nugget will come in handy. Sometime soon, you'll drown one too many of those precious surlyn pellets fresh out of the box and start reaching for the oldies. You're just going to lose them anyway. Why waste the good ones?

Finding golf balls recently took on a whole new meaning. I was visiting a friend in Myrtle Beach, South Carolina. He lives near a course. (Okay, everybody in Myrtle Beach lives near a course.) We were out for an evening stroll with Rover and, lo and behold, there it was: A sparkling white, slightly used, top-of-the-line ball in the right rough, about 220 yards from the first tee. What a find! Have you priced these things lately? Fifty-four bucks a dozen if you can get them! A little quick math says that's $4.50 a ball minus depreciation, which in this case was probably one swing.

"You want this?" I said.

"Naw, you take it," my friend said. "I've got a garage full of them."

I doubted he knew exactly which ball I'd found, but took it anyway. Walking on, we found more. Not all the same type, but mostly high-end balls with few battle scars. I was excited. I was hooked. Wouldn't you be if you just found $5 bills lying around? It was like a golfer's Elysian Fields. I wanted more. "This is great!" I said, "I wish I could do this at home."

He said, "You probably can. Not as much competition back in Charlotte. We've got to get out early down here before the retirees get 'em all."

He was right. How many other people living in an upscale golf community would spend (or waste) time looking for balls? "Pardon me, Barfield, that's not a used ball you're playing, is it?" I needed a cover. I needed a disguise. I needed a plan. So I stunned my wife by announcing, "Honey, I need more exercise. I think I'll start taking a walk in the evenings."

I waited until Monday. The course was closed so I wouldn't be running into any late-afternoon golfers. Besides, with a full weekend's play just finished, the woods should be teeming with dimpled fruit ready for picking.

I put on a hat and sprayed myself with bug repellent to ward off ticks and mosquitoes. I wore long shorts and high socks to minimize poison ivy exposure. I grabbed a 6-iron — ostensibly to ward off angry dogs, but perfect for swatting snakes — stuffed a plastic bag in my shorts and headed out.

Moving briskly, I planned as I went. I would have rules. No traipsing around in the neighbors' backyards. They paid big bucks for a course lot and deserved any stray balls on their property — yuppie mineral rights. Lakes were off limits; even I can't bring myself to buy a ball retriever, and it would blow my cover.

I would have to be selective. Unsold lots were fair game, but the prime hunting ground was the right side of hilly holes. You've got to go where slicers lose balls and fear to tread, and be willing to put up with a few hazards like Lyme disease, venomous serpents and twisted ankles.

The plan worked like a charm. My friend was right; I had no competition. I came home with ten balls. The next morning, I lovingly washed and sorted them: Shags, Kids, Everyday and Tournament. It was like Christmas. The next day was better still; my hunting skills had improved.

I have continued "walking" and have never come up empty. Several times, I've found two dozen balls. Not always perfect, but eminently playable. Many are only one bad swing and a little mud removed from the pro shop. For a guy who gave up golf gloves as an economy measure, this was a windfall. That feeling of extravagant but imitation wealth is back. I gladly suffer the opulent burden of choice. "Which of the $50-a-dozen balls shall I play today?"

I even make better grillroom conversation. "That brand is soft, but I prefer the lower spin of this one off the driver," I might muse. "Still, nothing beats this third one for holding its line on putts." I've become a golf ball connoisseur.

My buddies envy the luxury of playing different balls. They wonder if their own games are refined enough to discern such subtle differences. They marvel at my fearless calm as I execute lengthy carries from precarious lies without the temptation to reach for a water ball. My waist-line is thinner, my wallet is thicker, and both my cholesterol and scores are lower. Life is good.

Now if I could just figure out where everyone is tossing those new drivers.

~Henry Lawrence
Chicken Soup for the Golfer's Soul, The 2nd Round

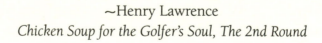

The Golf Maniac

I'm a golfaholic, no question about that.
Counseling wouldn't help me. They'd have to put me in prison,
and then I'd talk the warden into building a hole or two
and teach him how to play.
~Lee Trevino

We rode in and out pretty often together, he and I, on a suburban train.

That's how I came to talk to him. "Fine morning," I said as I sat down beside him and opened a newspaper.

"Great!" he answered. "The grass is drying out fast now and the greens will soon be all right to play."

"Yes," I said, "the sun is getting higher and the days are decidedly lengthening."

"For the matter of that," said my friend, "a man could begin to play at six in the morning easily. In fact, I've often wondered why there's so little golf played before breakfast. We happened to be talking about golf, a few of us last night—I don't know how it came up—and we were saying that it seems a pity that some of the best part of the day, say from five o'clock to seven-thirty, is never used."

"That's true," I answered. Then, to shift the subject, I said, looking out the window, "It's a pretty bit of country just here, isn't it?"

"It is," he replied, "but seems a shame they make no use of it—just a few market gardens and things like that. Why, I noticed along here acres and acres of just glass—some kind of houses for plants or something—and whole fields full of lettuce and things like that. It's a pity they don't make something of it. I was remarking only the other day in the train to a friend of mine that you could easily lay out an 18-hole course here."

"Could you?" I said.

"Oh, yes. This ground you know, is an excellent light soil to shovel up into bunkers. You could drive some big ditches through it and make one or two deep holes. In fact, improve it to any extent."

I glanced at my morning paper. "Look at this," I said, pointing to a headline, "'United States Navy Ordered Again to Nicaragua.' Looks like more trouble, doesn't it?"

"Did you see in the paper a while back," said my companion, "that the United States Navy is now making golf compulsory at the training school in Annapolis? That's progressive, isn't it? I suppose it will have to mean shorter cruises at sea; in fact, probably lessen the use of the Navy for sea purposes. But it will raise the standard."

"I suppose so," I answered. "Did you read this article about the extraordinary murder case on Long Island?"

"No," he said. "I never read murder cases. They don't interest me. In fact, I think this whole continent is really getting over-preoccupied with them. "

"Yes, but this one had such odd features. "

"Oh, they all have," he replied, with an air of weariness. "Each one is just boomed by the papers to make a sensation. "

"I know, but in this case it seems that the man was killed with a blow from a golf club."

"What's that? Eh, what's that? Killed him with a blow from a golf club!"

"Yes, some kind of club. "

"I wonder if it was an iron—let me see the paper—though, for that matter, I imagine a blow with even a wooden driver. Where does it say it? It only just says 'a blow with a golf club.' It's a pity the papers don't write these things up with more detail, isn't it?"

"Have you played golf much?" I inquired. I saw it was no use to talk of anything else.

"No," answered my companion, "I am sorry to say I haven't. You see, I began late. I've only played twenty years, twenty-one if you count the year that's beginning in May. I don't know what I was doing. I wasted half my life. In fact, it wasn't until I was well over thirty that I caught on to the game. I suppose a lot of us look back over our lives that way and realize what we have lost.

"And even as it is," he continued, "I don't get much chance to play. At best I can only manage about four afternoons a week, though of course I get most of Saturday and all Sunday. I get my holiday in the summer, but it's only a month, and that's nothing. In winter I manage to take a run south for a game once or twice, perhaps a little swack at it around Easter, but only a week at a time. I'm too busy — that's the plain truth of it." He sighed. "It's hard to leave the office before two. Something always turns up."

And after that he went on to tell me something of the technique of the game, illustrate it with a golf ball on the seat of the car, and the peculiar mental poise needed for driving, and the neat, quick action of the wrist (he showed me how it worked) that is needed to undercut a ball so that it flies straight up in the air. He explained to me how you can do practically anything with a golf ball, provided you keep your mind absolutely poised and your eye in shape, and your body a trained machine.

So, later in the day, meeting someone in my club who was a person of authority on such things, I made an inquiry about my friend. "I rode into town with Llewellyn Smith," I said. "I think he belongs to your golf club. He's a great player, isn't he?"

"A great player!" laughed the expert. "Llewellyn Smith? Why, he can hardly hit a ball! And anyway, he's only played for about twenty years."

~Stephen Leacock
Chicken Soup for the Golfer's Soul

The Sermon
on the Mound

The greatest discovery of my generation is that
a human being can alter his life by altering his attitudes.
~William James

My heart sank. The last person I wanted to see right then was Tommy Lasorda. What could he want? I wasn't sure I wanted to know. In fact, with a 2-2 record and a 6.20 earned run average, I was pretty sure I didn't.

But Ron Perranoski was the boss. When the pitching coach tells you the skipper wants to see you in his office, you don't stand around wondering what to do. "What does Tommy want, Perry?" I asked. I hoped against hope it didn't mean a trip back to the minor leagues.

"He'll let you know."

Uh-oh. "You goin' with me?"

"I'm invited, just like you. That's how Tommy works, you know. He wouldn't tell you anything without me there."

"Well, that's good. I guess. I hope."

It was early May 1984, during my first full year in the big leagues, and I was a Los Angeles Dodger relief pitcher trying to hang on for dear life. I couldn't get anything going, couldn't maintain any consistency. I might get a guy or even two guys out, then I'd get too fine, too careful, and walk somebody. Tommy hated two-out walks. Almost as much as he hated two-out runs. And two-out runs too often followed my two-out walks.

I'd get even more careful, and before you knew it, someone had doubled up the alley. I'd be yanked, aired out for not doing what I was paid to do, and then I'd sit, wondering what was happening to my brief career.

As a rookie, I was pretty much a non-entity with the Dodgers. I didn't have that casual relationship with the coaches that the veterans did. I wasn't consulted about strategy. Nobody cared what I thought was the right pitch in a specific situation. If I offered an opinion, it might just as likely be ignored as disputed. I was proving on the mound that I couldn't execute the pitches, even if I knew what they should be. Everyone said I had potential, the most frustrating label any player can have. I'd been hearing that since the day I signed.

Because I was young and looked younger, and because I was thin and wore glasses, and because I was known as a Christian athlete, I got the feeling people assumed I had no guts. Hershiser was too passive, too nice, too mellow to get the job done.

I was intimidated by Tommy Lasorda. Loud and brash and a real veteran baseball man, he was a manager any player would want behind him. He could be an encourager, but I didn't know where I stood. I feared I was on the bubble. There had to be guys in triple-A who could do better than I was doing.

And now he wanted to see me and my pitching coach. What could that mean? What could he want? Perry wasn't saying much. Did that mean he didn't know? Or worse, that he did know? Though the walk to Tommy's office seemed to take forever, I wished we hadn't arrived so soon. This was like being sent to the principal's office, but the stakes were much higher. I'd sure rather stay after school than be shipped back to Albuquerque.

Perry knocked, and Tommy waved us in. My mouth was dry, and I noticed Tommy wasn't smiling. He pointed to a couple of chairs, and Perry and I sat down. Tommy sat on the edge of his desk and looked down at me. I didn't take my eyes off him, and if I blinked I wasn't aware of it. I was prepared to agree with whatever he said, no matter what. I wondered if he could hear my heart.

"I invited you here with Ronnie because I never talk to a player without his individual coach present."

"Yes, sir, I know. I appreciate..."

He continued as if I hadn't said anything. "I wanted to talk to you about your game, the use of your ability, your mental approach to pitching."

I nodded.

"You remember how mad I was about how you pitched to Cruz the other day against Houston..."

I nodded again. Did I ever. It was one of those two-out situations with two men on. Jose Cruz was a great contact hitter, a dangerous RBI (runs batted in) man.

"You throw low and away, ball one. Low and away, ball two. Low and away, ball three. He's takin' and you finally get a strike over, luckily, 'cause that one could'a been called low or outside, either one. He knows you can't afford to walk him, so he's sittin' on your three and one pitch, and what do you do?"

I didn't want to think about it, and I sure didn't want to talk about it. The worst thing was, Tommy was getting himself upset all over again just rehashing it. He grew louder. His face reddened. He leaned closer.

"You laid the ball in for him! Boom! Double and two runs! Hershiser, you're givin' these hitters too much credit! You're tellin' yourself, 'If I throw this ball over the plate, they're gonna hit it out.' That is a negative approach to pitching!"

I knew. I felt small and young and stupid. Sitting there nodding, I finally knew what he thought of me. My worst fears had been confirmed. I was hopeless. And, if it was possible, Tommy was getting louder. He was in my face now, those eyes bulging, his cheeks crimson. Sweat broke out on my forehead and the back of my neck. I didn't dare move even to wipe it off.

"You don't believe in yourself! You're scared to pitch in the big leagues! Who do you think these hitters are, Babe Ruth? Ruth's dead!

You've got good stuff. If you didn't, I wouldn't have brought you up. Quit bein' so careful! Go after the hitter! Get ahead in the count! Don't be so fine with him and then find yourself forced to lay one in!"

As he sped on, louder and louder, something registered with me. Was that more than an airing out I just heard? Did a compliment slip by, disguised as a tongue lashing? I've got good stuff? He believes that?

Tommy continued, "If I could get a heart surgeon in here, I'd have him open my chest and take out my heart, open your chest and take out your heart, and then I'd have him give you my heart! You'd be in the Hall of Fame! If I had your stuff, I'd a been in the Hall of Fame!

"I've seen guys come and go, son, and you've got it! You gotta go out there and do it on the mound! Take charge! Make 'em hit your best stuff! Be aggressive. Be a bulldog out there. That's gonna be your new name: Bulldog. You know, when we bring you in in the ninth to face Dale Murphy and he hears, 'Now pitching, Orel Hershiser,' man, he can't wait till you get there! But if he hears, 'Now pitching, Bulldog Hershiser,' he's thinkin', Oh, no, who's that!? Murphy's gonna be scared to death!"

We're nose to nose now, and I could use a towel on my face, but I don't even swallow, let alone move. "I want you, starting today, to believe you are the best pitcher in baseball. I want you to look at that hitter and say, 'There's no way you can ever hit me.' You gotta believe you are superior to the hitter and that you can get anybody out who walks up there. Quit givin' the hitter so much credit. You're better than these guys."

Part of me resented anyone thinking that I needed a nickname to make me tough and aggressive. No question I had not learned a proper approach to pitching. But I didn't think I needed a new name to make me stronger. Still, I couldn't get over that Tommy Lasorda felt I was worth this much time and effort. It hurt to hear him say what he said, but beneath it there had been a foundation of confidence in me. He believed I had more than potential. He believed I had big league stuff.

He was right that I had been treating big-league hitters in a special way. I believed they had special ability. Which they did. What Tommy was telling me was that so did I. I wasn't some minor-leaguer who had lucked his way up to the big club because it was a thin year for pitchers. I belonged on that mound just as much as the hitter belonged in the box.

Two days later against the San Francisco Giants the Dodgers needed a reliever in a difficult situation. The bullpen was full of tired, sore-armed pitchers, me included. The call came, "Can anybody down there pitch?"

I volunteered, despite a tender elbow and an arm weak from overwork. I strode to the mound reminding myself what a pleasant surprise it had been to learn that Tommy believed in me, thought I was special, needed me, thought I would be successful with an adjustment in my approach. I didn't know what I could do with my arm and elbow in the shape they were in, but my attitude was finally right.

From the dugout Tommy hollered, "C'mon, Bulldog! You can do it, Bulldog! You're my man, Bulldog!"

I challenged the hitters, kept the ball low, got ahead in the count on nearly every batter. In three innings, my arm feeling like a rag, I gave up only one run. Tommy's talk had worked. (He calls it his "Sermon on the Mound" and says he wishes he had taped it. "It'd sell a million, Bulldog!")

With my performance against San Francisco, I became a believer. I told myself that if I could do that when my arm felt terrible, think what I could do when I felt great. I still didn't like the nickname (I still don't), and I was still chagrined that anyone thought I needed it. But that day I became a big-league pitcher. My attitude was revolutionized. I believed I deserved to be there, competing with big leaguers because I was a big leaguer. (The legendary Branch Rickey once said, "A big-leaguer is a minor-leaguer with a chance to play there.")

I learned years later that assigning a nickname to a player was Tommy's unofficial way of welcoming him to the big leagues. Until you showed him you could compete at that level, you were called by your given name. Franklin Stubbs was just Stubbs until Tommy decided he was worthy of a nickname. Then he became Cadillac. Mike Marshall was just Marshall until Tommy christened him Moose. Neither Tommy nor I knew then that he was right and that I could succeed at this level. But within two months, we had more to go on.

An injury to Jerry Reuss thrust me into a start on May 26th. I joined the starting rotation for good June 29th against the Chicago Cubs, when I began the longest consecutive scoreless inning streak in the National League that year (332/3 innings). I pitched four shut-outs in July alone (and was named Pitcher of the Month), tied for the league lead in shutouts for the year, and finished third in ERA (earned run average), sixth in complete games, and eighth in strikeouts. I was third in Rookie of the Year voting.

My game had become focused. And the concentration, moti-vated by the confidence Tommy instilled in me, remains a key to my success today. Do you wonder how a pitcher could have had a 1988 like I had? Do you wonder how we Dodgers could have been moti-vated to maintain our intensity all through the season and the post-season, in spite of injuries and setbacks? We owe a lot of it to Tommy, of course, because he is a true motivator, encourager, cheerleader.

Knowing he believed in us allowed us to focus our energy, to eliminate distractions, to major on the fundamentals that outweigh everything, no matter what the task or pursuit. I benefited from real-izing that there was too much to think about, too many variables, too many distractions if a pitcher tried to stay on top of every nuance of the game all the time. In my mind I narrowed my emphasis and priority to one thing and one thing only: the pitch.

~Orel Hershiser
Chicken Soup for the Baseball Fan's Soul

Who Is the Greatest Golfer?

My body is here, but my mind has already teed off.
~Author Unknown

For the first time in my personal golfing history I had broken 90. Because of it, I couldn't sleep. In the midnight darkness, I nudged my sleeping wife, "Can you believe it?" I cried. "I'm no longer a duffer! The secret of golf is simply a matter of..."

"...Of beginning your downswing with your shoulders instead of your hands," she muttered.

"How did you know?" I asked, amazed.

"Only because that's what you've been muttering all night." She felt my brow to make sure I was not delirious. "Try to get some sleep now, darling. You've got a big day coming up, remember?"

She was right. I should have been asleep hours ago. In a few hours, I would play my first-round match in the club tournament against my arch golfing enemy, Steve Galloway. I chuckled into my pillow sadistically. With the secret of the game now locked in my breast, I would humble him at last.

I shut my eyes and ordered my mind to go blank, but to no avail. It insisted that I again replay each stroke of my day's round. During the first two holes, my smile all but illuminated the night shadows of the room. But when I again found myself missing that twenty-inch putt on the 3rd green, my smile turned itself off. That putt had hurt.

So had the four other short ones I had muffed later on. If I had sunk them instead, I would have completed my round in 84.

Nor were those missed putts the only additions to my score that should not have happened and most certainly would not happen again. If one of my drives hadn't sliced out of bounds, costing me two penalty strokes, I would have toured the links in a sizzling 82.

Or might not I have scored better still? The supposition caused me to gasp aloud, waking my wife with a start. Now that she was no longer asleep, I could find no reason for not sharing my joyous discovery.

"I had some tough breaks today, not of my own doing," I explained. "A perfect pitch shot to the 9th green took an astounding hop into a bunker, and my drive on the 12th freakishly scooted beneath a bramble bush. And on the 17th hole, my caddy sneezed at the top of my backswing, all but causing me to miss the ball completely. Wouldn't you agree that because those were obviously non-recurrable accidents, I should further reduce my score by that same amount?"

"Why is it," my wife interrupted, "that a man can recall for a week every shot of his last game but can't remember for five minutes that the screen door needs fixing?"

I lay back in the pretense of sudden sleep. But my subconscious kept busy subtracting those three strokes from my hypothetical round of 82. On arriving at the amazing answer of 79, my body seemed to float toward the ceiling.

"Good Lord," I cried, "I'm a championship golfer!"

Every shred of evidence now pointed to my being able to par even the toughest holes on the course, and should it be my good fortune to slap in an occasional birdie—and, after all, why shouldn't I?—well, the implications were downright staggering.

Ever so carefully, so as not to cause my wife to phone a psychiatrist, I slithered from bed and stood beside it, my hand gripping an imaginary driver. For a moment I waggled it back and forth in delicious anticipation, then powerfully and smoothly I swept my body through an entire swing. Had the situation been born in reality, the ball surely would have zoomed into orbit. I drew in my stomach and threw out my chest and, in the utter darkness of the bedroom, exuded more confidence than ever before in my life.

Confidence, that was the key... confidence born of my new mastery of technique. How incredible to realize that in all these years I had simply conducted an endless series of tiger hunts on the golf course, violently beating the earth with my clubs, exhausting myself with my very ineptness. Not once, in fact, had I gotten past the first round of the club tournament. But tomorrow would be vastly different. Poor, unsuspecting Galloway!

At 2 A.M., I begged my mind to let me sleep. My plea was in vain. By three o'clock I had won the club championship. An hour later, I captured the U.S. Open. Dawn was creeping over the windowsill before I divested myself of an armful of phantom trophies and tumbled into a canyon of sleep.

My wife and I and the Galloways sat together on the golf club terrace, watching the sun call it another day on the fickle fortunes of man. Now that my tournament match was over, I wished I were alone, like Napoleon, on Elba Island. Not even on Boy Scout timber hikes had I met up with so many trees. No doubt about it. I would have scored better with an axe. What could have gone wrong to lead to all that abject, humiliating agony? My wife reached over to pat my knee. "Didn't you remember to keep your eye on the ball, sweetie?"

Her question was so ridiculous that I refused to answer. Without looking up, I felt the sting of Steve Galloway's mocking glance. This time I was through with golf for good. Should I give my clubs to some deserving caddy, I wondered, or instead salvage a scrap of retribution by wrapping them around my opponent's neck?

My wife was talking again—a far too usual procedure—and I was trying not to listen. I chose instead to gaze out over the course where the evening dew already had tinted the fairways with silver and where, on either side, the terrible towering trees now slept, harmless and serene, as a moon tip rose above them into the night. It seemed impossible to believe that this gentle pastoral scene had, by daylight, proved itself such a violent battlefield.

I poured myself another drink and downed it quickly. Somehow it made me feel better. I reclined in my chair, my eyes again drawn back to the lush and quiet fairways. The course was beckoning me now like a temptress in the shadows. "Come conquer me," she seemed to whisper. "You can, you can."

I closed my eyes, but the voice refused to go away. When I refilled my glass and drank deeply from it, I began feeling surprisingly relaxed. Much the same as I had felt yesterday when I had shot my 89.

Ah, so that was it — relaxation! Not how you gripped the club or pivoted your hips or snapped your wrists, but simply how well you relaxed. No wonder Galloway had trounced me so completely. My mind had been gorged with a jumble of mechanical DOs and DON'Ts. By taking it smooth and easy, wouldn't those technical elements fall naturally into place?

Yes, yes, I saw it clearly now. After years of huffing and puffing on the links, I caught the message at last. Silently, almost breathlessly, I started out over the vastness of the golf course, lost in wild surmise. What, I wondered, should I wear while competing in the British Open? A touch of heather, perhaps? I could only hope I would not be so relaxed as to drop my trophy on the toe of the queen.

Pulling myself back to the present, I tried not to sound condescending as I turned to Steve Galloway. "How about a return match next Saturday?" I asked.

"But darling," my wife protested, "that's when you promised to fix the screen door."

For a moment her words buzzed near my ears like mosquitoes, then mercifully took flight when Galloway's voice chose to lead him to slaughter. "In the mood for another licking, eh?"

I only smiled in the dark. Already I was growing joyfully tense just contemplating the wonders of relaxation.

~Graham Porter
Chicken Soup for the Golfer's Soul, The 2nd Round

11

Becoming
True Fishermen

Most summers, my extremely busy retirement schedule permitting, I travel to the beautiful Rocky Mountain town of Telluride, Colorado. The Sheridan Arts Foundation has an ongoing effort there, helped by a willing contingent of well-known celebrities, to restore the historic Sheridan Opera House and support its theatrical training program. Another part of the Foundation's program is its annual Wild West Fest.

Each summer the Sheridan Arts Foundation, in partnership with the Boys and Girls Clubs of America, brings a large number of inner-city and underprivileged children to Telluride for a magnificent week of Wild West activities. As part of the program, which includes mentorships in theater, horsemanship, art, music and Indian hoop dancing, they offer the kids an opportunity to learn how to fly-fish. I have been very fortunate to be involved with that program, helping these great kids learn some of the secrets of my favorite pastime.

One of my fondest memories occurred a couple of summers ago when I was teaching a young inner-city boy from Atlanta how to fly-fish. At one point, I was so taken with our beautiful Western Colorado surroundings that I asked, "Have you ever seen mountains prettier than these?"

He looked at me and said, "Sir, I have never seen any mountains."

It suddenly made me realize how blessed are we who have enjoyed the sport of fly-fishing in beautiful, natural surroundings.

Later on that day I was conducting a mentorship discussion with the kids, and I publicly asked my young fishing partner how many fish he had caught. He proudly stood up among his peers and announced he had caught four fish. That immediately caused several other kids to jump to their feet claiming five, six, seven and so on. Needless to say, when I asked how big, claims were made of every size from minnows to tiger sharks and everything in between.

It was at that moment I proudly realized these kids had become true fishermen.

~General H. Norman Schwarzkopf
Chicken Soup for the Fisherman's Soul

12

Sunday Drivers

*Golf combines two favorite American pastimes:
taking long walks and hitting things with a stick.*
~P.J. O'Rourke

We have to make a lot of choices in life. Do I want the Big Mac or the Whopper for lunch? Will I sit in the recliner or lay on the couch to watch the game? Should I get up at 6 A.M. on Sunday morning and head off to the golf course for our weekly Duffer Tournament, or should I put on my Amazon outfit and finally mow the lawn enough so that we can see out the windows again?

As luck would have it, the mower was somewhere in the yard, and even after a full two-minute search I couldn't find it. I took this as a sign. I was sure my wife would agree, but being a gentleman, I didn't wake her to ask.

The sun was already coming up when I arrived at the golf course, so by the time I parked and rummaged through the trunk until I found both golf shoes and a pair of socks that weren't too stiff, the West Coast Duffers were already at the 1st tee, choosing up. Twelve guys and serious bragging rights on the line. The conversation went something like this....

Skip: "Okay. Me and John take on Jim and Pete; Rich and Willie, you're up against Vern and Tommy; Ernie, you and Joe-Joe play Bobby and Big Mike. We're giving two strokes on the front nine, even on the back."

Big Mike: "I don't wanna be with Bobby. He has gas."

Bobby: "I told you that was a medical thing."

Rich: "Since when has frijoles been a disease?"

I rummaged through my bag and found two golf balls, both dented and covered with tree marks. "Anyone got any extra balata balls?" I asked.

Jim: "What? The squirrels ain't happy with your range balls anymore?"

"I think I sliced all my range balls right back into the range the last time we played." I searched the bag again.

Joe-Joe: "I think it should be me and Big Mike. We haven't played together since July."

Big Mike: "That's okay with me, but my back's out a little, so I'll need to shoot from the white tees for it to be fair."

Jim: "Yeah, right. And what about my wrist? I've got carpal tunnel syndrome."

John: "The way you were tossing 'em back last night, it's a wonder you ain't got carpal head syndrome."

Tommy: "How 'bout Pete and me?"

Pete: "No way, Tommy. Ever since you got that Pennzoil cap, you're a psycho with a golf cart."

Tommy: "Well, if you could hit the ball in the same direction twice in a row, we could drive slower and still finish before the moon comes out."

Luckily I found a few balls. I also found half a Snickers bar stuck to my divot tool. "Anyone got any extra tees?" I asked, gnawing on the Snickers. Big Mike threw me half a dozen of his wife's pink tees. They matched my left sock perfectly.

Skip: "Pete, how 'bout you and Vern?"

Pete: "Okay, but Vern's a lefty, and this is a righties' course, so we'll need a couple of strokes."

Vern: "Sounds fair to me. We'll take on Skip and Ernie."

John: "I thought I was with Skip."

Big Mike: "You've been really hot lately, John, you gotta be with Rich."

Rich: "What's that supposed to mean, you shanker? Your handicap is higher than your annual salary."

Skip: "Willie, you and Jim?"

Willie: "I guess so, but no eating in the cart, Jim. The last time, it took me ten minutes to get all the french fries out of my spikes."

Skip: "So. We got John and Rich. You guys are with me and Ernie. That leaves Jim and Willie up with Joe-Joe and Big Mike, and Pete and Vern with Bobby and Tommy. Any other problems?"

"I need a ball marker," I said. Ten ball markers hit me in the head.

Pete: "We got a right-hander's wind going today, too. Vern's gonna need a stroke or two for that."

Tommy: "Why doesn't the poor guy just have an operation and become a normal player?"

Vern: "I'll show you who's normal, Buddy. Let's make the odds straight up."

Pete: "Oh, swell. Who do I make the check out to?"

Jim: "Make a check out to Ernie so he can afford to buy his own stuff next week."

"Hey, you guys. It's not my fault. This isn't my regular bag," I said defensively.

Willie: "No kidding. You borrowed it from me three months ago."

"Oh yeah. I think mine is in the yard somewhere near the mower."

The loudspeaker announced that we were up on the 1st tee.

Skip: "Okay, then we're all set. Now... who's gonna go first?"

An awkward pause ensued as we all looked at each other.

Tommy: "I'm not going first. It's bad luck."

Willie: "I went first last week."

Vern: "Lefties should never go first."

Rich: "I call last."

Jim: "I already called it."

Rich: "No, you didn't."

Jim: "Did too."

Rich: "Did not."
Next week. The lawn. I promise.

~Ernie Witham
Chicken Soup for the Golfer's Soul, The 2nd Round

Tales OF Golf AND Sport

The Sporting Family

*Call it a clan, call it a network, call it a tribe, call it a family. Whatever
you call it, whoever you are, you need one.*
~Jane Howard

What Sports Is All About

Sports is human life in microcosm.
~Howard Cosell

My boy is only three years old, but I know the day will come when he asks me about the birds and the bees. That task, I will graciously leave to my wife, bless her. But in return, I will share with him a few of life's other important lessons.

The conversation might go something like this....

"Dad?"

"Yes, son."

"Why do you like sports so much? I mean, what's it all about for you?"

"That's easy, son. It's about eye-black, stickum and pine tar. It's fourth and goal, first and long, and John 3:16. It's about tapping in a sixteen-foot putt for an eagle on the eighteenth after seventeen holes of triple bogeys. It's about divots, brush-burns, rally caps, the Miracle On Ice, and Lions, and Tigers and Bears (Oh my!).

"It's Goose Gossage, Bear Bryant and Catfish Hunter. Sweaty gym socks, the Boston Red Sox and the penalty box; ballpark franks, checkered flags and if you ain't rubbin', you ain't racin'. It's about sudden death, extra innings and being behind the eight ball; the Green Monster, Wrigley ivy and Yankee pinstripes; goal-line stands, the terrible towel and the Dog Pound. RBIs, FGs, HRs, TDs, FTs and the 7-10 split.

"It's about tying flies, slimy worms, baiting the hook and having fun whether you catch a fish or not.

"It's about '...and down the stretch,' 'Let's get ready to rrrumble,' 'How ya hubba' and 'Holy cow.' Cans of corn, blue darters and playing pepper in the backyard until the sun goes down and you can't see the ball anymore.

"It's about the Music City Miracle (even though the Bills lost), the Immaculate Reception and the Drive.... The Thrilla in Manila, No Mas, and floating like a butterfly and stinging like a bee. It's about Any Given Sunday, The Fish That Stole Pittsburgh, and Rocky I through V (although V wasn't all that good)... mashed-potato mouthpieces, Little League baseball, Pop Warner football, face masks, shin guards, shin pads, the stand-up slide and natural grass... sunflower seeds, chewing gum and Gatorade.

"It's about driving the lane, finding your line and being in the zone; press boxes, dugouts, sidelines and that peanut guy who can hit you between the numbers from twelve rows down and hand you your change before you can open the bag.

"It's about still being in your seat long after the game is over because we were having too much fun to realize the game was over... grand slams, Hail Marys and the suicide squeeze... hearing swoosh before the buzzer, slap shots, wrist shots, sand traps, Ping Pong, aces high and bull's-eyes.

"It's about tailgates, the tale of the tape and knocking a leaner off with a ringer; starting blocks, tackling dummies and spring training. The boys of summer, the rope-a-dope, who's on first, what's on second, and I don't know — third base.

"It's about Go Army, Beat Navy and how kids scream 'car' during street hockey games to let the goalies know they need to move their nets. It's about playing umpteen games of P-I-G and Around the World in the driveway until you finally beat your older brother.

"It's about cutmen who can make Frankenstein's monster look like Christie Brinkley, first basemen who can scoop up a dirt ball like it were rocky road and goalies who guard their nets like Fort Knox.

It's about slumps, streaks and standing Os... the Ice Bowl, the Super Bowl, Lord Stanley's Cup, the Heisman and Touchdown Jesus.

"It's about the smell of your first baseball glove, the feel of your first lucky bat and the sound of your mother cheering at your first football game.

"In short, son, it's about the thrill of victory, the agony of defeat and everything in between.

"But most importantly, it's about passing all this on to your son one day as my dad did to me and I am to you."

~William Wilczewski
Chicken Soup for the Sports Fan's Soul

A Baseball for Dad

Many hot summers ago, when I was in elementary school in California, I fell in love with an idea, a game, a dream. I fell madly in love with baseball.

I soaked in baseball. I threw, hit, ran, read, felt baseball. I would throw without a ball, hit home runs in my head, be a hero, be a bum. I loved it all.

For a while, baseball was bigger than even my dad. I saw that he had a hero. How could my hero have a hero?

My dad's hero was Stan the Man. Stan Musial from Donora, Pennsylvania, who played for the St. Louis Cardinals. At the time, St. Louis was the closest major-league team to Los Angeles. All major-league players were heroes in my eyes, but Dad told me that Stan was the greatest of his time.

There were others who could hit the ball harder, run faster, field better or even put on a better show than Stan the Man. But Dad said that Stan was special.

God had given Stan the tools and he used them well. But that was only a small portion of what made him great. He was all the things that my father valued. He was the embodiment of all that life stood for.

I wanted to be like Dad and I felt that Dad wanted to be like Stan Musial. I knew I couldn't go wrong trying to fit into those shoes.

This particular summer was special because my dad and I were going to the place where my father grew up—St. Louis. Just the two of us. It was hot and humid in what seemed like a foreign land where the people were pale and talked slightly off English.

In California, everything was new. In St. Louis, everything was old. Only the people were young.

Our mission was to meet Stan the Man. I almost didn't believe it. There was a part of me that didn't really think that these idols were real people. To me, they only came to life as legend, like Paul Bunyan or Robin Hood. But the closer I came to the meeting, the more obvious it was that Mr. Musial was a real man. Newspapers said so, all my relatives said so, and most important, Dad reassured me.

Through some good fortune, I got a ball autographed by Musial. An injured rookie was at the hospital where my grandmother worked. She told him my story and he got Stan's autograph on the ball. The ball was living proof that Stan was for real.

That night, the Cardinals were playing the Brooklyn Dodgers and we went. I held onto my ball so tightly that I elicited an inquiry from the guy next to me.

"New ball?" he asked.

"Yep, with an autograph," I teased him.

"Who?" he prodded.

"The Man," I bragged.

"No."

"Yes."

"I don't believe you."

"Here," I handed him the ball.

"Wow! I'll give you $20 for it right now!" Twenty dollars to a ten-year-old boy in 1955 was a pot of gold.

"Nope, let me have it back," I demanded.

"You've got a dream in the form of a baseball," he said. "Take good care of it!"

I shoved it deep into my pocket and resolved that the ball was the most important thing in my life.

The next day was the big day. We would be meeting the Man. As Dad and I walked up the walk to the door, I was in a state of shock. "He'll be here," Dad said, knocking.

Sure enough, the door swung open, and there stood Stan the Man in his robe and slippers. My dad introduced himself then me to Stan, and explained that the ball he had signed earlier was for me.

He was just as I had imagined him: sincere, kind, strong. He looked at me in a way that only a few adults look at kids, and we knew that we had a common bond — baseball.

He inquired about my baseball playing. I bragged. Next to Stan, I felt that it was necessary. I thought that I was some great baseball player. He understood.

Getting back to Los Angeles couldn't happen fast enough. When I told everyone about my experience in St. Louis with Stan Musial, nobody believed me. Such a reality didn't exist, my friends insisted. I knew that it had happened, though, and that the ball, the meeting, the feeling would always be mine. The older I became, the less I revealed my treasure.

The seasons paraded by. Teams won, players got traded. There were retirements, rookies, home runs, other kids and other idols. My father died. As in life, he wished to carry on in death. His last request was that in his casket there be a deck of cards, a bottle of Jack Daniel's and, most important, a baseball. He knew that, wherever he was going, he ought not be ill equipped.

On the day he was buried, the whiskey and the cards were ready. The last item was a baseball. I decided it should be my twenty-year-old autographed treasure.

Since my father had been responsible for me meeting Stan Musial, I felt it most appropriate that it should be with my dad. I would miss it, but it belonged with him. Some people thought that it was a sacrifice. I did my best to assure them that it was not. The ball was where it belonged.

Spring trainings, long hot Julys and thousands of extra innings later, my sister, Kathie, asked me to stand in for Dad at her wedding. I was flattered. I was honored to give my sister away, to stand in the shoes of my dad.

On the eve of my sister's big day, we went to an elegant French restaurant for the rehearsal dinner. As the evening went on, the impact of the occasion seemed to build to an emotional crescendo. The speeches were many. I became aware that something special was happening.

My sister is an airline stewardess and had flown with the Los Angeles Dodgers for part of the 1984 season. After dinner, she thanked my younger brother for his participation in her wedding by giving him a baseball autographed by all of the Dodgers and dedicated to him by Tommy Lasorda.

I was next for a gift.

She told all of us about flying with Lasorda, about how, on the way to spring training, she had told him the story of my Stan Musial baseball.

She said she'd had a difficult time completing the story, stopping again and again to recapture her composure. She said she had been amazed to learn that Tommy Lasorda knew exactly what she meant.

"I'll get that baseball back for you," he told her.

Later during the flight, Lasorda told my sister that he, too, had had a magical relationship with his father, and that when his father had been laid to rest, a baseball accompanied him.

Lasorda told my sister that his life in baseball, his success in baseball and his love of baseball, had all come from his father.

Being a friend of Stan Musial, Lasorda called and told him the story of the baseball. Musial responded with a new autographed baseball and sent it to Lasorda. The ball was then mailed to my sister.

I looked up to see her holding the ball. "I got you another one," she said, throwing it to me.

I was a child again, coming home. I heard the distant crack of bat on ball and the roar of a crowd. I heard that man sitting next to me in St. Louis in 1955. "New ball?" he asked.

"Yep, with an autograph," I teased him.

"Who?" he prodded.

"The Man," I bragged.

"No."

"Yes."

And then: "You've got a dream in the form of a baseball," he said. "Take good care of it!"

And so I will.

~Patrick Thomson
Chicken Soup for the Baseball Fan's Soul

Golf Balls in Heaven

One of the most fascinating things about golf is how it reflects the cycle of life. No matter what you shoot — the next day you have to go back to the first tee and begin all over again and make yourself into something.

~Peter Jacobsen

My dad first taught me how to golf when I was three years old. He was an accomplished golfer and had a room full of trophies to prove it. Unfortunately, I can attest that golf skills aren't always passed on genetically, though it wasn't for lack of trying.

Dad would take me out to the driving range on most Saturdays in my childhood, and he eventually started taking me out on the course with him as well. And while our driving range experiences felt to me like forced practice sessions, the days I spent with him on the course were the ones I looked forward to. Since Dad ran his own business and worked long hours, he didn't have a lot of spare time, so it meant a lot to me when I would have him all to myself out on the course for nine or eighteen holes. So much of the best of our relationship, from the mutual encouragement to sharing the little victories together, was forged on the golf course.

I'll never forget one summer during my junior high school years. Twice a week, Dad would wake me before dawn and we'd head off to Glendover, the local municipal course that my mom had helped save from developers a few years earlier. Those dewy mornings, when we were the first golfers to walk the course together, are things of beauty in my memories of Dad.

Dad died suddenly and unexpectedly of an aneurysm on June 9, 1999. My wife and I had a golf date set with him for the Fourth of July. It was a difficult time for the whole family, but arrangements for the funeral had to be made nevertheless. As we discussed what to do about my dad's final resting place, we weighed several options, including the cemetery outside of town where some of our family members were interred. Just then my mom and sister had the same idea: Wouldn't it be great if Dad was buried in a cemetery close by so we could visit him as often as we wanted? Well, the only place close by that we knew of was a private cemetery that we thought was full.

I called them on a whim the next morning. A delightful woman, whose family had managed the cemetery for years, informed me that contrary to popular belief, they had plenty of space. She went on to tell me of the beautiful mountainside setting, the amazing views, and "Oh, by the way, we're right next to a beautiful golf course." I took it as a sign, and made an appointment for all of us to meet with her the next morning at the cemetery.

The sky was a clear blue as we pulled into the picturesque grounds. We immediately noticed the golf course adjoining the property and the driving range that actually bordered one side of the cemetery. My eyes followed the fifty-foot-high net that protected the grounds as it ran up to the tee area of the range, and I noticed that it was devoid of life on this early weekday morning. As the caretaker reverently guided us through the headstones, we quietly talked about what a beautiful setting this was. What little doubt remained about this being Dad's perfect resting place was erased a moment later. As our guide brought us to a halt in what we later agreed was the most beautiful spot in the cemetery, she gestured to the area she had in mind. And as she pointed to the spot where my dad would spend the rest of his days, a single golf ball fell out of the sky and rolled to a stop. We all looked back up toward the tee area, and seeing it was still empty, knew that Dad had given us his approval.

After the funeral service a couple of days later, our family gathered for a very special and private final farewell. We opened Dad's casket and gave him back the golf ball he had used to let us know he was still with us. We love you, Dad, and hope you're in a place where the fairways are always green and your scores under par.

~Mark Donnelly
Chicken Soup for the Father's Soul

Remember When

"You know, Mom, a person's true character always comes out on the golf course. Since you never played golf, you really didn't know Dad—Pat Gardner, the golfer—now did you?" This was one of the toughest things I'd ever said to my mother. It was a calculated risk I had to take.

My eighty-five-year-old mother glared at me, slowly shaking her head, her stern look signaling me to stop. She wanted no part of this. We—my mother Goldie, sisters Evelyn and Marge, brother Don, and my daughter Jill—were sitting in the Schmitt Funeral Home in WaKeeney, Kansas, putting the final touches on my Dad's funeral, scheduled for the next day. Dad, who had suddenly died of a heart attack, was lying in an open casket about fifteen feet from us.

Because two other funerals were scheduled that weekend, the atmosphere was morbid to say the least. So I decided to lighten things up a bit.

I began telling a story about my dad's crazy antics on our golf course. He had taken up golf late in his life and never quite got the hang of it, playing to a 30-something handicap. "One day, Mom, when we were teenagers," I said, "Dad actually hit a drive in the fairway—it was the first one I'd ever seen. Huh, Don?" Don nodded, grinning, knowing what was coming.

"When we got to where his ball was supposed to be, we couldn't find it, which got Dad all riled up.

'Okay, where is it? I hit it right here!' he barked. Then he stopped dead in his tracks. He had spied his ball about two feet down a ten-inch-wide gopher hole, sitting on a dirt ledge. 'Shut up, you two, and don't move,' he scolded.

"Heck, Mom, we weren't talking or moving. Right, Don?"

"That's right, Mom," said Don, mischievousness dancing in his eyes. Mom narrowed her eyes, still glaring at me.

"Then, Dad got down on his knees and carefully reached for the ball with his 5-iron. Hope soared within him as he hooked the ball with the club face. Holding his breath, he gently lifted the ball upward, hand over hand, delicately holding the club by his thumbs and fingertips. Sweat beads appeared on his forehead. His hands were really shaking now, and he winced each time the ball nearly slipped off the club. It was painstaking work.

"'Keep quiet, you two,' he whispered. 'I've just about got it.' After what seemed like an eternity, he finally pinned the ball near the top of the hole and ever so tenderly reached down with his left hand to retrieve it. Just as his fingers approached the ball, two more balls fell out of his upper shirt pocket and slammed into the first ball, causing all three balls to disappear down the gopher hole, lost forever. Dad flew into a rage. He jumped up, kicked the hole a few times, then beat the hole half to death with his club. Don and I were dying laughing on the ground."

As Mom gave me that dreaded old schoolmarm look that she had perfected in one-room schoolhouses out on the prairie where she had taught for forty years, the family exploded into laughter. My plan was working, the gloom lifting.

Dad had demonstrated a great sense of humor all his life and loved a good belly laugh. I was banking on Mom understanding this, and I was looking for some help from the rest of the family. Just then, Don chimed in.

"Remember the time, Bud, when we were sitting on the bench behind the raised tee box on the third hole, and Dad was getting ready to hit his driver? Now, Mom, I'm not trying to degrade Dad in any way. You know he was a great baseball player, who played a mean first base and hit cleanup for the WaKeeney town team and even played against the great Satchel Paige once. Remember?"

Mom, warming up a bit, nodded at Don.

"Well," continued Don, "standing over his ball that day, he told us he really felt like clobbering a drive. Bud and I glanced at each other but kept quiet as Dad addressed the ball. Then he swung with all his might. He stared down the fairway, yelling at us. 'Did you guys see it? Where in the devil did it go?'

"The truth is, Mom, he had swung so hard he overshot the ball and just nicked it with the heel of his club, causing it to trickle between his feet and slowly meander off the tee box and down the hill behind him. Don and I couldn't hold back. We laughed so hard we fell off the bench into an anthill.

"Seeing our predicament, Dad bellowed, 'Serves you right, you galoots! Now where's my ball?' When he saw it still trickling down the hill, he realized how silly this all was and cracked up, too."

The whole family roared at that one, which brought a brief smile to Mom's face. She quickly regained her serious composure, but we were on a roll and couldn't stop now.

"Another time, Mom," I recalled, "Dad, Don and I played in an out-of-town golf tournament. When Dad's foursome was called to the first tee, Dad pulled the head cover off his wood driver and threw the club to the ground in disgust.

"'What's the matter, Pat?' asked one of his playing partners.

"'Would you look at that?' snapped Dad. 'See all those white marks on the top of my driver. Darn it, my kids have been using my clubs again.'

"His buddies all sympathized as he addressed the ball. Dad made a ferocious swing at the ball—which he had teed up way too high—and whipped the club head right under the ball, sending it straight up into the air. Then things got real serious as everybody scattered when the ball came crashing down in the middle of the tee box, leaving no doubt who had been putting the white marks on that driver."

The twinkle in Mom's eye told me I was doing the right thing.

She had finally realized I was just trying my level best to help us cope with the loss of Dad. We then told a few more golf jokes about Dad, which seemed to lift the spirit of our family at this mournful time. A few minutes later, Don asked Jill and me to accompany him over to Dad's casket. Dad was dressed in his best gray suit with a matching tie. "Bud, take a close look at Dad's tie," urged Don. I couldn't believe it. It matched all right, but the words on it caught my eye. It had "Happy Anniversary," scrawled repeatedly on a diagonal its entire length.

"And watch this," said Don, as he reached for the tie. He pressed a small button on the back of the tie and out jumped a classic song. I couldn't believe it.

"Who chose this tie?" I asked when the last note had faded away.

"Mom did," said Don. "I gave Dad that tie as a joke years ago for one of their anniversaries. I guess Mom was too numb over Dad's passing to know what she had done."

Knowing my dad had a great sense of humor, I believe he would have gotten a big chuckle out of watching this scene unfold. Just then, I heard Mom laughing at something my sisters had said. It was music to my ears.

The next day during Dad's funeral, I was extremely nervous. I had agreed to do Dad's eulogy on behalf of the family. I had done only one other eulogy for a dear friend, which I had mishandled badly. I had lost control and cried throughout my entire presentation. So, I wasn't sure I could pull this one off; after all, it was my Dad's final hour. The family was counting on me. The funeral home was crowded with about seventy-five family members and friends. I was so shook up, I asked my daughter, Jill, to accompany me to the lectern—and to finish reading my prepared statement if I began to cry and lose control. She agreed.

Then it was time. The minister nodded, and Jill and I moved to the pulpit. I thanked everyone for being with us to honor Dad's life and then began to read my statement. About a third of the way through, my voice cracked and tears began streaming down my face. I paused, then started reading again. I choked up again as tears spilled onto my papers. I was about ready to have Jill continue for me when she slipped something into my left hand. I felt an old familiar friend—a golf ball. At that instant, an overwhelming wave of relief washed over me, followed by a serene peace. Just then I understood the depth of Jill's unconditional love for me. I was thankful she had made the long trip from California to Kansas to be with me. That ball—a symbol of joy and love—and Jill's reassuring smile gave me the courage to finish one of my greatest challenges.

~Bud Gardner
Chicken Soup for the Golfer's Soul

A Father and Son's Fall Classic

The everyday kindness of the back roads more than makes up for
the acts of greed in the headlines.
~Charles Kuralt, On the Road with Charles Kuralt

There will be many memorable moments from this year's World Series—moments that baseball fans will talk about for years.

For a father and son who live in Lima, Ohio, though, it will be hard for anything that happened on the playing field to match the World Series moment that unexpectedly came to them.

Don Bruns is forty-three; his son Aaron is ten. Aaron loves baseball, and the Cincinnati Reds in particular. He broke his arm in a bicycle accident last summer, and missed the last part of his Little League season. For a birthday present, his dad decided to take Aaron down to Cincinnati for the first game of the World Series. They had no tickets.

"I was hoping that we could find some scalpers who would sell us tickets," the father said. "I explained to Aaron that there was no guarantee we would get into the game. But just being around a World Series, even if we didn't get in, would be exciting."

So they drove the more than two hours from Lima to Cincinnati—Lima is in the northern part of Ohio, Cincinnati is all the way south. For two more hours they walked the streets—Aaron wearing a Reds cap.

"There were a lot of scalpers, all right," the father said. "I didn't realize how much tickets cost. The cheapest ones we were offered were $175 apiece. The most expensive were $300 apiece. I couldn't do that, and I explained it to Aaron. He understood."

Then, the father said, they were approached by a man who asked if they were going to the game.

"He told me his name, and he told me that he was staying at the Omni Hotel," the father said. "I explained about our trip to Cincinnati, and I said that I couldn't pay what the scalpers were asking.

"He pulled out two tickets. He said that my son reminded him of himself fifteen years ago. He handed me the tickets.

"I asked him how much he wanted. He said there was no charge. He said the tickets were free.

"I thought that maybe this was part of a scam or something. I kept waiting for something tricky to happen. We were waiting for the guy to play us for fools.

"But he just said that he hoped we would enjoy the game, and he left. We went to the stadium. The tickets were wonderful. I had never been to a World Series game, and of course my son hadn't. The World Series! It feels different than any other baseball game. The intensity, the emotional high, the excitement level... and this guy had just handed us the tickets and walked away.

"During the game my son and I must have turned to each other thirty times and said to each other: 'I can't believe this.'"

Here is the story of the man on the street:

His name is Michael Teicher; he works as an account executive for a company called Phoenix Communications Group in South Hackensack, New Jersey. The company markets TV shows about base-ball—the syndicated *This Week in Baseball* and ESPN's *Major League Baseball Magazine*, among others.

Teicher seemed surprised when I tracked him down in Oakland, where he had traveled for the second leg of the World Series. I explained what Don Bruns had told me.

"Here's what happened," Teicher said. "I work for a man named Joe Podesta. He hadn't missed a World Series in sixteen years. A month ago, though, he had a mild heart attack, and he's not at the Series this year.

"I guess like a lot of people who have heart attacks, he felt some kind of new appreciation for the preciousness of life. He told me that he wanted to make some people happy. So he told me that when I was at the World Series I should take two tickets and give them to people I thought would be thrilled by going to the game. That's the only ground rule he gave me—give the tickets to people I thought would be thrilled."

Teicher walked around town for some time before seeing Don and Aaron Bruns.

"I had seen a lot of people on the street who I thought might just take the tickets and sell them," Teicher said. "This guy and his son, though—the father was carrying a sign that said 'I Need Two Tickets.' His son was this nice-looking, skinny kid with glasses, and he looked very disappointed.

"I followed them and I heard the father telling the son about how much the scalpers wanted for tickets. I heard the father say they wouldn't be going to the game.

"I looked at them and they reminded me of my dad and me when I was a kid. I would have died to go to a World Series game with my father. But I never did.

"So I went up and I gave them the tickets and I told them to enjoy themselves."

Because of his work, Teicher has begun to regard going to World Series games as almost routine. "I go to all of them," he said. "That makes you forget how important going to the World Series can be."

How important was it to Don Bruns and his son? Here is what Bruns said: "This is the most memorable thing that has ever happened to us. My boy and I will never forget that night."

After Michael Teicher had handed the tickets to the father and son, he watched them walking together toward the stadium.

"The little boy," he said, "it was like all of a sudden he had a bounce in his step."

~Bob Greene
Chicken Soup for the Baseball Fan's Soul

The Ace Man

Luck is when opportunity knocks and you answer.
~Author Unknown

I consider myself an incredibly lucky man, possessed of a wonderful, interesting and eclectic life. I have a remarkable wife and life partner, Ewa, a fantastic and truly unique step-daughter, Nikki, a wonderful twin and mother, and, thanks to a truly mystical golfing adventure, a magical dog that enhances all of our lives.

The Charlotte Golf Links is an expertly crafted layout carved from the rolling farmland outside Charlotte, North Carolina. It has often been the scene of peaceful late afternoon walks, one of the few courses where you can still walk nine holes at dusk. That, as well as its obvious ties to the traditional roots of the game, has made it a place where we sometimes can feel a connection to the deeper, more spiritual side of things. We were, however, unprepared for what was to happen one eventful morning.

On a clear, beautiful Thursday, Ewa (who shares most everything in my life, including a passion for golf) and I had an early tee time. I felt completely at ease warming up, and had, surprisingly, become aware of and was able to repeat a simple swing thought that was allowing me to hit the ball better than I had in quite a while. I hoped the thought would stay with me.

The course was serenely uncrowded, rare nowadays, especially on such a gorgeous golfing day. We began the round in a relaxed and unhurried mood, both grateful, as we often are, for the kind of lives that allow us to be out on the course together.

I was +1 after six holes (not bad for a 10 handicap), and Ewa and I were laughing as we went to the seventh hole, a long, uphill par-3 whose tee is surrounded by tall, heather-like grasses, waving in the breeze. As we turned to approach the tee, we cleared the tall grass, and there, standing at the tee, was a small dog staring straight at us. We all seemed to pause for a second, and then, being unabashed dog lovers, Ewa and I said hello to this funny, playful, reddish-coated pup. A mixture of long-haired dachshund and something resembling a fox (with no tail), he rolled around on the tee, licked us a few times and stood watching as we hit away.

We said, "See ya later," and proceeded up to the green. Before we got there, our little friend ran up to the green and picked up my ball in his mouth, looking child-like and full of mischief. After we stopped laughing, Ewa and I bogeyed the hole, but before we could leave the green, there he was again, this time with his head entirely in the cup, looking, no doubt, for the deeper meaning of the game.

We proceeded to the next tee, followed of course by you-know-who, who jumped into our cart (sadly you must ride early in the day) and climbed into Ewa's lap. The eighth is a dogleg left (of course) par-5, and I snap-hooked my drive into the trees lining the fairway left, feeling my score slipping away a bit. I heard no contact with wood, so I presumed my drive was out of bounds. I re-teed and hit a provisional ball, trying not to think too much about losing a good round's score. On returning to the cart, I found our new friend asleep in my wife's lap, and chuckled at this strange new golfing partner.

After Ewa hit her tee shot, we drove out to the fairway, and lo and behold, about two hundred yards out, dead in the middle, was my first tee ball. Incredible, I thought, and turned to Ewa and said, "It has to be the pup. He's lucky. That ball never touched a tree." I proceeded to hit a flush 3-wood, then a really crisp 8-iron to about three feet, and made the putt for birdie. Back to +1, and really laughing now.

The ninth hole is an uphill par-3 that was playing 167 yards that day. I took a look at the still-asleep, gentle face of my good-luck charm and suddenly was reminded of the swing key I had used earlier in the round. I hit a pure 5-iron at the flag, the bottom of which was hidden by the elevated green. I watched the ball in flight, and, as we are wont to do after a feel-good strike on a par-3, yelled "Go in the hole," or some such brilliantly worded phrase. As I walked back to the cart, Ewa remarked on the seeming ease of my play that day, and we both looked again at the dog. I said, "If the ball is in the hole, we're keeping the dog."

Ewa hit her tee shot, and as we approached the green, there was only one ball visible. Still in a playful mood, I asked Ewa to go pick my ball out of the hole, and I sat with a now wide-awake, furry-faced pooch staring at me. I looked up in time to see Ewa jumping up and down, a beaming smile on her face, saying, "Yes, yes, yes...." I ran up to the green, followed by, you-guessed-it, and, somewhat in shock, picked the ball out of the hole, the first time in eighteen years I ever had that privilege.

It wasn't much of a choice after that. His name is, naturally, Ace, and along with our other two, Stella and Raquette, he is now an integral part of our home and lives, and is, I think, a symbol of all the reasons that golf is the greatest game—he gives us joy and constant surprise. Although he is often frustrating and difficult, when we pay attention and allow him to teach us, he rewards us with unending gifts.

~Mitch Laurance
Chicken Soup for the Golfer's Soul

19

The Pitcher

Love is the most important thing in the world, but baseball is pretty good too.
~Greg, age 8

My father was always "permanent pitcher" in our backyard baseball games when I was growing up.

He got this special honor in part because no one else could pitch well enough to get the ball over home plate. If we had any hope of moving a game along at a fair pace, we needed him to do the pitching.

But he also pitched because, with one wooden leg courtesy of Adolf Hitler, he didn't do too well in the field. Running after a fly ball that got hit into the cornfield out back just wasn't his strong suit.

And so he stood under the hot sun throwing endless numbers of pitches to my sister, brother and me, while we took our turns at bat and in the field.

I never questioned the rightness of it.

"Fathers pitch," was a fact of life I'd internalized without giving it any real thought. When I'd play ball in other children's backyards, it always seemed odd to me that their fathers played the outfield and ran the bases. It was somehow childish, the way fathers were sprinting around out there.

Fathers pitched.

He ran our games with the authority of a Yankees team manager. He was boss of the field, and there were requirements if we wanted to play. We had to chatter in the outfield. I must have said, "Nobatternobatternobatterno-batter," 5,000 times growing up.

We had to stand properly, too, both in the field and at bat. And we always had to try to outrun the ball, no matter how futile it might seem. This was baseball, by God, and there was only one way to play it. The way the Yankees played it.

Going up to bat against my father was not exactly like playing T-ball. None of this self-esteem stuff for him, trying to make kids feel good about hitting a ball that's standing still.

It was perfectly fine with him if he struck me out, and he did it all the time. He never felt sorry about it at all.

"Do you want to play ball, or don't you?" he'd ask, if I began whining about his fast pitches.

I wanted to. And when I'd finally connect with one of his pitches—oh, man—I knew I deserved the hit. I could tell by the feel of it. And I'd be grinning all the way down the first-base line.

Then I'd turn around to look at my father standing on the pitcher's mound. I'd watch as he took off his glove and tucked it under his arm. And then he'd clap for me.

To my ears, it sounded like a standing ovation at Yankee Stadium.

Years later, my boy was to learn those same rules about baseball from my father.

"Grandfathers pitch," was his understanding. By then, though, his grandfather was pitching from a wheelchair. By some medical fluke, my father had lost his other leg sometime between my childhood and my son's.

But nothing else had changed. My boy was required to chatter from the outfield. He had to stand properly at bat and in the field. He had to try outrunning the ball, no matter how futile it might have seemed.

And when he whined that the ball was coming at him too fast—my father could still get steam behind it, even sitting in a wheelchair—he got the ultimatum: "Do you want to play ball or don't you?"

He did.

My boy was nine years old the spring before his grandfather died. They played a lot of ball that season, and there was the usual litany of complaints about my father pitching too hard.

"Just keep your eye on the ball!" my father would holler at him.

Finally, at one at-bat, he did.

He swung the bat around and connected with the ball dead center. Then the ball headed back out where it'd come from, straight down the middle. Straight and hard at my father.

He reached for it, but it got past him. And in the process, his wheelchair tilted backward. In ever such slow motion, we watched him and his chair topple until he came down on his back with a thud.

My boy stood stock still halfway to first.

"You don't ever stop running!" my father roared at him from the ground. "That ball's still in play! You run!"

And when my boy stood safe at first base, he turned to look at my father lying on his back on the pitcher's mound. He saw him take off his glove and tuck it under his arm.

And then he heard his grandfather clap for him.

~Beth Mullally
A 5th Portion of Chicken Soup for the Soul

20

The Miracle Ball

There is no shortage of testimony to the power and magic of the Titleist golf ball, which is far and away the number-one choice on the PGA Tour. As guys like Phil Mickelson, Davis Love and Ernie Els relate in a current television commercial, the Titleist was present for all their special tournament moments.

None of their Titleist success stories, however, is as heartwarming as that of young Samuel Rachal. Sam would qualify as Titleist's youngest spokesman, except for the fact that at less than six months old he's still pretty much into baby babble.

So we'll tell the story for him.

Born five weeks premature on March 15, 2001, to a couple of Port Arthur, Texas, natives—Tom and Denise Rachal, who now live in Dallas, Texas—Sam started life with what in golf terminology would be an unplayable lie. His heart arteries were crossed, meaning he would need something called an arterial switch to survive.

The surgery proved successful, but Sam's handicap was a heart so weak that he had to be put on a heart-lung machine. Then a kidney problem developed. Much agonizing followed for Tom, the son of Pat and Mary Helen Rachal, and Denise, the daughter of Sam and Billie Jo Henry.

Baby Sam, though, was not about to WD from this high-stakes game to which he'd just been introduced. Helped along by faith, prayer, hope and a Titleist 1 that remained in his bed throughout the entire ordeal, he overcame the life-threatening obstacles in his path and is expected to live a normal life.

Now about that Titleist 1.

Tom, an avid golfer, had spotted the ball in his car on the way to the hospital for Sam's delivery and thought he would stick it in his pocket for a good luck charm. Later, on a whim, he put the ball in Sam's bed at the hospital.

For the next eight weeks, while Sam was transferred from Presbyterian Hospital to the Children's Medical Center of Dallas, the Titleist 1 was his constant companion. Day after day, week after week, as he battled through a series of hazards tougher than Pete Dye could conceive, the Titleist 1 was always there.

"It's hard to explain but that golf ball kind of became a focal point for everybody," says Tom. "The doctors and nurses would always look for that ball when they came into his room. The ball was just sort of a symbol of hope."

Now that Sam is home, healthy and happy, the Titleist 1 sits on Tom's desk as a constant reminder to him and Denise of what they went through. One of these days, if Sam desires to give golf a try, Tom has already decided it will be the first ball he hits.

But it certainly won't be the last Titleist at his disposal.

Thanks to George Sine Jr., Titleist's vice president of golf ball marketing and strategic planning, Sam is well stocked. After receiving a letter from Tom relating how the Titleist 1 proved to be a positive symbol during his son's crisis, Sine responded with a heartfelt letter, 144 Titleist 1 balls personalized with Sam's name and birthdate, and a pair of baby FootJoys.

"It was really a nice touch on his part," Tom says of Sine's letter. "We were so surprised when that care package arrived."

Sine, a father of four young children, was obviously touched by the story about Sam. He wrote, in part, "While I am confident that it was your faith, prayer and hope that resulted in Sam's wellness, not to mention a dedicated medical team, the fact that a single Titleist 1 was along for the journey is indeed a proud moment for the brand.

"The round which you have described is unparalleled by any

major championship, coveted trophy or record score, as it was not a game of honor but rather a game of life at stake... So that you may permanently enshrine the now famous Titleist 1 which accompanied Sam on his journey, I am enclosing a supply of new No. 1s.

"The enclosed are personally imprinted for that first occasion when you and Sam approach your first tee box, place the tee in the ground and cherish what is certain to be your first of many father-and-son moments sharing not merely a game but rather a milestone together that will not be forgotten."

Sounds like Titleist needs to get baby Sam and his dad under contract for what could be a powerful TV spot.

~Bob West
Chicken Soup for the Golfer's Soul, The 2nd Round

21

Dad's Magic Clubs

My father died last month. He was eighty-six, in poor health, and his passing was not unexpected. His funeral was marked by an outpouring of affection and accolades. If novenas, Masses and prayers mean anything, then Dad is already a consultant to St. Peter. Ironically, this outpouring of adoration was not fully appreciated by his children.

My father was a medical doctor, and by all accounts, a good one. His specialty was bringing babies into the world, and he loved it. He came from a generation that believed that the doctor an expectant mother saw throughout her pregnancy was the one who should be there at the birth. Many a seashore excursion, vacation or special occasion was delayed, curtailed or postponed because Mrs. So-and-so's baby was due at any moment.

I was always amazed by how many parents named their sons Joseph, after my father. Patients loved him. He had a way of making each individual feel like the most important person in the world. He was also a man of the people outside the office and hospital. His Irish heritage, of which he was immensely proud, his love of poetry and his sense of humor made him a sought-after speaker for public and private affairs. In short, he was a charming man. Unfortunately, his children believed that wherever he parked his car each night was the same place he parked his charm.

Dad was a strict and demanding parent. He was the oldest of five in hard economic times, and his childhood was purposeful, tough and short. In turn, he expected his children to think and act like adults. Our dinner table was not always a happy place.

Having said that, it was my father who introduced me to golf. In the late 1940s and early 1950s, sports to a male teen meant baseball, football and basketball. I did not know another teenager who played golf. My friend, Frank Costello, and I were recruited to caddie for Dad and his friends. The bags were heavy, the pay pitiful, and we were expected to find balls in places where no golf ball—much less human—should go. Frank and I soon discovered it was good sense to have something else planned for Wednesdays and Saturdays.

As a caddie, I learned about the quality of golf scores. I knew that anybody who could regularly break 100 was a good golfer. And if they could score in the 80s, they were great golfers. It never dawned on me that an amateur could shoot in the 70s.

Then my father joined a golf club—Upper Montclair Country Club, a quality 27-hole layout a dozen miles west of New York City. We had a family membership, and I was encouraged to play. I did so only as an activity of last resort. I usually played by myself and only nine holes. I rarely broke 50 and only did so with the help of mulligans, generous gimmes and a few should-have-beens.

Playing with my father made Latin seem easy. From him, I learned almost nothing about how to play golf, but everything about the game of golf. My first lesson was in the proper pace of golf. Slow play was sinful. To this day,

I am uncomfortable when groups behind us have to wait, even when we are not at fault.

A golfer never steps to the tee without at least two balls in his pocket. If you need to hit a second ball, it is bad manners to make everyone wait while you return to your bag. Dad was a stickler for preparation. Have enough tees and know where your ball marker is. He would be appalled at the condition of my sons' golf shoes. His were always clean and shining. I suspect, at age sixty-three, I am one of the few left who regularly take polish and brush to their golf shoes.

He disdained practice swings, and his view on winter rules was simple: They are for cheats. Through the years I have played with generals, admirals and politicians, many of whom can give great speeches on honor, duty and country but think nothing of moving the ball all over the course.

Dad was scrupulous about the accuracy of his scores. In later years, when he knew his memory was failing, he would ask his fellow golfers to help him keep track. To Dad, the difference between a seven and an eight was important. I learned that some of the most boring people in the world are those who have to relive every shot after the round. Dad said, "What was done was done, and since most golfers dwell on their bad shots, who cares?"

Dad always had a bet, if only a modest one, but to him competition and survival were synonymous. All of this I learned about golf long before I could play it.

After graduating from college, I went off to a career in the Air Force. Early on, I caught the golf bug, and thanks to Uncle Sam, I had the opportunity to play around the world and throughout the United States. Thanks to Dad, there was never a doubt about how to play the game. As my handicap drifted in the low teens, I put into practice every one of my father's rules of golf. During those years, I rarely played with Dad. Until my last assignment, we were never closer than one thousand miles, and often our trips home to New Jersey were not compatible with golf weather.

At thirty-eight, I gave up golf for nine years. My wife and I were blessed with seven healthy, active children, and their many activities left little room for golf. When, on his own, my oldest son Michael took up the game, I was lured to golf again. This time the bug hit hard. In 1984, I bought my first semi-custom-fit clubs—Ping woods and Ping Eye Two irons, the blue dot model. New clubs, a back operation and the resultant compact swing brought new vigor to my game and handicap. It also brought a return to playing golf with my father.

Residing in Virginia, I was able to make regular trips north to New Jersey. Dad was now in his mid-seventies and his golf game weak. In his prime, he was thrilled to break 100 and broke 90 only once in his life. But his zest for the game never diminished. We always played for a bet, but his 36 handicap drew a surplus of strokes and he always won. And despite the quality of my handicap, by now a 5, I never played Upper Montclair at my best. Losing to my father I accepted, but Upper Montclair was something else. No matter how well I played, I could not break 80. Shooting 80 or 81 was easy, but I could not get through the barrier.

In late summer of 1991, I headed north to play what turned out to be my last rounds at UMCC. On that glorious weekend I shot 76 and 74. I was pleased beyond measure, but what surprised me the most was the great pleasure my father took in my accomplishment. At age eighty, he made more of a to-do about it than I ever could.

For me, that weekend was the culmination of a forty-year golf odyssey—from a disinterested teenager to a competent amateur golfer. Shortly thereafter, my father fully retired from his medical practice and moved to Hilton Head, South Carolina. We played a number of times at his Moss Creek course, but because of his declining health, we could never relive the magic of that day at Upper Montclair. Through the years, I have come to realize that my father had an appreciation and love for golf that few ever realize.

To him, golf was not just playing eighteen holes; it was the whole experience: the preparation, the wager, the good holes and the bad, the occasional par, the traditional cold potato soup and beer afterward, the discussion of world events, the hot shower and clean clothes. All were integral parts of a golf day, with each segment to be enjoyed to its fullest. The score was important, but only briefly and a small part of the picture.

After that weekend in 1991, my game continued to improve. By late 1992, I was taking myself seriously. Modest success in several one-day senior events led me to believe my golden years would be spent collecting golf prizes.

And then I got greedy. Deciding that my 5 handicap needed to be further lowered, I fell prey to modern technology. Never mind that with my trusty Pings I was playing the best golf of my fifty-eight years. I needed to do better. I gave my clubs to my son John, who is now playing the best golf of his life.

Technology has done wonders for me. Five years and five sets of clubs left me with a 14 handicap and a mechanical hack of a swing.

And then my father died. After the funeral, I remained in Hilton Head for a few days to help Dad's wife settle his affairs. Our mother had died suddenly many years ago, and we had come to love Dad's second wife, Louise, dearly. She offered the love and care that few men receive once in a lifetime, much less twice.

One of my tasks was to do something with Dad's golf equipment. He had a garage full of odds and ends, unopened catalog-company packages containing "magic" putters and wedges. At age eighty-five, Dad was still looking for that par-saving club. All of those were given to junior golf, with one exception: Dad's final and little-used set of irons were Ping Eye Twos, the blue dot model.

I took them back to Virginia, having no idea what I would do with them. Shortly after my return, I participated in a local three-day tournament. My play was indifferent, and I failed to make the third-day cut.

During the ensuing week, discouraged with golf, I played with my father's clubs. What happened was mystical. In an eleven-day period I shot 76, 75, 73, 75, 74 and 75. Conventional wisdom says there is no way an honest 14 handicap can play that kind of golf. The next few rounds were not as impressive, but there is no doubt my game has taken an amazing turn. My handicap is plunging, and my swing is easier and more fluid than it has been in years.

Golf is fun again. Why? I only have a clue. For his entire life, my father was considered the consummate charmer. In his lifetime, I received little of that charm. In his clubs, he gave me my share.

~John Keating
Chicken Soup for the Golfer's Soul

Creating a Dynasty of Values

Weave in faith and God will find the thread.
~Author Unknown

When I was born, Mother and Daddy lived with my grandmother and granddaddy. There were three brothers and four sisters all living in the same rural house with no running water or electricity. We had twelve or fourteen people living beside the shop. We were poor, but we didn't know it because all the neighbors were the same way.

My little brother, Maurice, and I were always getting into scrapes with each other. I've got scars all over my head, and he has scars all over his. Our social lives were completely different, but when we were at home we played together and worked together.

I played football and basketball in high school. Most of the guys who played ball stayed after school for practice and games, then went home to plow a field or milk a cow or something. I'd go home and work on a race car.

My dad was pretty stern with us, but he could be very compassionate. In business dealings, he didn't have contracts. He gave his word and made sure he got it done; it didn't make a difference how much of a hardship it was on him. He taught us that you are responsible for what you say and for what you do.

Mother was a peacemaker. She tried to keep the home fires

burning while Dad was out racing or doing other things, and she got us off to church every Sunday morning.

Daddy was always a mechanic. He had a bunch of trucks and hauled anything for anybody. He did a little truck farming, too, with a few things he raised. In 1949, when the NASCAR Winston Cup Series first started, he got his first race car—a '37 Plymouth with a straight 8 Buick motor in it. People came from Daytona, Atlanta and all around to race. It was big money even back then. Dad read in the paper that Bill France was having a race in Charlotte. Dad hung out at a service station on the south side of Greensboro with some of his buddies. One of them had a '47 or '48 Buick. It ran really fast on the road. Dad and his brother talked the guy into borrowing the thing so we could race it in Charlotte.

We drove that car over to Charlotte and pulled into a Texaco station, put it on a lift, changed the oil, greased it and got ready to race. That's all there was at the time to make a race car. Dad got about halfway through the race when the sway bar broke. The thing turned over with them, tearing off all four doors. We had to thumb a ride back with my uncle to get home. Even after all that, my dad said, "You know, I think I might like this racin'." He went out and bought the smallest car he could, which was a 1949 Plymouth Coupe. It didn't even have a back seat. I think it went for $890 and they could win $1,500, so it was a great deal.

I don't think that Mother thought a lot about what Daddy did when he sold his truck and trucking business and stopped farming the land. He said, "Okay, we're goin' in the racin' business." This was a new venture, and he didn't know if it was going to work. The first year they only ran about eight races, but he had made the commitment. He was probably the first one to say, "I can make a living out of this if I watch what I do." It was a family business from the beginning. We didn't have help, and Daddy did all the work. As long as we got enough money racing on Sunday to get back to the race the next week, he was happy. When we first started racing, he was not that fast. He figured out that there were 200 laps, and he wanted to make it to the end of the 200 laps. If he led for 195 laps and then fell out, he wouldn't make it back to race the next week. They called him "Mr. Consistency." He might not win first, but he wound up winning more races than anybody at that time. He was always second, third or fourth. He won enough money to get us something to eat so that we could go to the next race.

I started working on the cars when I was about eleven years old. I wasn't really interested in driving them. I graduated high school and went to King's Business College in Greensboro. I took an eight-month business course, but it took me two years to get though it. I went four months during winter, and then when the '57 season started I came back and started working on the race car. Even when I went to school, I'd go during the day and work on the car at night. When we had to start going to the races, I couldn't go to school at all.

When I turned eighteen, I went in one day and said, "Okay, Dad, I want to drive a race car." He said, "You're too young." I told him, "Buddy Baker's driving." But he said it didn't make a difference. He told me I couldn't race until I was twenty-one. "You'll do a lot of growing up between the years of eighteen and twenty-one," he said, and he was right. I got out into the world and experienced a lot more during those years.

I walked in one day and said, "Okay, I'm twenty-one." He said, "There's a car over in the corner. Get it ready." It was a convertible. Dale Inman, Red Myler and I loaded it up and headed for Columbia, South Carolina. I had never been in a race in my life, but they threw me right out there and away I went. It took me a long time to learn to drive, but we finally brought in a winner.

I met Linda early in my racing career. We dated a couple of years, but I was out of town a lot. One night I told her, "You know I love you, and if we are ever thinking about getting married, we need to do it now because I'm not going to have time later." She said, "Okay." We went to South Carolina and got married one night. When we came home she didn't tell anybody besides her parents that we were married; not even my parents knew. It took about three months for me to get up the money to buy her a ring. After I gave her the ring, she told everybody.

A little over a year later, we were living with Mother and Daddy when Kyle was born in the same house that I was born in. Linda and I saved up some money and bought a mobile home and put it in their front yard. Within twelve months, our daughter, Sharon, came along, and that place seemed to get even smaller. We didn't have air conditioning in the trailer, but we had a '60s Chrysler with air conditioning. We'd eat supper, put the kids in the car, and go out and ride around until they went to sleep. Then we'd come home and put them in bed.

When I was home, we did things together, like playing ball or taking them to the movies. When I was on the road, Linda took care of things. In the summertime, we took the family with us everywhere. I had one of the children in each hand, and Linda would have the third one along with the diaper bags. We put the little ones in the back seat, and we went because that was our family. We just did it the way my mother and daddy did it.

I was fortunate to be with NASCAR Winston Cup racing as it was growing. We were driving an offbeat car—a Plymouth. We won twenty-seven races in one year, and people screamed for us to win more. Right at the time that my career was taking off, Dad's was winding down. He won the championship in '58 and '59. He was third or fourth in the points standing in '60, and then I think he won only one race in '61; then he got hurt at Daytona, and that was basically the end of his career. He and Johnny Beauchamp got together right at the end of a 100-mile race, and they went through the fence and turned the car over, demolishing everything. They carried him off to the hospital with a punctured lung, a torn-up knee and a broken leg. A bunch of people came in to donate blood. For two or three days he laid there, and they just tried to keep him alive. I went in, and he said, "Come here." I leaned over. "You and Maurice go on home and go up to Greensboro and buy another car. Mother and me will be home about Friday." He was home on Friday—about four months later. That's how badly he was hurt, but he was ready to go. "Let's go racin' again."

I've had some bad wrecks and been beaten up pretty badly, but if I can wake up and see the ceiling, I know that it's okay. After some of the wrecks, I could remember everything that happened, and with others, I could only remember part of it. I think that the good Lord has got a little mechanism in us that, when you get close to death, causes you not to remember. It seems like he blocks that out of your memory so that you don't wake up in the middle of the night screaming with the terror of it. The big wreck at Daytona in '88 was spectacular. But I felt like a guardian angel said, "This is going to be a bad wreck," then took me out of the car, turned it over and then stuck me back in. I know this has happened more than once because I've seen some of the wrecks and I say, "No way are you going to get out of there without getting hurt." I'm usually conscious of what's going on, and most of the time I can get out of the car by myself. At Daytona I remember the doctor coming to the side of the car and asking, "Are you okay?" I said, "Yeah, I'm okay. I just can't see anything." I was blinded for probably five minutes, but the doctor said my sight would come back, and it did. It wasn't until after I had seen the films of the accident that I knew that the car had turned over.

Linda came to the hospital, and I could tell she had been crying. Once she knew everything was fine, though, she was mad. She had gotten over the hurt part and moved on to anger. All the times we talked about racing and accidents that happened, we had reached an agreement. I always told her, "When we are not having fun anymore, I'm not going to do this." She came in there gritting her teeth and said, "Are we having fun?" Everybody just broke up laughing, and any hurting I had just went away.

It hurts a lot more to see someone you love hurt than to be hurt yourself. When Kyle was hurt in Talledaga, Linda and I went in to see him. I felt like we were hurting even worse than he was, and we couldn't help but wonder who was to blame.

After Kyle's son Adam was killed in the accident, we got hundreds and hundreds of letters from fans. One lady wrote, "Never put a question mark where God has put a period." I settled right down after I heard that. I said, "Okay, I'm not going to question anymore." We have to go forward with our lives.

One thing I've never questioned is who's responsible for my making it in this business. The racetracks have never paid Richard Petty a penny; the sponsors have never paid me anything. If it weren't for the fans, I wouldn't be out there in the first place. After my first race I signed one autograph; my second race I signed two. I have always looked at the fans as the guys who were paying the bills. Every time I sign an autograph, it's like saying, "Thank you for letting me do what I want to do and make a living out of it."

I thank God for my family.

I thank God for my fans.

~Richard Petty
Chicken Soup for the NASCAR Soul

23

A Measure of Love

Even as an adult I find it difficult to sleep on Christmas Eve.
Yuletide excitement is a potent caffeine, no matter your age.
~Carrie Latet

It was the afternoon of Christmas Eve, and I had just finished wrapping the last gift for my family when Greg, my sixteen-year-old son, came into the bedroom after returning from shopping with his dad.

"Mom, you are not going to believe what Dad got you for Christmas!" he announced. "It's a gift that shows how much he loves you."

My mind immediately envisioned a diamond ring or gorgeous tennis bracelet. Without giving away my idea of a "love" gift, I responded with the question, "Do you think I got Dad enough for Christmas?"

After a few moments of thoughtful consideration, Greg answered, "Gosh, Mom, I don't know. You might want to run down to the hardware store and buy him that tool chest he's been wanting. It's going to be hard to match what he got you though."

With a teaser like that, I found it as difficult to sleep on Christmas Eve as I had when I was a kid. Visions of rings and bracelets danced in my head and I was the first one up in the morning. I eagerly gathered Greg, my other son Jeff, and my husband Randy for the ritual of opening gifts. As each one took his turn opening, we oohed and aahed over the selections each had made to show our love. I opted to open my gifts last, saving the moment when I would see the gift that would be the measure of my husband's love.

Finally, it was my turn. The first gift I opened was a blender. Next, I opened a set of pots and pans. I took each one out of the box and carefully looked inside them, on the handles, and even in the packing for anything that resembled a piece of jewelry. My next gift was some cologne, my favorite kind. Still, I didn't see any evidence of the spectacular gift for which I had been preparing myself to be surprised and overwhelmed. My last gift from my husband was a pretty gold nightgown and robe (in the wrong size).

Hiding my disappointment, I good-naturedly thanked Randy for the gifts and planted a big kiss on his lips. Mentally, I was trying to determine which gift in a sixteen-year-old's mind had deserved the assessment that it showed how much he loved me. I decided probably the pots and pans!

We started to clean up the mountain of wrapping paper, bows and boxes. Randy came up behind me as I was stuffing them into the trash bag, put his arms around my waist and navigated me into the living room where we had another Christmas tree. My deflated spirits took wing, and I fully expected to find the ring or bracelet decorating one of the branches. Instead, he took me over to the tree and pointed behind it, where I saw a golf bag filled with shiny, new clubs.

My face fell as I tried to figure out how a new set of golf clubs for Randy was going to show how much he loved me. I already knew how much he loved golf, so he certainly didn't need to convince me on that point.

My boys said in unison, "She doesn't like them, Dad."

Randy, so secure in his choice, calmly reassured the boys, "Don't worry, guys. I knew she'd react like this. It's just going to take some time for her to learn the game and enjoy it like I do!"

"They're not yours?" I dumbly questioned. "They're for me?" I was now becoming indignant. "I can't believe that you think I would want to play golf alone!" Randy, an excellent golfer who consistently shoots in the 70s and always attracts a gallery of spectators even on the driving range, had often expressed his frustrations with women golfers who slowed the play down because they weren't very good. I, a woman with no athletic ability, had only swung a club once or twice. With a giant stretch of the imagination, I would not even fit into the category of "not very good."

Randy, undaunted by my less-than-enthusiastic reaction, said, "I thought this would be something we could do together. When the boys and I go out, we could have a foursome, and I know you'll grow to love the game like we do."

"You're serious, aren't you?" I asked incredulously. Things were starting to make sense. To take me on the golf course was a true measure of love to Randy. To allow me, a woman who was totally incompetent at golf, to play with him really was a sign of how much he loved me. And in the months that followed, his patience and perseverance in taking me to the driving range and enrolling me in lessons had proved that his gift was a gift of love and not a mere whimsy or desperate last-minute purchase for Christmas.

Because we are both teachers, we spend our summers at the beach in San Clemente, California, camping and now going to the golf course. With our sons grown and busy with their own lives, we have something that we can share as a couple that will keep us active and young. Randy still loves to play competitive golf and he is awesome, but he takes the time and patience to help and encourage me and keep me motivated to participate in what I have found to be a very challenging and alluring activity.

Greg, the sixteen-year-old who prepared me for the gift of love seven years ago on Christmas Eve, married recently. I gave him a little womanly advice on gift giving to take with him into his marriage. I looked him in the eyes and said, "Son, when you want to show Sarah how much you love her, go for the bracelet or the diamond ring in the first five years. Save the golf clubs for later when she can fully appreciate how much love that kind of a gift shows."

~Judy Walker
Chicken Soup for the Golfer's Soul

24

Best Seats in the House

We are inclined that if we watch a football game or baseball game,
we have taken part in it.
~John F. Kennedy

The best thing I ever bought was the season ticket. Actually, it was three season tickets.

I was thirteen years old at the time and a rabid fan of the New York football Giants. They were called the football Giants in those days to distinguish them from the baseball Giants, who had just moved to San Francisco.

How does a little thirteen-year-old boy gather enough spare change to spring for three season tickets? With his wits.

My bar mitzvah was looming, and everyone in my rather large family was calling and asking what I wanted for my present. I knew exactly what I wanted, but I also knew that no one was going to give it to me. So I proposed the following deal to my father: I would buy as many season tickets as I could with whatever money I got as bar mitzvah gifts if he would promise to renew the tickets every year until I was old enough to hold down a job. My father agreed. After all, he was a Giants fan, too. Then I told everyone in the family that I wanted cash.

When the big day was over and I totaled up the take, it came to three season tickets and about fifteen dollars left over. I half expected my father to make up the difference and purchase a fourth ticket to sort of round things out, but he didn't. A deal's a deal, I guess, and I suppose he thought he was teaching me something. Anyway, when the 1958 season came around, we had three seats in the upper deck on the five-yard line at the closed end of Yankee Stadium.

That was the year the Giants played the famous overtime championship game against the Baltimore Colts, the first sudden death in NFL history. Professional football exploded after that, and suddenly all the big-shot lawyers and account execs wanted tickets. But they couldn't get them anymore. The Giants were sold out, and season tickets would now become something like heirlooms, to be passed down from father to son. And I had three. Well, we had three.

For the first several years, the threesome was always me and my father and my best friend Richie, and then my best friend Bob, and then my best friend Philly, and then my best friend Richie again. But always, it was my father and I.

We wore Giants-blue sweaters before people sold such things. Grandma knitted them for us. We were boosters, my father and I, yelling ourselves hoarse on days at the stadium. I don't know if those were cold years or if I was just underdressed, but I remember shivering through those winter games even with the sweater. We tried everything. Hot coffee. Wool blankets. A can of Sterno burning at our feet. I had my first nip of brandy from a flask. I loved those games with my dad.

Then the war came—Vietnam—and I rolled off in a tank with the Third Armored Division. Guess what my dad did? He gave the three tickets to my cousin Bernie! Not to keep, just to hold until I came back. We never talked about this, my father and I, and so I don't know whether he was being superstitious or whether he just didn't want to go to a game if I wasn't there.

Not long after I came back, I got married. And we took the tickets back from Cousin Bernie. The Sunday gang became me and my father and my wife. Actually, my father, my wife and I coming along with a picnic basket and endless questions.

It wasn't the happiest of times for the three season tickets, because the Giants were in the midst of a long slump. In fact, they stunk. My wife couldn't understand why my father and I put ourselves through the agony of defeat week after week, especially when it was cold. My father couldn't understand how my wife couldn't understand.

Somehow we survived this. My father loved my wife, and although she didn't care much for the game, she loved us. She knitted a pair of Giants scarves, one hundred percent wool with a snappy team logo that my late grandmother had never even attempted. People would actually stop by our seats and ask us where we got the scarves. We would point at my wife, and they would ask her if they could order one.

Then I had a son. Ivan came to his first football game when he was six years old. He spent half the game sitting on my father's lap and half the game sitting on mine. Without a doubt, this was the finest period for the season tickets, the three generations sitting in the upper deck—still on the five-yard line, but now we were in the Giants' new stadium in the Jersey Meadowlands, and the team was beginning its march toward two Super Bowls.

Every Sunday we gathered together, grandfather, father, and son, either at the stadium or in front of one of our TVs (if it were an away game). And we rooted. And we cheered. And we talked about the players.

What is it about men, men of six or thirty-six or sixty-six, that they find it easiest to share their intimacies not directly but through a protective shield of old stories and third-person assessments? By which member of the team we admired (the quarterback, the linebacker, the wide receiver), we told each other who we thought we were or, more likely, who we wished we were. By reacting to referees' calls that went against us, we spoke to each other about our sense of fairness, our belief that the world was just or unjust. By sticking with the team when they were playing badly, we informed each other, and ourselves, of the importance of loyalty and trust.

Once I remember booing a Giants player who had taken himself out of the game. I did this in order to communicate to Ivan (or maybe to my father) my belief that a real man always plays through the pain.

Another time, the three of us proved our power to stay with the team by remaining in our seats during a driving hailstorm. We were heroes after that one, boy, and when the Giants beat the Eagles that day we felt as much a part of the team as any cornerback.

Then there was my father's heart attack. Giants-Rams, 1984. It was bitter cold that afternoon, and in the second quarter I noticed that my father's lips had turned purple.

"Are you all right?" I asked.

Slowly, as if not to break something, he shook his head no. I turned to my nine-year-old son and said quietly, "Grandpa is having a heart attack. I want you to help me."

And Ivan did just that. As I helped my father to the men's room where he could get warm, Ivan went to the security staff. He returned with two burly guards and a wheelchair.

We wheeled my father down to the training room, where a doctor was waiting. I was right; it was his heart. We put him in the ambulance that usually runs broken players to the hospital for X-rays. I brought the car around to follow the ambulance. My son climbed in with my father. As they pulled out, Ivan flashed me the thumbs-up sign, and I smiled through my gathering tears.

My father pulled through, but he would never go to a game again. He was afraid of the cold. And he was afraid of the long climb we had to make to get to our seats.

For the next few years, whenever the Giants were on the road, we congregated at my father's house to watch the game on TV. At the stadium, the third seat was filled by my sister and a rotation of friends. But we all watched Super Bowl XXI together, my father and my son and I. When the Giants beat the Denver Broncos, we whooped and hollered and hopped around the room.

My father died soon after that—another heart attack. My son and I have shared the three tickets ever since, rooting and reminiscing and exchanging those protected intimacies across the past nine seasons.

Now my son is leaving for college, and it suddenly strikes me that for the past thirty-five years these three tickets, these magic tickets, have been a kind of special connection, first for my father and me; then for my father, me, and my son; and then for me and my son together. This year, for the very first time in the history of the three season tickets, there will be only me.

I find myself wondering what it was that made my father give the tickets to Cousin Bernie during the years when I was away at war. And I think I might give the tickets to my cousin Sam.

But then Ivan notices that he'll be home for one of the Giants home dates. He says, "I can go to that one, Dad!" And I think perhaps I'll just hold on to the tickets for maybe one more season. Maybe one more game. Maybe.

~Barney Cohen
Chicken Soup for the Sports Fan's Soul

Tales OF Golf AND Sport

Wisdom of the Game

It's what you learn after you know it all that counts.
~John Wooden

25

My Best Friend

The language of friendship is not words but meanings.
~Henry David Thoreau

The agony of the final round set in off the first tee. It wasn't Sunday. There was no tournament. It was just me and Matt, my golf partner of three years, not to mention my best friend since the third grade.

We had entered the world of golf as two youngsters with cheap clubs, inspired by our fathers' stories of birdies, three-hundred-yard drives, and near-holes-in-one. For some reason these tales failed to hold true when we played with them.

Expecting to go out and conquer the game, Matt and I were quite surprised (not to mention angry) when we found ourselves humbled by a little white ball. Over time though, our swings became more controlled, good shots became more frequent, scores lower and our friendship stronger.

That summer, we entered a junior golf tour. We soon realized how much we had to learn, and how much we wanted to win. We had been in the game for two years already, and we figured all we needed was some fine-tuning to give our game the extra edge.

We played almost every day after school that year with the hope that the hard work would pay off with victory on the tour next summer. Then we got the news.

"Andrew, my dad's being transferred to Charlotte right after school," Matt said when he broke the news to me. He was moving away following our freshman year and right before the golf season would start. We had only a month left together, so we decided to make the most of it. Golf was the only way we knew how to enjoy ourselves without facing the sorrow of separation. No matter what is going on, golf helps you forget by making you concentrate on the task at hand—beating the guy you're playing with—and that was good enough for us.

We played and the time flew, and soon we found ourselves in what we realized was our final round together. We had tried to ignore it for so long, but now it hung over us. The only way to shake it was to continue the eighteen.

When all was said and done, we finished the game. Our scores were average. He beat me by three strokes.

Matt had to be home so he could wake up early in the morning and head out. We stood at the practice green waiting for his mother to come get him. Finally, she arrived.

"It was a pleasure playing with you." I held out my hand. He shook, and then I half-hugged him, like boys do when they want to be men. I saw him off the next morning.

He played on a tour at his new home, and I competed also. One day, I received a letter in the mail. It was a scorecard and a picture of the leader board. Matt was atop it. He finally won.

Over the years, I received many scorecards from Matt (unfortunately more than I sent him). I keep them in my golf bag for good luck.

I guess the magic of golf isn't the course, or the swing, or the sound you hear when you hit a solid 3-iron. It's the feeling you get when you beat your best friend, or lose to him, for that matter.

And sooner or later you realize that you didn't play every week because you were golfers; you played because you were friends.

~Andrew Galanopulos
Chicken Soup for the Golfer's Soul

26

Home vs. Visitors

People who don't cherish their elderly have forgotten
whence they came and whither they go.
~Ramsey Clark

My grandmother was a gentle soul. She came from a time when life was simple and uncomplicated. She would shy away from anything that was new. Every Sunday morning, she would take me to church, where she felt at home with the familiar surroundings. Because her vision was poor, we always sat near the front facing a tack board that would indicate how many home parishioners and visitors had attended the Sunday service.

As I grew older, I realized how sheltered her life had been and encouraged her to try new things. One evening as I was getting ready to attend a local basketball game, I asked her to join me. To my surprise she agreed to come along. I knew she had never been to such an event before and I tried to explain the game to her. She listened intently and pretended to understand.

Actually she seemed to enjoy it, and got caught up in the excitement of all the cheering. After the game was over, we met my mother for coffee and my grandmother began telling her about the high points of the evening. Turning to my mother she said, "You should have seen all the people there. Why, there were more present than at our church service on Sunday."

"How could you tell?" Mom asked.

Innocently, my grandmother replied, "Well, there was an

attendance board at the end of the gym, just like the one at church, and it said, 'Home 134 and Visitors 120.' Why, we only had 122 home members attend last Sunday, and heaven knows we've never had that many visitors!"

~S. Turkaly
A 5th Portion of Chicken Soup for the Soul

Way Above Par

One afternoon I had the chance to meet a couple of friends on the course for a quick nine. We were paired together for a scramble at our church the next weekend and we admittedly needed the practice. As I was driving to meet them, I started reflecting on my marriage. After seven years, we had become too predictable. No itches mind you, but more than enough rashes and hives from the children. With the kids, the mortgage, the bills and, of course, the job to pay for all of the above, we had landed in a sand trap.

In college, it seemed like everything enjoyable in life centered around our time together. People always said that we were the ones who lit the fires, but it seemed like we had forgotten the matches.

Golf was an escape for us. I'd chase that stupid white ball around a deep green golf course and would never get any better. My wife drove the electric golf cart, always wearing a shorts-and-tank-top set, dark sunglasses, and a white golf visor. For ten yards in either direction, you could smell the unmistakable scent of cocoa butter. The only reason she went was to get a suntan.

If the truth were known, the only reason I went was to watch her.

One afternoon, she studied my golf swing more intently than ever before. Finally, on the seventeenth hole, she came out with her notion.

"Let me try to hit one."

At first, I thought it was a novel idea. Then I changed my mind. Golf was a man's sport, or so I thought. "You? You can't hit a golf ball. You're a girl."

"Thanks for noticing. Just the same, I think I can lose golf balls as well as you can."

A very true observation.

I handed over my 3-wood and dug the tee into the hard clay at the tee box. Without even a practice swing, she promptly knocked the ball straight down the middle of the fairway. When we got to our balls, her drive was five yards further than mine. From that day on, she started playing golf.

Some of the best times we shared early in our marriage were on the golf course. We'd go in the mid-morning before the temperature would climb. The time we spent together laughing and teasing under the sun cemented our relationship. As I pulled into the parking lot outside the clubhouse, I realized how much I missed seeing her on a golf course.

All the guys at church looked forward to playing our annual tournament. Mike and Danny, a couple of fellow church members, were going to play on my team along with a mystery partner. Hopefully someone who could drive and putt, our collective shortcomings.

Every team invited someone outside our church to play. Sort of a community involvement thing. What I always found amazing was how all these strangers could hit the cover off the ball and always straight down the middle! Let's face it, there are more ringers in a church golf tournament than in the children's bell choir.

When I got to the practice green, I saw Danny and his wife, Beth, pulling out Danny's clubs. A second golf bag was resting on the side.

"Whose clubs are those, Danny?" I asked, expecting him to say that next week's mystery golfer was already inside the clubhouse, paying for our tickets.

"Why, they're mine," said Beth as she threw them across her shoulder.

"Yeah, she's my secret weapon today. She tees off from the women's tee box, you know. With her drives, we are guaranteed at least a good one."

I snickered at the thought of a woman playing golf, then I caught a whiff of cocoa butter.

The three of us spent the afternoon chasing balls, hitting horrible iron shots and missing almost every putt. Danny and Beth didn't care. They enjoyed playing golf together in a way that I suddenly recalled.

It's not the winning but the losing together that matters most.

As we were starting to leave, the conversation came to the tournament. Danny asked, "Well, do you think you can find a fourth player by Saturday?"

"Yeah. Playing this afternoon reminded me of the perfect partner."

I came home to find my wife in the kitchen. She smiled and asked, "Did you play well?"

"Nope. Just as hopeless as usual."

"How did the others play?"

"Hopeless as well. We need a fourth player for the tournament and I think I found one."

She looked up at me with those bright eyes and asked, "Really, who?"

"You."

Surprise grew across her face. "Me? I haven't played golf in years. I can't help you win."

"Can't help us lose either. But it sure would be nice to see you out there again."

That next Saturday, the four of us played golf on perhaps the most beautiful spring day that I can recall. We laughed and teased all over the course as shot after shot missed the mark. On the last hole, we finished with a score of 79, seven shots above par, buried deep in last place.

Afterward, the awards were handed out and we got the prize for having the roughest day, a kind way to say we lost. Each of us received a sleeve of shiny pink golf balls for our hard day's work. On our way back to our table, I put my arm around her shoulder and whispered, "These guys just haven't figured out who really won!"

~Harrison Kelly
Chicken Soup for the Golfer's Soul

Start of a Love-Hate Relationship

They say golf is like life, but don't believe them.
Golf is more complicated than that.
~Gardner Dickinson

Apologies to the property owner on South Mountain, the one who must've wondered if a comet had crashed through the drywall. Honestly, I didn't know a little white ball made so much noise when hitting a house.

Apologies to the man who came into view just after I made contact, the one who suddenly appeared in my fairway and came within inches of not finishing his life, much less his round. I really must learn to say "Fore" a little earlier.

And sincere empathy goes out to a certain female, the one currently wondering about the return policy on husbands.

Yes, I did a very bad thing on vacation. I learned how to play golf.

I'm not sure what precipitated such madness, but one day, I was scanning the Internet, printing out pages on how to swing a golf club. The next few days were spent in a ridiculous cocoon: Trips to the cash machine, trips to the driving range, midnight swing sessions in the driveway. And then, the binge.

Eleven rounds, nine different courses and, oh, the things I've seen.

I have tasted the euphoria, the intensely satisfying moment when the swing is true and the ball sails forever. I have been slightly alarmed by my shortcomings, especially when the result lies somewhere past a warning sign regarding rattlesnakes in the immediate vicinity.

I have seen a woman stand aghast in her backyard, resentful of the ball that just plunked her tile roof, as if a golf course had suddenly sprouted around her home.

I have barged onto a hidden green, unaware that a foursome hadn't completed the hole. After apologizing profusely, I proceeded to hit one of their balls.

I have played a round in two hours and five minutes. Alone. An exhilarating day when it seemed like the course was empty and I was the only person alive. Naturally, on this day the planets were aligned, the clubs were wands and I was the maestro—a day I craved for witnesses.

Another time, I made the turn after nine holes in three and a half hours, stuck behind a legion of slow-playing foursomes. A tortoise parade that would qualify as golf purgatory.

I have seen men examine long-distance putts for five minutes, only to hit the ball six inches.

I have seen a friend hit the ball sideways, nearly decapitating another friend sitting in the cart. I have willingly raked sand.

And just when you think you're the biggest and only doofus on the planet....

One afternoon, while I walked to my ball, which teetered on the last blade of grass separating land from lake, a diver emerged from the black. In full scuba gear. Carrying about six thousand errant shots.

Yes, misery loves company.

And yes, golf is a lot like life. Humbling beyond reason. Laced with a rich bouquet of hope. And in the end, it gives you just enough to keep going.

To be honest, the intent of this experiment was born from curiosity and a desire to become socially equipped. Living in Arizona and not learning to play golf is like living in Paris and not speaking French. I still maintain that any endeavor requiring a collared shirt is not a sport, but for a recreational skill, golf is addictive. Much better than Ping Pong, and much more than a good cart ride spoiled.

Fascinating game, really. Intoxicating in its solitude, decadent in its consumption of time, a wonderful reminder of how nice it is to walk on grass.

Granted, I still don't get the extensive volumes of etiquette, and I'll never forget the look on my friend's face when I arrived for our initial golf date in a T-shirt. But I quickly learned to love the game, and now I'm ready for the next step.

Because I'm starting to hate the game.

On Friday, I hit three excellent shots in succession, leading to a six-inch putt and the first birdie of my life.

On Saturday, I stepped up to the tee, swung at a ball and missed.

And now I get the joke.

Why do they call it golf? Because @!#@ was already taken.

~Dan Bickley
Chicken Soup for the Golfer's Soul, The 2nd Round

Lost and Found

From the satchel on my office desk, forty ungraded compositions whispered at me in grammatically incorrect urgency. But after two days of torrential rainfall, a radiant sun enveloped the local greens in a golden Sunday embrace. After a quick shower, I was off for a lone round before trading in my pitching wedge for the proverbial red pen.

The attendant at the clubhouse greeted me with an only slightly disgruntled countenance; rising early to watch others play golf is apparently not without its limitations. The sign-in sheet indicated only one other gentleman had begun his round. Good. The golf would be quick, private and unhurried.

After sticking my wedding ring in my front pocket for safekeeping (it causes blisters if I leave it on), I astounded myself with my first drive, a sweet whistle down the center of the fairway. I lovingly replaced the head cover on my driver.

By the sixth hole, it was becoming increasingly apparent, even given my poor math skills, that I was having the round of my life. Not that Tiger Woods has to worry just yet; after five holes I was one under, thanks in part to holing a slippery twenty-footer.

Addressing my ball, I peered down the sixth fairway, a beautifully designed par-5 that loped around a kidney-shaped pond fronted with flowering water plants and cattails. Poking around with his ball retriever was Mr. Early. This is what I dubbed him, unable to recall his name from the logbook I had hastily scribbled my signature into less than an hour ago. Hair whiter than a freshly opened pair of tube socks, with a posture that suggested firsthand recollections of the birth of the game, he did not notice my growing impatience on the tee box. Finally, rationalizing that I was playing too well this morning to actually hit him (and feeling the ever-increasing weight of those essays bearing down on the remaining hours of my shortened weekend), I teed off with a shank that would make Sir Murphy and his Book of Laws proud.

Old fart, I grumbled to myself, thrusting the ill-fitting head cover over my driver. Eager to make the turn alone, I promised myself not to engage this feeble duffer in conversation. Trouble is, in my disgust over the missed hit, I had failed to track my ball with any degree of precision. All I knew is that it had sculled somewhere near where Mr. Early was still searching.

"Quite the morning, isn't it?" he asked as I approached.

"Yeah," I said, avoiding direct eye contact. Old folks are like animals, I reasoned, they can see the weakness in your eyes.

"We seem to have lost ourselves in here somewhere," he said, waving his ball remover over the tangled grass in which we waded.

Just as it seemed I was destined to spend my Sunday morning chaperoning a member of the geriatric unit around the links, I spied a dimpled sphere buried deep in the rough.

"Here I am," I said, reaching for the first thing in my bag. A rotten stick would have done.

"Are you sure?" he asked. "I was hitting a Titleist."

"Me too," I said, rolling my eyes in exasperation. Or was it a Top-Flite? Who cares, I finally decided. The ball was mine.

And I was gone.

But the image of the old man staring at me as I made my way around the lake kept me from concentrating. My game suffered. I grew angrier and angrier.

Following another chunked drive, I slammed my driver into the bag, resolved never to grip its evilness again.

My iron game left me as well, literally. On the thirteenth hole, I went to my bag to retrieve my 7-iron, only to find it was not there. I groaned, realizing what I would be forced to endure. Mr. Early was still behind me, and most likely in possession of my club.

Unfortunately, he was gone. Apparently, nine was enough for him this fine Sunday morning. Probably off to church, I steamed, heading for the clubhouse, my round destroyed.

The clubhouse was still empty as I entered, the overhead fan doing little to cool me off. The attendant gazed at me with that same sleepy boredom with which he had greeted me earlier.

"Did anyone else come in here?" I asked.

"Older guy? Head of white hair?" he asked, yawning.

"Yeah," I said. "Did he leave anything behind?"

"Yup. Said you'd be looking for it. He set everything over on the bar."

"Everything?" I asked.

"Look, it's on the bar. That's all I know," he said.

I walked over to the mahogany counter, the clicking of the cleats ringing in my ears. There on the bar was the cover to my driver, my 7-iron and a golf ball. Reaching for the ball, I felt my face flush red. Top-Flite. It even had my personalized markings, three dots with a permanent red pen. Then I noticed a drink napkin amidst my returned equipment. Set in the middle, shining as bright as the day on which my wife had slipped it on my finger, was my wedding ring. It had fallen out of my pocket somewhere on the golf course. A miracle itself that he had found it. Even more astonishing that he had somehow known it was mine and to return it, with everything else. My throat tightened as I raced for the parking lot.

Mr. Early was just pulling out as I skidded to a halt in front of his car. I slowly made my way to the driver's-side window, which he was already rolling down.

"My stuff," I said. "You returned my stuff. Even after... the ball... your ball... I stole your ball."

"Let me see it," he said, gazing up at me.

I almost ripped my pants digging for that ball I still had in my front pocket. With shaking fingers, I slipped it into his palm.

He peered at the ball, turned it in his gnarled hands and sucked on his teeth. After a long moment, he reached the ball back out the window and said, "Nope. This isn't mine. I was hitting a Titleist 3. This here is a Titleist 1. You keep it, son. You found it."

In a daze, I retrieved the ball from his hand. "But my stuff, you found all the stuff I lost," I stammered.

"Not everything," he replied with a slight smile. "Not everything."

"What do you mean?" I asked.

He put his car in gear and eased it forward. As he rolled up his window, he said, "You lost the one thing even I can't get back for you, son. Go read the napkin on the bar."

And then he was gone.

Back in the clubhouse, I made my way to the bar. Turning the napkin over, I read in Mr. Early's scrawled handwriting the following words:

YOUR TEMPER

~Greg R. Bernard
Chicken Soup for the Golfer's Soul

30

Golf, Like Midlife, Is Absolutely Unfair

*"Play it as it lies" is one of the fundamental dictates of golf.
The other is "Wear it if it clashes."*
~Henry Beard, Golfing

When I turned fifty, I discovered three essential facts of middle age: periodontics, bifocals and golf.

Golf? Did she say golf?

Let me explain. I once assumed golf was a sport for elderly Country Club Republicans. The sort of men who wore green pants with whale belts and protected their clubs with fuzzy duck-head covers.

Golf was Dwight David Eisenhower. My family was Adlai Stevenson.

In my twenties, I thought golf was God's way of telling you that you had too much time on your hands. In my thirties, I decided a low handicap was admissible evidence of child neglect in any custody dispute. In my forties, as a fairly decent tennis and squash player, I couldn't imagine hitting a ball while it was standing still.

Quite frankly, it seemed unfair.

But somewhere along the way, somewhere between Bill Clinton and Big Bertha and Tiger Woods, between chiropractors and knee surgery and Advil, I had an epiphany (that's something close to a muscle spasm) that said: "Golf is my next sport. To wit: my last sport. I better learn it now."

This was a decision aided and abetted by a quirky nine-hole golf course in Maine where people still stroll and stop to look at the view.

It was also aided and abetted by a quirky husband (more Bobby Kennedy than Adlai Stevenson) who enthusiastically gave me all his clubs. This was an act of generosity I didn't immediately recognize for what it was. A ploy for him to get new equipment.

Now, as I approach Columbus Day weekend with a full set of clubs and big plans, I feel fully qualified at last to offer up my views on why golf begins at fifty. Yes, I know one sign of a new and erratic duffer is the penchant for turning golf into a good walk through midlife spoiled. For reasons that remain unclear, golf has spawned more philosophical rambles than fairways.

Nobody compares tennis to life. A love game? Ken Burns and several million fans talk about baseball as the collective field of youthful dreams, but there's no senior tour on the diamonds.

Today there are, I hasten to add, some 25 million golfers and 16,010 golf courses. There are speed golfers and networking golfers and boring golfers. There is even, for reasons that escape me, a golf channel. All golf, all day long.

There is a business writer who actually correlated the handicaps of CEOs with their stock performance. And there are the very, very serious golf professionals who sit around discussing whether they should ban new, improved clubs because they are making the game too easy. Say what? But from my perspective, golf is the midlife sport of choice for very different reasons. First of all, it's easier to reach your goals. In midlife, after all, it's a snap to have a handicap below your age and a score below your weight. And getting easier all the time.

Golf is like midlife because only now do you realize the course you have set upon is governed by rules so vast, so arcane and so arbitrary that the average person—you—will never figure it all out.

Golf is like midlife because it is absolutely unfair. As a young person, you carry the illusion that if you do your homework, study and work overtime, you'll get it all right. By middle age, you know every time you've got it all together—work, family, putt, pitch—some piece is about to unravel. I promise you.

Golf, like midlife, is played against only one opponent: yourself. By the time you reach fifty, you had better figure out that doing well doesn't depend on others doing badly. You don't have to wish them ill. They're not the reason you are shanking the ball.

Golf is like middle age, because—ah, you knew this was coming—in these years, you really do have to play it as it lies. You don't get to start everything all over again. The most you get is a mulligan. If it's an unplayable lie, everybody sympathizes, but you still have to take a penalty.

On the other hand, golf, like midlife, also offers another chance.

No matter how badly you hit one ball, you can still recover on the next. Of course, no matter how well you hit one ball, you can always screw up the next.

Finally, golf is like midlife because at some time on a beautiful October day, when you are searching for a ball, or for that matter your swing, you look around and realize for the first or fiftieth time that, in this game, you're the one keeping your own score.

~Ellen Goodman
Chicken Soup to Inspire a Woman's Soul

31

"Those Kids"

Things do not pass for what they are, but for what they seem.
Most things are judged by their jackets.
~Baltasar Gracian

The switch from a small, private Christian school to a public eighth grade had been difficult for my son. Now he faced the challenge of a new high school, with his new friends zoned to attend another school.

"Can I please repeat junior high?" Jim begged. "Everyone thinks I'm in seventh grade anyway. I won't know anyone at my new high school."

"Best to push him through," his junior high principal advised.

My heart ached, but my husband and I agreed to force our son to face his deepest fears—another new school and making new friends.

The first day I picked him up, he waved goodbye to a kid with short dark hair, baggy pants, an earring and tattoo.

"Who's your new friend?" I asked, trying not to sound alarmed.

"Just some kid named Jerry." I could tell his first day in a school with over two thousand kids hadn't been easy.

"Still planning to go out for football?" I asked. It had always been his dream.

"Yeah."

Then you'll find better friends, I thought, and not hang around with these kids who probably get into trouble.

When football sign-ups came, I dropped him off at the school, and week after week I picked him up after freshman practice. One day while doing laundry, I noticed his football clothes looked brand-new. As did his football cleats.

A quick phone call to the coach confirmed what I had suspected: Jim was staying after school, but he wasn't on the football team. He was hanging out with his new group of friends until practice was over, then timed it just right to meet me at the curb.

"I called your coach today," I said after picking him up.

"Yeah?"

"I understand you're not playing football."

Silence.

"What's going on?"

"I tried to go out," he said. "I just couldn't. The other kids were better than me. And I didn't know anyone. I just couldn't do it."

"So you hang out with your new friends during practice?"

"Yeah."

"Doing what?" I could only imagine. Smoking? Shoplifting? Skipping classes? How could my son be hanging out with "those" kinds of kids?

"I'm sorry, Mom," he said. "I'm sorry I lied."

The decision not to hold him back in junior high ate at my heart. We should have listened to him. Another year and he would have had more confidence. Then he would have gone out for the football team. Then he wouldn't be with "those" kids.

The following years were no different. I'd drop him off for spring football tryouts, but he'd come home defeated. "I'm not good enough," he'd say. "I should have played my freshman year. It's too late now."

My heart ached.

By his senior year, his dream to play football seemed over. To our surprise, Jerry, one of "those" kids, knew his desire and understood the fears and insecurities that had held Jim back.

"You're going to do it this time," Jerry insisted on the day of tryouts, as he walked Jim to the locker room. "This time you're going to stay!"

Jim worked out with the varsity team daily, coming home with his cleats and uniforms covered with grass stains and mud.

"I'll never get to play in a game," he said. But game after game, he suited up, ran onto the field with the other varsity players and cheered them in victory or defeat.

Near the end of the season, his school played the cross-town rival in their homecoming game. As floats were driven off the field and the band settled, my husband and I wedged in among the packed parents sitting in the visitors' section. Blinding lights filled the night sky.

By the fourth quarter, our team held a twenty-point lead. Suddenly, a low chant rose from among the varsity players on the sidelines. Some picked up towels, turned to the stands, started waving to the crowd and shouting, "Jim, Jim, Jim, Jim... "

The crowd joined the chant, and other mothers turned to me, smiling with tears in their eyes.

With four minutes remaining on the clock, the coach signaled out the starting quarterback and motioned Number Sixteen, my son, into his first varsity game. The crowd went wild. I looked around and saw Jim's friends, the kinds of kids who don't normally attend football games, on their feet and crazy with excitement.

It was because of "those" friends that Jim was on the team.

The crowd jumped to its feet clapping and cheering as Jim threw his first pass. No, it didn't end in a touchdown, but his determination and courage prevailed.

A few months later, the varsity players, coaches and parents met for the Annual Awards Banquet. After three hours of speeches and acknowledgments, the head coach stood.

"Finally, we come to the most important award of the evening, The Most Inspirational Player. This award is selected by the team, not the coaches, and goes to the player who has most influenced his teammates."

The coach opened a piece of paper and read, "This year The Most Inspirational Player Award goes to Jim Pallos."

Jim stumbled to the podium in a stupor, grinning from ear to ear.

After the ceremony, one of his coaches approached me. "When Jim first came out for the team," he said, "I wanted to laugh. A senior who has never played football wanting to be a quarterback? He was so bad at catching the ball that we had to hand it to him during practice. But he taught me one thing: I'll never again laugh or make fun of any kid who wants to play football."

And I knew I'd never again judge a teenage boy by the clothes he wears, the rings in his ears or the tattoos on his arms. I smiled at my son, who was surrounded by his teammates.

Now I wished "those kids" were here.

~Jeanne Pallos
Chicken Soup for the Mother and Son Soul

32

Golf Carts Do Not Have Four-Wheel Drive

The revelation that golf carts do not have four-wheel drive came to me one morning as I tried to find my ball in the mud, which I found out later was actually not part of the golf course at all but rather the site of a pending condo project, half a block away. I must have missed the out-of-bounds marker when I was crossing the freeway. It was just one more lesson in the complex world of golf.

I remember the first time I played. My twosome was paired up with another twosome. After my tee-off on the first hole went somewhat awry, landing on the clubhouse roof, one of the other players asked if I had a handicap. I thought his joke in poor taste and threatened him with my 9-iron. Now, of course, I realize that having a handicap is a good thing, even if it is 52.

Learning the rules and language of golf is crucial. It separates the obvious beginner from someone just having another bad day. Therefore, I have from experience compiled a few lessons that may help other novices.

If the instructor tells you to address the ball, do not take out a pen and write "to green" on the ball.

Try not to stand on asphalt in the summer while wearing golf shoes, unless you are with a very strong friend.

The easiest way to find a lost golf ball is to ask the guy limping in the next fairway.

Never insist that your spouse golf. It can lead to only two results. One, she/he plays really badly, complains for four hours and ruins your whole day. Or, he/she plays really well, offers four hours of suggestions on how you might do better and ruins your whole day.

A double bogey is not a strong drink from the movie *Casablanca*. It means two over par. And not a bad score at all. If they have a name for it, it's a good score. There is no name for a fifteen.

A chip is not something left behind by a foraging cow. That's a flap. A chip is a carefully choreographed half-swing that often goes further than your original drive.

A divot is a lump of grass that flies up from where the golf ball used to be. A damnit is a lump of grass that flies up in your face as you hit two feet behind the ball.

A slice is a ball that curves to the right. A bad slice is a ball that lands behind you.

A tough lie has double meanings. It's when you have to come up with an excuse — for the umpteenth time — as to why it took six hours to play nine holes and why your breath smells like nacho chips and beer. It also refers to a difficult spot to have to hit your ball from. For instance, the base of a tree, the crook of a tree or the upper branches of a tree.

Heavy rough is the area along the edge of the fairway just before your ball is legally out of bounds. A good rule of thumb — if the guy beside you is barbecuing, you're probably out of bounds.

And finally, Club Rules imply that you are not penalized by foreign objects on the fairway. Therefore, if you knock out a tourist with your drive, you are allowed to move your ball one club's length from the body.

Now that you understand some of the basics, you should be able to better appreciate the game. And, you can focus on some of the more intriguing idiosyncrasies of golf, like if it's completely made out of metal, why do they call it a 3-wood?

~Ernie Witham
Chicken Soup for the Golfer's Soul

The Ten Inevitabilities of Hacker Golf

I t never fails....

1.   You're standing in the fairway 220 yards from the green. The group in front of you is still on the green. You know that if you hit the ball you will fly it to the green, send that group scattering, and once again have four angry golfers waiting for you at the bar. So, you wait until they completely clear, then you duff the shot and end up 75 yards short.

2.   You're wearing your lucky hat, your lucky socks and your lucky underwear. Things are in your favor. And even though you typically shoot 90, you've had a really good back nine and you are at 76 with only two par-4s to go for your best score all year. Correspondingly, you triple bogey both holes, your only triple bogeys of the day, to end up shooting—you guessed it—90.

3.   After careful consideration you decide to hit a high soft lob shot onto the elevated green just like Tiger might do, but you hit it flat with your wedge and line drive it over the green. On the next hole, faced with a similar shot, you decide to bounce it on with a

9-iron like Sergio might do, but instead hit it straight up into the air and leave it three feet short of the green.

4. After muffing the tee shot, sculling the approach, pitching it into the sand trap and taking three shots to barely get it out and onto the green, you make a forty-five-foot, double-breaking, downhill putt that you couldn't make again if your life depended on it.

5. You place your tee shot right behind a tree so large that it should be named after a president. By some miracle not only do you get your iron shot around the thing, but it hooks right back into the middle of the fairway. On the next tee shot you land fifty yards behind a three-foot-tall sapling no bigger around than your finger. Using a lofted fairway wood, you hit the little tree dead on, the ball pops up into the air and lands five yards behind you.

6. You are playing really well and, therefore, decide to dole out a "bit of advice" on someone else's game. Instantly, your game goes south faster than a Canadian goose in late November.

7. You decide to wear your brand-new, birthday-gift golf shoes to a course you've never played even though they are not broken in yet. Upon arrival, you find out the club has a cart-path-only rule and, subsequently, you end up walking more miles than Lewis and Clark did exploring the Dakotas.

8. You are on the driving range and your buddy lets you try out his five-hundred-dollar driver. You have never, ever hit the ball as far or as straight. So you buy one for yourself. The first time you play with it, your cogolfers nickname you Water Boy, because you shank drives into the lake, the creek and a resort swimming pool next to the course, before you put the thing away and go back to your fifty-dollar garage-sale driver.

9. After tossing some grass into the air to check the wind, you see

that it's blowing left-to-right, so you alter your grip, play the ball back in your stance to keep it low, aim a little left to be safe. Then, after two great practice swings, you hit a wicked slice way up into the wind that lands two fairways to the right.

10. The course is busy, and they are backed up at the 195-yard par-3. The group on the green waves you up. You know the odds of hitting that green with everyone watching are slim-to-nil. So you decide to lay it up. Then you proceed to hit a wicked worm-burner that just keeps going and going, finally rolling up onto the green and stopping just inches from the hole. A dead bug and several blades of grass fall off the ball. The crowd cheers—and, of course, laughs.

What's the good news about these inevitabilities? You get asked to play often, because you are just so darned entertaining!

~Ernie Witham
Chicken Soup for the Golfer's Soul, The 2nd Round

The Almost Home Run

A happy person is not a person in a certain set of circumstances,
but rather a person with a certain set of attitudes.
~Hugh Downs

He stepped up to the plate, a tanned, sturdy six-year-old, for his first time at bat, in his first Peewee baseball game. Jeff shouldered the bat, longer than he was tall, with the composure of a seasoned major-league hitter.

The first pitch went wide. The second, too high. When the third pitch headed straight for him, my heart flip-flopped. He swung the bat, connected with a resounding crack and sent the ball sailing over the second baseman's head.

Flinging the bat to the ground, my son headed for first base, his chunky legs churning. He rounded second, passed third and was almost home when someone yelled, "Jeff, you didn't touch third base!"

With that, he spun around, heading back to third. But before he got there, the third baseman caught the ball. So Jeff dodged him and ran toward second. The ball beat him there, too. Then, not knowing what else to do, the gutsy little guy started running all over the infield, hunting a safe place to land—halfway to the pitcher's mound, a sharp left toward first base, back to third. By now the crowd was laughing so hard, they barely heard, "You're out!"

Talk about no joy in Mudville. I couldn't even enjoy the rest of the game worrying about how I would console my fledgling Peewee.

Was he devastated? Would he refuse to talk about it? Quit baseball forever? And what could I, his athletically challenged mother, possibly do to help?

After the game, I gathered up my plucky little player and his older brother and headed for the car. As we pulled out of the parking lot and started down the road, the boys discussed the game, never mentioning the out. Then, on the verge of delivering my pep talk, I glanced in the rearview mirror and saw Jeff grinning broadly, his blue eyes shining.

"I hit that ball, didn't I, Mama?"

"Yes, Jeff, you sure did."

Enough said.

~Nancy J. Knight
Chicken Soup for the Mother and Son Soul

One at a Time

*If profanity had an influence on the flight of the ball,
the game of golf would be played far better than it is.*
~Horace G. Hutchinson

My introduction to the game of golf came as a teenage caddie at an exclusive country club near our home. The $3.50 I was paid for eighteen holes of carrying singles and $5.75 for doubles was a welcome wage for my first job outside our home. My blue-collar family could never afford to belong to a club like this, so my duties were also my entry inside the gates that we so frequently passed. Every Monday was "caddie day," which meant we could play the course for free.

I had always been an above-average athlete. I expected I would do as well with golf. Never having taken even basic lessons, my transition from a baseball bat to a 5-iron was not pretty. My ability to deal with this fact was uglier still. My frequent shots hit out of bounds, whiffed at or drubbed thirty feet up the fairway generally led to a loud, blue stream of cursing. More than one golf club was left to decorate some elm tree, having been thrown and caught up too high to retrieve. At eighteen, even I was mature enough to realize that I needed to either get serious about my golf or give it up. Shortly thereafter, college pursuits gave me little time to play, and a new job meant I would have to pay real greens fees. The "pleasure" I derived from playing made not playing an easy decision.

At the age of thirty-five, I found myself the father of two

boys—eight and ten years old. Their friends in our Iowa neighborhood all played golf. So one summer, our boys took group lessons at a public course near our home. They were both quickly hooked. The lessons they took and a "kids play all day for five dollars" program at a short course in town made for a great summer. About this time, my new job was requiring some very long hours, and my wife suggested that I take up golf as a way to spend time with the boys. I quickly confessed my "dark past" with golf and that I didn't think I would enjoy it any more now than I did then. In the end, her motherly instincts and wifely persuasion won out. "Free Lessons with Every Purchase of a New Set of Clubs" caught my eye, and armed with my credit card I trekked down to the discount golf store.

Much to my surprise, it was different this time. Same basic instruction... the grip... the setup and stance... backswing and follow through... all helped me focus more on the process than necessarily just the result. After many hours on the driving range, I was still not breaking 100 but I enjoyed the experience of learning something new. It propelled me out of the office and into the fresh air of the Iowa heartland. And it did give me more time with my boys. It was interesting, though, to see how their own impatience and lack of maturity caused problems on the course. The ebb and flow of good moods and bad determined what kind of an outing we had. Both boys had inherited my competitiveness. After each hole, they would argue about the accuracy of the score reported by the other sibling. While I was older and more patient than when I first took up the game, I still did my share of carping about lost balls and their slow play as other foursomes waited behind us. Back at home, I was usually greeted by my wife's insightful, "Well, how did it go this time?"

It bothered me that our time together on the course was not creating the father-son bonding experience that my wife and I had envisioned. In my earlier years, I might have become discouraged and vowed not to take the boys out anymore. But giving up is seldom the answer, and some of my favorite memories were of my own dad's love of sports and the way he taught me to play by playing with me. At times like this, if we can only discard discouragement and replace it with a search for new possibilities, we can often rekindle an earlier dream.

I decided to take the boys out one at a time. I also decided to relax and let them play their game at their pace without regard for the result. If they lose a ball, we'll buy another. When they say their score, I'll just write it down. After all, it is their score not mine. I would also take half-days away from the office so we could play during slow times and maintain our own pace. But above all, I remembered, be encouraging, no carping and no criticism. The time we spend together will be our goal and our reward. And it worked! I have great memories now of times on the course with the boys. My best Father's Day gift was when my oldest son took me for a free round of golf at a course where he worked.

I am forty-seven now. My scores are not much lower than they were in the past. But I can play all day and not care. So what has changed since my first set of clubs and the frustration of those early years? Golf has taught me much about life, even as life has taught me much about golf:

1. Relax—the easier you swing, the farther the ball will go. A white-knuckle grip and a harder swing will probably only increase the tension and reduce the joy—with poor results to follow.

2. Get some basic instruction from the experts... better yet, find a mentor and vow to have a listening, teachable spirit.

3. Focus on people. Choose to play with people you enjoy, people who you've found that lift your spirit. Head out to the course on your own sometime and practice showing interest in whomever fate may place you with that day. Look for ways to be an encouraging and uplifting gift to their day.

4. Refresh yourself by learning something new. New experiences will help to keep you young, will rekindle your interest, your vitality and your love for life. Find a partner who shares your interest in learning and in experiencing new things.

5. Look for the positive possibilities in every challenging situation. Very seldom will you have no shot at all. Even when you do,

you may be able to take your drop and scramble back into play. Go for it.

6. Realize that life, like golf, has its ups and downs... its bunkers and fairways. Ride it out. Beyond each bunker is a well-groomed fairway or green. It only takes one shot to put it back in play.

7. Sharpen up your "inner game." A smooth, relaxed swing—like a smooth, relaxed life—begins in your mind and heart. Learn to stir and rekindle the human spirit by stopping to "smell the roses" along the way. Take a deep breath. Look around at the beauty of the course and get the most from the experience.

8. Tempo is important. Get in touch with your feelings. A good swing has a distinct and gratifying feel. Developing a feel for the game is as important as the mechanics.

9. Above all, have fun—enjoy the journey and the process and let the results take care of themselves.

~Larry R. Pearson
Chicken Soup for the Golfer's Soul

My Uncle and Me

My uncle Ben Diamond was a draftsman, and it was the perfect job for him. He had a clear, logical mind and an esthetic sense to go along with his devotion to detail. He dressed in a preppy way—navy blazer and gray flannel slacks—and his gestures were mesmerizing. A courtly man, he seemed to move a beat or two slower than others.

When I was a boy in Fairfield, Connecticut, I would walk to his place for breakfast every morning. I left early, before my parents began their daily argument. My father was a gambler, and life in our house was at the mercy of his dark moods. So I'd escape to my uncle's childless apartment, which was always as quiet as a church.

I would sit at the dining room table, surrounded by Aunt Ada's knickknacks and little boxes of violets, while Uncle Ben made our breakfast. (Aunt Ada always slept late, it seemed.) It was an elaborate ritual, and always the same—orange juice, two pieces of buttered toast, one soft-boiled egg and a cup of coffee (mine mostly milk). It was certainly not the usual breakfast for a child, but Uncle Ben made it sound like a king's feast.

He explained how he squeezed the oranges by hand in a cut-glass juicer, never grinding them too hard or there'd be too much pulp in the juice. The toast had to be a perfect shade of tan, he'd say, holding out a slice for me to see. Then he'd lay a pat of warm butter on top, let it melt and spread it evenly over the toast. The egg was cooked for exactly three minutes and brought to me in an eggcup. He showed me how to tap around the shell's circumference with the side of my spoon to remove the top half.

Uncle Ben had a way of singing the praises of the most mundane thing so that it became something of wonder to a child.

While we ate, for instance, he read the major-league baseball scores from the newspaper out loud. We were Yankee fans because the Yankees had many Italian Americans like us: Raschi, Berra, Rizzuto, Crosetti and, of course, Joltin' Joe DiMaggio. I clapped my hands softly at his mention of their success and dreamed of being a part of that someday.

After breakfast, I helped do the dishes. When we finished, Uncle Ben would take a tiny porcelain Buddha from Aunt Ada's china cabinet and let me rub its belly for good luck. Then we'd go play catch in his narrow driveway.

He'd lay a piece of folded cloth on the pavement as a plate and get down stiffly into his catcher's crouch, pinching the knee of each pant leg. Then I'd pitch to him. We made believe I faced the mighty Yankees. After each pitch, he would bounce out of his crouch and fire the ball back. "Attaboy, Paddy!" he'd say. "You got him!"

He was always tough on me, until I got behind in the count on Joltin' Joe and he saw my face flush with panic. Then he'd give me a break on a pitch even I knew was off the plate. "Strike three!" he'd call, then fire the ball back so hard it stung my hand. I always pitched a perfect game with Uncle Ben.

Like many childless adults, he didn't have to feign having fun with children. He really did. Adults, with their neuroses and duplicities, made him nervous. Children, in their innocence, calmed him, which was why he jumped at the opportunity to be our town's Little League baseball coach when it was offered to him.

The job came open every couple of years because the coach was usually the father of one of the players.

He'd coach until his son graduated from Little League, then he'd quit. It was assumed that Uncle Ben would coach for the two years I was eligible to play and then quit. But twenty years later, after I married and had children of my own, he was still our Little League coach.

Uncle Ben was harder on me than he was on the other players. We both knew this was a ruse to hide his obvious affection. On the field he called me Jordan, not Paddy, and he made me carry the heavy canvas bat bag from his car. At batting practice he grunted a little harder when he threw me his fastball and he never told me when his curve was coming, as he did for others.

I was the team's star pitcher, and no matter how hard he tried, my uncle could never really hide his pleasure when I was on the mound. It would be the final inning of a one-run game, with a runner on third base and two outs. He would pace back and forth, yelling encouragement. "Come on, Paddy! You can do it!" (I wasn't Jordan then.) I would get two strikes on the batter, and before I delivered, I'd give my uncle a wink then get strike three. He would charge out to shake my hand.

Uncle Ben ran constant herd on us to act like men. I remember the one time he ever really spoke harshly to me. It was before a game I was not scheduled to pitch. I was fooling around, showing off for the benefit of some twelve-year-old girls who had come to flirt. I put my cap on backward, and my shoes were unlaced in a deliberately sloppy manner to elicit laughter. "Fix your hat and shoes, Jordan!" my uncle barked at me. "Look like a ballplayer!"

I sulked for the entire game. Afterwards, as my uncle drove home, I sat in glum silence. I felt humiliated. He tried to explain why he had snapped at me over such an inconsequential matter.

"It's important how you look, Paddy," he said. "Details, like wearing your uniform just so, add up. They count. If you do all the little things right, then when the big things come it'll be easier to handle them. And sometimes the little things are all you have in life. You can take great satisfaction in those details."

As a child of twelve, I only vaguely understood what my uncle was talking about. I understand now, of course. He was talking about pride in oneself. He was talking about his own life really.

People came from all over the state to see me pitch that year. In the six games I pitched, I threw four no-hitters and two one-hitters. And our team also won when I wasn't pitching.

My uncle's secret to success was to know the limits of his boys, never push them beyond those limits. He kept things simple and orderly. Other managers overextend their players by concocting elaborate plays that always seemed to backfire and humiliate the boys in front of their parents. Those managers wanted to show the fans how much they knew. My uncle always managed in a way that kept the attention on us, not him.

We were a heavy favorite to win the state championship on our way to the Little League World Series at Williamsport, Pennsylvania. But we lost our final game and were eliminated. I pitched a one-hitter that day before three thousand fans. But I threw wildly on a bunt attempt early in the game, which let in what proved to be the only run. After the game we were presented trophies at home plate. When my name was announced, the crowd rose and gave me a standing ovation. My uncle walked out to the plate with his arm around my shoulder. I began to cry, and he was crying, too.

We drifted apart as I became a teenager. He still saw me as a child. I began to see my uncle as lovable but eccentric. He seemed fussy and enmeshed in the myriad details he felt were so important. His interests seemed trivial.

When I was eighteen, I signed a thirty-five-thousand-dollar bonus contract with the Milwaukee Braves and went away to the minor leagues. After three years of diminishing success, I was released by the farm club. I went home, depressed and confused by this first failure of my life.

My bride and I were living, temporarily, at my parents' house near the ballpark where I had had so many youthful successes. My parents had offered us the use of their house until, as my mother put it, "you get back on your feet."

But I couldn't get back on my feet. I spent most of each day lying on the bed in my old room, staring straight ahead. The sun came in through the window, illuminating in a dusty haze the mementos of my career arranged on the bureau: bronzed trophies from Little League, scuffed baseballs from notable high school successes. What had gone wrong?

I stared at those mementos for hours, not really seeing them, but rather lost in a kind of lassitude that made even the simplest tasks—dressing, reading the newspaper, going down to dinner, talking with my wife—seem superfluous.

Downstairs in the kitchen, I could hear whispering voices.

"What's wrong with him?" my mother said.

"I don't know," my wife answered, sobbing softly.

Then one day my uncle called. "Paddy, it's me, Uncle Ben," he said, as if I could ever forget his voice. "Why don't you come over tomorrow for breakfast?"

"I'll see," I said. I had no intention of going, but my mother insisted. "It will hurt him terribly if you don't."

It was just the way it had been when I was a child. The orange juice. The perfect toast. Uncle Ben showing it to me before he buttered it. "See," he said. "Tan." He wasn't trying to humor me; he was just transporting me back to that simple time of my childhood.

After we did the dishes he smiled and said, "I've got something for you." He went into the dining room and opened Aunt Ada's cabinet. Returning with her Buddha, he said, "Remember this, Paddy?"

I smiled. He held it out to me. I rubbed its belly for luck.

Maybe it was the Buddha. Maybe it was just seeing my uncle still take such pleasure in the little details of his life. But I was all right after that. It dawned on me that my life, far from being over, was just beginning. I had a wife. I was twenty-two years old, and there were so many things out there for me to do. I went back to college. Had children. Taught school. Became a writer. Filled my life with a host of things that give me pleasure.

Then, suddenly, my uncle was gone. I was stunned. I thought he'd always be there. And in a way he is.

I think a lot about my uncle these days, especially when I begin to feel sorry for myself. He never allowed himself to indulge in self-pity, even in the face of the one great disappointment of his life—not having a child of his own.

For Uncle Ben, happiness was never a given. It had to be worked at, created. He was a master at finding joy in life's details. He showed me how to take delight in small, everyday pleasures. Like perfect, buttered toast.

~Pat Jordan
Chicken Soup for the Baseball Fan's Soul

The Substitute Caddie

They throw their clubs backwards, and that's wrong.
You should always throw a club ahead of you
so that you don't have to walk any extra distance to get it.
~Tommy Bolt, about the tempers of modern players

An unusual experience occurred at the L.A. Open, where I came out of retirement from my previous job to caddie. My husband Tom Lehman's longtime caddie, Andrew Martinez, was injured the night before the tournament, and Tom asked me to fill in. I agreed under the condition that I did not have to carry Tom's TaylorMade tour bag, which is huge. We struck a deal, and they got me a much smaller bag.

My first duty as caddie was to meet Tom on the driving range so he could warm up before his round. Other players and caddies were stunned to see me. I proceeded with my job like any other caddie — marking balls, cleaning his clubs and getting the towel wet.

Things went smoothly, and Tom played okay, but the whispers and comments from the gallery as I passed by were amusing. The only rather tense moment came on Sunday on the sixteenth hole. Tom had been having a very, let's say, trying day as far as golf. But I was proud of him because his temper was under control.

When Tom three-putted for bogey, I noticed his putter in mid-air, sailing into the middle of the pond. The crowd gasped and looked at me for my reaction. I just smiled and walked with Tom to the next tee.

As we walked, I whispered to him, "That's fine. At least you didn't swear. But now I get to pick which club you'll be putting with on the last two holes."

Tom went along with it.

The seventeenth hole started with a drive down the middle, and his second shot landed just over the green. He proceeded to hit a sand wedge and left the ball six inches from the cup. I told him to putt out with the same club, and the crowd loved it. Especially when he made it.

The eighteenth hole, a par-5, started with Tom's driver straight down the middle, and his second shot got him in position for an easy approach. I handed him the wedge that had just served as his putter. He almost holed it (that would have eliminated the putting problems), the ball rolling to six feet.

Just for effect, I handed him his driver. After the crowd figured out that he didn't have a putter anymore, they were all eagerly awaiting a birdie with the driver. He missed it. But ending on two pars was not such a difficult lesson to learn.

~Melissa Lehman
Chicken Soup for the Golfer's Soul

Tales
OF Golf AND
Sport

The Roar of the Crowd

*We can't all be heroes
because someone has to sit on the curb and clap as they go by.
~Will Rogers*

38

The Clown Prince of Golf

Pro-ams take two basic forms: the normal week-to-week events populated by local businessmen who fork over the fee to play with Greg Norman or Nick Price—or players far less famous but, they often find, just as much fun. Then there are the celebrity Pro-Ams that mix business people with actors, politicians and athletes. These tend to be major yuck-fests, personified in recent years by Bill Murray, who has become the dominant figure at Pebble Beach.

Several years ago, Jeff Sluman found himself in Murray's foursome. A big Murray fan, Sluman was looking forward to the experience. It was a memorable week for Sluman but, he admits, he had some trying moments. "On the first day I three-putted three holes on the front nine," he says. "I just kept missing short ones. We get to the eleventh hole (at Poppy Hills), and I hit my tee shot about forty feet above the pin. As we're walking off the tee, I hear Bill say to [partner] Scott Simpson, 'Now we're really going to find out about him.' I knew I was in trouble."

Sluman left his first putt about six feet short and could feel the yips coming on as he lined up his second putt. He got over the ball and was about to draw the putter back when he heard Murray say, "Ladies and gentlemen, I need some love for this man. Right now, can you all say 'love!'"

Sluman stepped back while the crowd, coached by Murray, yelled, "We love you, Jeff!" several times. Sluman put his hand over his heart to show how touched he was, then began lining the putt up again. Sure enough, just as he was about to start his stroke, he heard Murray's voice again. "This man needs more love. More! Can I hear you, now!"

By now, Simpson had all but dissolved into a puddle of laughter near the edge of the green. This time, as all the love washed down on him, Sluman pretended to cry. The third time, much to his surprise, Murray let him putt. And, even more to Sluman's surprise, the putt went in. "I think I got a bigger roar than on the eighteenth hole when I won the PGA [Championship]," he says.

He deserved it.

~John Feinstein
Chicken Soup for the Golfer's Soul

39

Two Dreams Realized

One of the most poignant moments in Masters history came in 1992, when Fred Couples won the tournament—his first major championship.

After he signed his scorecard, tournament officials brought him to the CBS studio in Butler Cabin, where he would be interviewed by Jim Nantz and awarded the Green Jacket by the 1991 winner, Ian Woosnam.

What made the moment so special was that Nantz and Couples had been through this many times before in mock interviews. As suite-mates at University of Houston, Nantz—who dreamed of covering the Masters for CBS—would "interview" Couples—who dreamed of winning the Masters one day.

After CBS went off the air, Couples and Nantz embraced, both with tears in their eyes.

"The thing that is so amazing is that all those years ago, we always knew it was going to be the Masters that Fred would win," Nantz said.

~Don Wade
Chicken Soup for the Golfer's Soul, The 2nd Round

I Did Not Know That

Bristol, Connecticut. 1991. The dead of winter. The dead of night. Inside ESPN headquarters, only a skeleton staff remained: the 2:30 A.M. *SportsCenter* producer Tim Kiley, coordinating producer Barry Sacks, and a handful of production assistants helping with the wire copy, highlights and scripts for the program. Monitors that earlier blared out programs in progress all around the country were now silent. My partner for the 2:30 A.M. broadcast, Mike Tirico, was tossing out facts about the games and information we were about to deliver to the audience. It wasn't enough. We reviewed the video, scanned the box scores and gathered the research—we always want to know more.

At the end of the broadcast that night, we had time to fill. Mike Tirico came up with a gem of a fact, the kind of pertinent, resonant piece of information that totally satisfied the hunger for more. My delighted on-air response? "I did not know that." That is how one of my heroes outside the sports world, former king of late-night television Johnny Carson, used to respond to a great anecdote from a guest.

As soon as we went off the air, we huddled in the conference room, knowing we were onto something. Let's face it, sports fans are as competitive as the athletes they admire. Even if you're just talking about sports, you want the edge. You want to know more than the other guy.

Barry Sacks said we should throw out a great nugget every night on the 2:30 A.M. show. Production Assistant Edwin Van Duesen said we should make up a special graphic. Someone else suggested naming the segment "I Did Not Know That." Rather than using Carson's exact phrase, I proposed "Did You Know?" And a little piece of *SportsCenter* history was made.

The response was overwhelming. Whatever the top sports story that day, we'd compete to offer the best bonus piece of information. It wasn't that we were trying to outsmart the viewer. We were the viewer: ready to be surprised, eager to be informed, generous with what we knew. Viewers would send mail or call to give us their own items for "Did You Know?"—one of the first tangible links between the people who work at ESPN and our audience. Where else but *SportsCenter* could you learn that the only major-league pitcher to match his age in strikeouts in a single game was Bob Feller, who at age seventeen struck out seventeen batters in 1936? Or that the NFL record for fewest rushing touchdowns in one season was set by the Brooklyn Dodgers—the football Dodgers—in 1934?

I finally met Johnny Carson a few years ago, at a celebrity tennis tournament at UCLA. When there was a break in Andre Agassi's match, I approached the Hollywood legend and told him about his role in the creation of one of America's most beloved sports slogans. Without missing a beat, he smiled and said, "I did not know that."

~Chris Myers
Chicken Soup for the Sports Fan's Soul

Living the Dream

Follow your passion, and success will follow you.
~Arthur Buddhold

The name jumped out at me from the list of tournament scores in a national golf publication. It was printed in tee-ny-tiny type, and I caught it only because I'm in the habit of scanning the mini-tour results for past and future tour stars.

I didn't expect to see his name in italics, and it stopped me in my tracks and made me smile.

Darryl Staszewski.

I stared at the letters until they blurred, feeling pangs of nostalgia as I thought about an old high school friend and the paths we chose in life. I felt admiration for Darryl, and maybe a little envy, too.

Staszewski, a graduate of St. Francis (Wisconsin) High School class of '74—my class, my friend—had tied for seventh place in an obscure mini-tour event somewhere in the Northwest. He won $216.

Big deal, you say?

It is, if you knew Darryl twenty-five years ago. As a high school freshman, he stood probably four-feet-ten-inches, and couldn't have weighed much more than seventy-five pounds. By his senior year, he had sprouted to five-feet-six-inches and tipped the scales at about 120, soaking wet.

Naturally, he got teased about his size. His buddies, especially, were relentless with their wisecracks. He took it in stride, mostly, but

I'll never forget the day I snatched his driver's license out of his hand and loudly announced, with no small amount of glee, that Darryl was required to sit on a platform to see over the steering wheel.

In terms of teenage insults, I'd hit a 350-yard drive. Darryl laughed with the rest of us, but I noticed tears of humiliation welling in the corners of his eyes. It was the last time I ever teased him.

Darryl was a pretty good athlete, but he obviously was too small to play football, and after freshman basketball—he looks like a waif in the yearbook team photograph—he didn't make the squad as a sophomore.

So he turned to golf.

A left-hander, he swung in slow motion and barely managed to hit the ball out of his own shadow. He practically buckled under the weight of his golf bag. He didn't make the varsity team until he was a senior, and then only as the sixth man on a five-man squad, perhaps as a reward for his perseverance. Darryl played in few actual matches.

Back then, a few of us dreamed about becoming professional golfers, but we were eighteen and full of silly notions. Instead, we went off to college or to work, got married, had children. Ultimately, we fulfilled our destinies in golf: We became weekend hackers.

Except for Darryl Staszewski. He had the determination, the courage and the focus about which the rest of us only talked. Maybe the teasing he had endured made him tougher. Maybe he just wanted it more than we did. Maybe he just had more talent than we did, and it simply took a while to surface.

Not long after we graduated, Darryl moved to California to work on his game. Eventually, he became a club professional, and at some point in the late 1970s, I lost track of him.

Twenty years later, I was in the media tent at the Greater Milwaukee Open when somebody tapped me on the shoulder. I turned around and there was Darryl Staszewski—a lean, athletic six-footer.

He was living near Seattle, but was in town on vacation and had barely missed earning a spot in the GMO field in the Monday qualifier. We chatted for a while, and he gave me his phone number, saying it would be fun to get together and play a round if I ever got up to the Northwest.

And then I forgot about Darryl again until I found myself staring at his name in a golf magazine. It really doesn't matter whether he won $216 or $216,000, whether he finished seventh on the Cascade Tour or won the U.S. Open.

You see, Darryl is living the dream.

~Gary D'Amato
Chicken Soup for the Golfer's Soul

Quiet, Please!

She was sitting in the stands at the 15th hole lost in her thoughts. Maybe she was contemplating the previous hole. Or the beautiful Georgia day. Or perhaps she was praying that this would be the year Augusta National relented and allowed her husband to walk away with a green jacket instead of a broken heart.

Then Laura Norman heard those voices. Two men seated near her at the Masters were arguing... about her husband's hair. Was Greg Norman a real blond or wasn't he? It couldn't be real, could it? It was too perfect. Too white blond. Too much a part of the larger-than-life image of the Great White Shark.

"One of them said Greg must have stayed up all night bleaching it," Laura recalls, laughing. "They were like two catty women, the way they were going on. It was as if they were jealous of him."

One more crack and Laura had had enough. "It's real," she said.

They weren't buying it. "Yeah, right," said one of them. "How do you know?"

She smiled. "I'm his hairdresser."

Two jaws dropped. "You are? Well... uh... omigod... uh... okay."

Did that stop the thoughtless chatter?

What do you think? Want to bet those guys were at it again a few groups later?

The men and women who follow their spouses on the PGA and LPGA tours know the drill. Walking along outside the ropes with the gallery, they have an opportunity most of us don't have: They get to watch their spouses work. That has its benefits and its drawbacks. On the one hand, the husbands and wives don't have to wait until a spouse comes home and tells them about their day to know if a cranky or ebullient evening lies ahead.

On the other hand, they have to put up with the other people who are watching their spouses at work. People who let everyone know what they think they know. People who voice opinions without a worry about who might be listening. People who offer unsolicited advice to wives, husbands, mothers, fathers, even players—whether they want it or not. No wonder tour spouses generally tuck their "family" badges out of sight and walk alone.

Imagine hearing someone you don't know talk about your personal life, or listening to someone bad-mouth your wife for being last in the field or simply for not being on someone's short list of favorite players. Observing "true fans" is no better, if they are giggling about how cute your husband is or how he—and you—are headed for divorce court. Then there are the "experts" who love to disclose juicy details about the wild party you never threw, or your taste in furniture.

"Today, my daughter told me to hurry up and get over here," Sally Irwin says after walking a round watching her husband, Hale. "They were talking about our house in Arizona. About how big it was, what it looked like. They didn't have anything right."

They seldom do. Just ask Steve Stricker's wife, Nicki. In 1998, she found herself standing behind the 17th green at The Players Championship, five months pregnant and sandwiched between two guys out to impress their wives or girlfriends and each other.

"Steve walked up to the green and one of these fellows started telling the other, 'Yeah, his wife used to caddie for him, but they got in a big fight and now they're divorced,'" Nicki chuckles. "I stood there and thought about whether to say something, but I didn't. They were just trying to sound good for the women.

"When things like that happen, you have to evaluate the situation. Do you want to embarrass them? Or do you just walk away? I just walked away."

Others haven't. Ben Crenshaw's first wife, Polly, routinely joined in the fun. When someone would tell a story about Ben, she would lean in, without a hint of revealing her identity, and say, "Really? Tell me more."

Norman's mother once tired of hearing a fan belittle her son and hit the man with her umbrella. Another time, Irene Burns had had enough of one fan's disparaging remarks about her husband, George, so she wound up and hit him with her stick seat. Sue Stadler, whose husband, Craig, has always been a fan favorite and target, was subtler.

"It was at the Kemper Open, and Craig was playing on Sunday," Sue recounts. "These guys had been saying things all day and one of them yelled, 'C'mon Stadler, choke.' He was about four feet behind me when he said it.

"Later, we were all walking along, and I stopped and put my stick seat out. The guy ran right into it. It hit him right in the stomach." Oops. Pardon me.

Another time, Sue was less subtle. Craig was playing with Raymond Floyd when someone called him an SOB. "I held my temper in check and said, 'Excuse me sir, my husband is not an SOB,'" recalls Sue. "The entire gallery laughed at him."

It's even better when the player himself (or herself) responds. During the final round of the 1994 Masters, Jeff Maggert's first wife, Kelli, and his mother, Vicki Benzel, were at the 13th green waiting for him to hit his approach. Jeff was last and playing with a marker, so a few fans started in, calling him "Maggot" and other rude names. Kelli and Benzel were giving the fans a dressing down for insulting their husband and son when a ball hit the green and rolled into the hole for a double-eagle 2.

"I was just praying it wasn't the marker," Kelli says. It wasn't. Maggert had hit a 3-iron 222 yards for the third double eagle in Masters history, the first since 1967 and the first at the 13th. Everyone, including the Maggot men, cheered.

Even the most polite inquiry can be, well, annoying—and a little amusing. Consider the day Dale Eggeling's husband, Mike, was standing beside the 17th green at an event in East Lansing, Michigan. Dale was working on a career-low 63 and had just hit her approach shot eight feet from the flagstick. Just then, a reporter walked up and asked, "Does anyone know which one is Dale Eggeling?"

When Mike pointed her out, the reporter asked if he was sure. Mike said, that he was Dale's husband.

"Then with all sincerity, the guy—a reporter right?—says, 'Do you know she's leading the tournament?'" Mike recalls. "I was surprised a reporter asked that. I think I just said something like, 'Yeah, she is doing well.'" She won.

Some incidents aren't the least bit amusing. One day when he was in elementary school, Craig Stadler's son Kevin overheard someone in the gallery call his father a jerk. Tears came streaming down Kevin's face as he asked his mother why anyone would say that.

"It broke his heart. It's hardest on the kids," Sue says. "I told Kevin the man didn't know Daddy and that just meant that [the man] was the jerk."

She also taught Kevin and his brother never to root against anyone. Ever.

One scenario is so oft repeated that it's almost like an initiation rite: A husband or wife is walking along early in their spouse's careers when someone comes up and asks who is playing in the group, When the spouse rattles off the names, the fan responds, "Oh, nobody." If they are prepared, the spouse will turn and say oh-so-politely, "Hey, I'm Mrs. Nobody. And I don't appreciate that." If they aren't prepared....

"You have to grow thick skin," says Allison Frazar, whose husband, Harrison, turned pro in 1996. "People get excited about this or that, and they mean well. But sometimes I look at what they're criticizing, and see it as a problem I have to go home and help fix."

Which brings up another major hazard of watching someone in your family work: You tend to want to help. Melissa Lehman remembers one particularly tough week when every well-meaning family member turned into a critic or a teacher. They were all staying together, which made it especially hard on Tom.

Finally, Melissa exploded. "I said, 'From now on, Tom is the only person allowed to be elated or upset about any golf shot, understand?'" she said. And the second Tom walked in the door that night, she announced, "C'mon, we're leaving." And they did.

A fair number of stories, though, are just plain silly. Amy Mickelson overheard two elderly men who claimed that her husband, Phil, had broken both his legs in a skiing accident. "They both had to be amputated," the men went on. "And look how well he's walking."

Then there was the man who was seriously explaining why Dallas resident Frazar wore shirts with Byron Nelson's name on them. "You know, that's Byron Nelson's grandson," he said. "That's why he has Byron Nelson's name over his heart. Byron is his No. 1 fan." Of course, they're no relation. Frazar wears the shirts because he has a deal with E. McGrath, which makes the line.

Hal Sutton's wife, Ashley, overheard another man telling his companions that Hal had gone to school with his daughter at Arizona State University in the early 1970s. "I laughed at them," she said.

"If he did, he must have been sixteen." Hal went to Centenary College.

Trying to stay inconspicuous is often the best tack to take. Dottie Pepper's husband, Ralph Scarinzi, tries to lay so low that he usually stays about half a hole ahead of Pepper's group and doesn't even look at gallery members who approach him.

Melissa Lehman's favorite story may be one about her. One day, someone came up to her husband's caddie, Andy Martinez, and laid into Tom.

"The man said, 'I thought Tom Lehman was a nice Christian man,'" Melissa says, recounting the tale. "'If he is, then why was he clutching some babe behind the fitness trailer this afternoon? She was dark-haired and on a bike. And she was hot.'"

Yes, and she was Tom's wife.

Pardon me.

~Melanie Hauser
Chicken Soup for the Golfer's Soul, The 2nd Round

The Autograph

I t was 1963 in the Toronto suburb of Willowdale. I was eight years old and hockey-crazy. My next-to-nil skills had not stunted my passion for the game. Earning himself a reservation for a warm seat in heaven, my dad would stand shivering beside the boards of the outdoor public rink, watching me ride the bench in the Catholic Minor Hockey League. The Toronto Maple Leafs were, of course, my heroes, and their Bee Hive Corn Syrup photos plastered my bedroom walls in black and white. I had no idea that one of my most revered icons lived a mere three blocks away.

Back then, walk-a-thons and bike-a-thons had not yet been invented, so we raised funds the good old-fashioned way, selling something the public could actually sink its teeth into. In my school's case, it was the annual doughnut drive—Margaret's Doughnuts, big and doughy, choice of honey-glazed or chocolate-glazed, cheaper if you bought two dozen or more.

Door-to-door I went, clipboard in hand. Although it was long ago, I can still smell the Gestetner fluid on the freshly minted order form. I sold dozens of dozens; hardly a soul turned me down. Was the irresistibility in my product or my sales pitch? "After all, mister, EVERYBODY loves doughnuts." My sheet was almost full, and my stomach almost empty, when I reached Wedgewood Drive with its two modest rows of look-alike sidesplits. I went up the south side—no one home, no one home. The next house would be my last;

I had already stretched my parents' limit of a two-block radius, and dinner would be on the table in ten minutes.

I rang the doorbell and rehearsed my spiel while staring at the flamingo on the screen door. The bird swung toward me, and my next and indelible memory is looking up from a large pair of fuzzy slippers, way up, to the face peering down. Once it registered, I stood there speechless for what seemed an eternity, opening and closing my mouth like a fish out of water. Collecting my composure, but still unable to go into doughnut-talk overdrive, I told him something he already knew. "Yup, that's me," he replied with a nod and a smile.

Having successfully established a rapport, I followed with new information—that we shared our given name. I have a vague recollection of stammering through my "Please-buy-some-doughnuts-to-help-my-school" speech, and then a vivid one of him taking the clipboard from my hand. Of course, I had no way of comprehending the historical irony of the document he handed back to me. Flushed with pride from our first-name-basis farewells, I flew home clutching the clipboard to my chest. Nobody got a word in edgewise at dinner.

The next morning before the bell, I guardedly showed off the precious paper. In the classroom, my teacher grumbled good-naturedly as she copied out my orders on another sheet—no way would I let go of the form, no way was I giving up that autograph. Doughnut delivery day could not come fast enough, but my return to Wedgewood Drive was anticlimactic—his wife answered the door. There I stood, red-faced in my Maple Leafs sweater, as four school chums who had doubted my story taunted me from the street.

Fast-forward several years and several hundred franchises later: I wonder if the runt at the door was his inspiration. ("After all, EVERYBODY loves doughnuts.") In futile search, I've torn my folks' basement apart, but it seems I've lost that purple-lined piece of Canadiana, the testimony to a feat that is surely mine alone to claim: I sold Tim Horton a dozen doughnuts.

~Tim O'Driscoll
Chicken Soup for the Canadian Soul

Augusta Heaven

Always be a little kinder than necessary.
~James M. Barrie

I started to shake with anticipation as I hung up the phone. Could it really be true that I would be playing a round of golf at the hallowed ground of Augusta National?

The generous offer had been extended by my friend, Frank Christian, a world-renowned golf course photographer and the official photographer of Augusta National for the last thirty years. Each year, Augusta allows selected employees to invite two guests to play the course. Our date was to be just two weeks after the Masters.

I brought along my friend Tim Townley. Tim and I have been friends forever, but I have since found myself constantly reminding him that he will be indebted to me for just as long a period of time. Needless to say, the weeks leading up to our date seemed like an eternity. We talked every five minutes, sharing some nuance of Augusta history.

Frank Christian has a way to make people feel special and make his friends' trip to Augusta a once-in-a-lifetime experience. So it was when we arrived in Augusta.

Frank has a long-standing tradition that he invites you to partake the night before you play. You see, when the great Bobby Jones died, Frank was in charge of cleaning out Bobby's locker. In it he found a bottle of 1908 Old Rye Whiskey some three-quarters full. With permission, Frank cradled home his prize. Frank's preround ceremony consists of each member of the foursome taking a sip of whiskey from Bobby Jones's bottle. To this day, I get the chills thinking back on it.

I awoke before dawn the next morning in anticipation of the day that lay ahead. Finally the hour of our departure arrived, and we headed out to the course.

On approach, I had my first glimpse of the famed gate and the magnolia-lined drive. Just outside the gate stood a man and his young son craning their necks to get a peek inside. The young boy was attired in knickers and a tam o'shanter, just like Payne Stewart. Clearly golf was a passion the father had passed on to his son and now was being jointly shared. If I had the ability to let them inside the gates I would have, but alas, as we passed, I wished them luck in their efforts.

Everything was perfect, just the way I had always imagined it would be. Every blade of grass was perfectly cut, the gardens were brilliant and every shrub was precisely manicured. The golf course was very different than it appears on television. Namely, the course is distinguished by deep and numerous undulations and hills. Although the difficulties of the greens are well documented, I believe they are even tougher in person.

I have played St. Andrews, Royal Troon, Muirfield, Pebble Beach and many others, but Augusta National was without a doubt the best overall golfing experience I have ever enjoyed.

I have my own tradition whenever I play one of these great courses. I collect a small vial of sand from one of the bunkers and display it alongside its distinguished brethren. I pinched some sand from the famous bunker alongside the 18th of Augusta as my keepsake.

Arriving at the airport for my return home, I spotted the father and son I had seen at the gate to Augusta. I asked the little boy, whose name was Max, if he had a good time in Augusta, and he gave me a reluctant "yes." His dad mentioned to me that Max was really disappointed because he could not get in the gates of Augusta National to get a souvenir. Well, here I was just fresh from a round at Augusta wearing my new Augusta shirt and my new Augusta hat, and this little boy had nothing.

At that point I took off my hat and put it on his little head. I then reached into my bag and grabbed my vial of sand from the 18th hole and explained to Max what it was and how I got it. I told Max that this would be a great start for a new collection for him.

The look on his face was absolutely priceless.

As great as my golfing experience was at Augusta National, my most memorable moment was the look on Max's face.

~Jeff Aubery
Chicken Soup for the Golfer's Soul, The 2nd Round

The Day I Met the King

Gone golfin'... be back dark thirty.
~Author Unknown

I'll always remember how I first met him. It was in my rookie year of 1977. Coincidentally, it occurred at a tournament that has become very special to me through the years, the Bing Crosby Pro-Am. We had the Monday qualifying system back then, and I had missed the first two qualifiers at Phoenix and Tucson. I had finally made it into my first official PGA Tour event at the Crosby and was out playing a practice round at Monterey Peninsula Country Club, one of the courses used in the rotation at the time.

It was late Tuesday afternoon before the tournament, and I had played the front nine and was somewhere on the back side when I noticed a large cloud of dust billowing up in the distance. It was like in the old cowboy movies when there's a cattle drive or the posse's ridin' up on the bad guys, and I knew something important was happening. But I went about my business and, sensing I didn't have time to finish all eighteen holes, I cut over to the sixteenth tee.

As this was my first time on the course, I really didn't know the layout of the holes. I just knew I had about half an hour of sunlight left. So I hit a couple drives off the sixteenth, when all of a sudden, out of nowhere, an incredible throng of spectators emerged over the rise behind me and surrounded the back of the tee.

It was like when the entire Bolivian army encircled Butch Cassidy and the Sundance Kid and aimed their rifles at them. These people weren't armed and dangerous, but they were sure looking at me with expressions that said:

Who is this kid, and what's he doing out here?

And then the Red Sea parted, and who should walk through it but Arnold Palmer himself, The King. He couldn't have been more regal had he been wearing a robe and carrying a staff.

I felt a chill come over me. I was shocked and embarrassed. I mean, here was my boyhood idol, and I'd just cut right in front of him, and hit two balls no less. I wanted to crawl into the ball-washer and disappear. But true to his character, Palmer walked up to me, shook my hand, introduced himself and said, "How are you?"

I managed to squeak out a "fine," although I wasn't. And he said, "Could we join you?"

Now that was the first thing he ever said to me, and it struck me so funny because I was thinking, "Can you join me?" What I wanted to say was, "Can I have your permission to crawl under a rock and stay there for a day as penance for getting in your way?"

But, of course, I acted cool, considered his request for a long second, and said, "Sure, love to have you," like it was no big deal.

This was gut-check time, even if there was no money on the line, because in addition to meeting my idol for the first time, I also met Mark McCormack, who was Palmer's amateur partner. McCormack was head of IMG, with whom I had signed just a few weeks before, but I wasn't sure he even knew who I was.

Nevertheless, I was determined not to let the situation intimidate me, or worry about embarrassing myself. I've always loved the challenge of golf, whatever it may be, so I looked on this as just another challenge, and a darned good preparation for the coming week. After all, this was just a practice round, so I couldn't worry about future endorsements, or impressing these guys. My goal at that point in my career was simple survival. All I wanted to do was make some cuts, make some money and keep my playing privileges. I was recently married and I wanted to be able to make it to that Christmas and have enough money to buy my wife a nice present.

But back to the sixteenth hole. Arnold hit a nice drive, and I remember feeling good that both of my drives were past his. If I felt a moment of cockiness, however, it quickly evaporated when I snap-hooked a 7-iron into the bunker. Fortunately, I got it up and down, and that eased my nerves. On the next tee, Arnold asked me what kind of ball I was playing, and I told him it was a Titleist.

He said, "You ought to try one of these good balls," and tossed me a Palmer ball. I hit it and liked it, so he tossed me a three-pack and said, "As a rookie starting out, you need good equipment, and these might help you along the way." He was sincerely trying to be helpful, because it wasn't as if he needed the endorsement of an unknown kid from Oregon playing his golf balls.

As abruptly as the experience of playing golf with Arnold Palmer had begun, so it ended. After holing out at 18, Palmer thanked me, wished me luck in my career and disappeared into the madding crowd. When I looked up a few seconds after shaking his hand, everyone was gone. I mean everyone. There was no more Arnie's Army, only Peter's Poltergeists. I had to shake my head to make certain it had really happened.

~Peter Jacobsen with Jack Sheehan
Chicken Soup for the Golfer's Soul

Roger Maris and Me

It's nice to be important,
but it's more important to be nice.
~Author Unknown

I grew up in the shadow of Yankee Stadium, and just fell in love with baseball.

When Roger Maris came to the New York Yankees from the Kansas City Athletics in 1960, I was eleven. I had been burned in a fire in August, so I was laid up for a while and followed baseball even more closely. I remember a headline that said Roger Maris "rejuvenates" the Yankees. I had never heard the word before, but it made me think this Roger Maris was someone special.

For me, there was something about the way he swung the bat, the way he played right field and the way he looked. I had an idol. In 1961 the entire country was wrapped up in the home-run race between Maris and Mickey Mantle and Babe Ruth's ghost. I cut out every single article on Roger and told myself that when I got older and could afford it, I would have my scrapbooks professionally bound. (Eight years ago I had all of them bound into eleven volumes.)

I usually sat in section 31, row 162-A, seat 1 in Yankee Stadium. Right field. I would buy a general admission ticket, but I knew the policeman, so I would switch over to the reserved seats, and that one was frequently empty. I'd get to the stadium about two hours before it opened. I would see Roger park his car, and I would say hello and tell him what a big fan I was. After a while, he started to notice me.

One day he threw me a baseball during batting practice, and I was so stunned I couldn't lift my arms. Somebody else got the ball. So Roger spoke to Phil Linz, a utility infielder, and Linz came over, took a ball out of his pocket and said, "Put out your hand. This is from Roger Maris."

After that, my friends kept pushing me: "Why don't you ask him for one of his home-run bats?" Finally, when Roger was standing by the fence, I made the request. He said, "Sure. Next time I break one."

This was in 1965. The Yankees had a West Coast trip, and I was listening to their game against the Los Angeles Angels on the radio late one night, in bed, with the lights out. And Roger cracked a bat. Next morning my high school friend called me. "Did you hear Roger cracked his bat? That's your bat."

I said, "We'll see."

When the club came back to town, my friend and I went to the stadium and, during batting practice, Rog walked straight over to me and said, "I've got that bat for you."

I said, "Oh, my God, I can't thank you enough."

Before the game, I went to the dugout. I stepped up to the great big policeman stationed there and poured my heart out.

"You have to understand, please understand, Roger Maris told me to come here, I was supposed to pick up a bat, it's the most important thing, I wouldn't fool you, I'm not trying to pull the wool over your eyes, you gotta let me...."

"No problem. Stand over here." He knew I was telling the truth.

I waited in the box-seat area to the left of the dugout, pacing and fidgeting. Then, just before game time, I couldn't stand it anymore. I hung over the rail and looked down the dimly lit ramp to the locker room, waiting for Rog to appear. When I saw him walking up the runway with a bat in his hand, I was so excited I almost fell. I don't know what he thought, seeing a kid hanging upside down, but when he handed me the bat, it was one of the most incredible moments in my young life.

I brought the bat home, and my friends said, "Now why don't you ask him for one of his home-run baseballs?"

So I asked Roger, and he said, "You're gonna have to catch one, 'cause I don't have any."

Maris was traded to the St. Louis Cardinals on December 8, 1966—a dark day for me. That year, I went off to college at the University of Akron, in Ohio. My roommate had a picture of Raquel Welch on his wall, and I had a picture of Roger Maris.

Everyone knew I was a big Maris fan. My friends said, "You say you know Roger Maris. Let's just go see." So six of us drove two and a half hours to Pittsburgh, Pennsylvania, to see the Cardinals play the Pirates. It was May 9, 1967. We got to Forbes Field two hours before the game, and there was No. 9. It was the first time I had ever seen Roger Maris outside of Yankee Stadium, and I figured he wouldn't know me in this setting. I was very nervous. Extremely nervous, because I had five guys with me. I went down to the fence, and my voice quavered: "Ah, Rog... Roger...."

He turned and said, "Andy Strasberg, what the hell are you doing in Pittsburgh?"

That was the first time I knew he knew my name. "Well, Rog, these guys from my college wanted to meet you, and I just wanted to say hello." The five of them paraded by and shook hands, and they couldn't believe it. I wished Rog good luck and he said, "Wait a minute. I want to give you an autograph on a National League ball." And he went into the dugout and got a ball and signed it. I put it in my pocket and felt like a million dollars.

In 1968, I flew to St. Louis, Missouri, to see Roger's last regular-season game. I got very emotional watching the proceedings at the end of the game. I was sitting behind the dugout, and Rog must have seen me because he later popped his head out and winked. It touched my heart. I was interviewed by the *Sporting News*, which found out I had made that trip from New York City expressly to see Roger retire. The reporter later asked Maris about me, and Roger said, "Andy Strasberg was probably my most faithful fan."

We started exchanging Christmas cards, and the relationship grew. I graduated from college and traveled the country looking for a job in baseball. When the San Diego Padres hired me, Roger wrote me a nice note of congratulations.

I got married in 1976, at home plate at Jack Murphy Stadium in San Diego, California. Rog and his wife, Pat, sent us a wedding gift, and we talked on the phone once or twice a year. In 1980, Roger and Pat were in Los Angeles for the All-Star Game, and that night we went out for dinner—my wife Patti and I, my dad, Roger and Pat.

When Roger died of lymphatic cancer in December 1985, I attended the funeral in Fargo, North Dakota. After the ceremony, I went to Pat and told her how sorry I felt. She hugged me, and then turned to her six children. "I want to introduce someone really special. Kids, this is Andy Strasberg." And Roger Maris Jr. said, "You're Dad's number-one fan."

There is a special relationship between fans—especially kids—and their heroes that can be almost mystical. Like that time my five college buddies and I traveled to Pittsburgh to see Roger. It's so real to me even today, yet back then it seemed like a dream.

I'm superstitious when it comes to baseball. That day I sat in row 9, seat 9, out in right field. In the sixth inning Roger came up to the plate and, moments later, connected solidly.

We all—my friends and I—reacted instantly to the crack of the bat. You could tell it was a homer from the solid, clean sound, and we saw the ball flying in a rising arc like a shot fired from a cannon. Suddenly everyone realized it was heading in our direction. We all leaped to our feet, screaming and jostling for position. But I saw everything as if in slow motion; the ball came toward me like a bird about to light on a branch. I reached for it and it landed right in my hands.

It's the most amazing thing that will ever happen in my life. This was Roger's first National League home run, and I caught the ball. Tears rolled down my face. Roger came running out at the end of the inning and said, "I can't believe it."

I said, "You can't? I can't!"

The chances of No. 9 hitting a home-run ball to row 9, seat 9 in right field on May 9, the only day I ever visited the ballpark, are almost infinitely remote. I can only explain it by saying it's magic — something that happens every so often between a fan and his hero. Something wonderful.

~Andy Strasberg
Chicken Soup for the Sports Fan's Soul

Postscript: On August 3, 1990, I received a phone call from Roger's son Randy and his wife, Fran. They were calling from a hospital in Orlando, Florida. Fran had just given birth to their first son. Fran and Randy wanted me to know that they named their son Andrew and asked if I would be his godfather. To this day I still can't believe that the grandson of my childhood hero, Roger Maris, is my namesake and also my godson.

Tales
OF Golf AND
Sport

Against the Odds

"Impossible" only describes the degree of difficulty.
~David Phillips

Close to Home

I have found that if you love life,
life will love you back.
~Arthur Rubinstein

For six years, Bob and Nancy Mills celebrated their favorite week of the year—the week of the FedEx St. Jude Classic—with a house full of friends and clients. Overlooking the Tournament Players Club at Southwind's eighteenth hole, the Mills' home was a hotbed of activity for this family of golf-lovers who'd participated in the tournament for fifteen years.

But a week after the 1997 Classic, Nancy Mills walked out her back door not to join a party but to capture a quiet moment alone as she grappled with a parent's worst nightmare. Doctors had told the Mills earlier that day that their five-year-old daughter, Ali, had cancer. Incredulous, Nancy stared at the tournament's scoreboard across the lake that now read "The St. Jude Kids Say Thanks" and realized that Ali was now one of those children. The tournament the Mills had loved and been involved in for years was now to affect their lives in a larger way than they ever imagined—by benefiting their Ali.

During the tournament the week before, Ali's leg had begun to ache, and she lost her appetite and grew very pale. Nancy instinctively knew something was amiss, and she was right: Ali's bloodwork looked wrong and the doctor could feel something in her abdomen. She was sent to St. Jude, and by that afternoon the Mills family knew they were dealing with cancer. A grueling series of tests the next day confirmed Ali had a very rare and potentially deadly solid tumor called neuroblastoma. The tumor stretched from her abdomen to her neck, and had already spread to her bone marrow, the most advanced stage of the disease. The Mills were completely shocked.

"I thought, 'How did I miss this?'" Nancy says. "We were just numb. We couldn't think. You know there are bad things that can happen to your children, but I never thought of cancer. There's no history of cancer in our family at all. For the first week, I couldn't even say the word 'cancer.'"

St. Jude doctors moved fast to begin treating Ali because her condition was so serious. She began chemotherapy treatments the same night as her battery of tests and the diagnosis. Groggy from sedation to get her through the tests, Ali awoke the morning of July 4th in the hospital and learned she had cancer.

"She was very quiet—which isn't like Ali," Nancy says. "We told her she had a tumor and were very up front with her. She took it all very well. Even though she had just gotten her hair long, she was okay when it started falling out from the chemo. On her second treatment, she pulled it out and saved it in a plastic bag to give to the birds to use in their nests."

The Mills lived through tough days as Ali's doctors at St. Jude Hospital attempted to put her cancer into remission so she could have a bone marrow transplant—her only hope for a cure. Despite a year of various high-powered chemotherapy treatments and a surgery to remove the primary tumor, however, the cancer remained in Ali's bone marrow. At last, though, the Mills family received the wonderful news that for the first time Ali's bone marrow was free from cancer.

Ali had her bone marrow harvested the week of the FedEx St. Jude Classic.

"It's so hard to watch your child go through this, to know it's life-threatening," Nancy says. "You don't want to see them suffer, miss out on things, be stared at. We try to keep life normal."

Bravely soldiering through her treatments, Ali emerged from them with few outer signs of illness other than her bald head. A popular, bubbly presence at St. Jude, she entertains her nurses and doctors with songs and pranks. "She hasn't let her trials get her down," Nancy says.

In March, Ali went to see *The Lion King* on Broadway in New York. Her chemotherapy-induced baldness attracted the attention of another child in front of her. She heard the little girl say, "He doesn't have any hair!" Ali tapped her and told her, "A) I'm a SHE, B) it's called cancer, and C) it's the drugs." Then she leaned her smooth head toward the girl and said kindly, "Do you want to feel it?"

This is Ali's true spirit. She is known for bringing the St. Jude staff to tears with her favorite song, which says, "God doesn't see the same way people see. People see the outside of a person, but God looks at the heart."

It's Ali's beautiful, courageous heart that gives significance to the FedEx St. Jude Classic. This isn't lost on the Mills family, whose devotion to the tournament is ironically helping save their daughter's life.

~Bob Phillips
Chicken Soup for the Golfer's Soul

The Luckiest Golfer Alive

I'm not afraid of death.
It's the stake one puts up in order to play the game of life.
~Jean Giraudoux,
Amphitryon

No golfer worthy of his titanium driver would dare complete a round without complaining. The greens are always too hard, the pin positions too difficult, the rough too high and the sand traps too deep. The unwritten code of behavior dictates that every golfer must voice such complaints.

Either that, or admit the real reason for lack of success on the golf course: your own ineptitude.

But even while joining the griping session, I know deep down I am the luckiest golfer alive. I haven't holed a chip shot to win the Masters on extra holes. I haven't canned a sand shot to win the PGA. But I am lucky.

Just how lucky I am was brought home by an item in the *Golf Plus* edition of *Sports Illustrated*, which read:

"A golf course is the fifth most likely place to suffer a heart attack, but one of the least likely places to survive one—about 5 percent of stricken golfers survive."

But here I am. I twice beat the statistics. And on the same course. I had what was described as a cardiac arrest on the 3rd hole in February and on the 5th hole in November. Improved, huh?

I survived, I am convinced, because of having good friends. In the foursome immediately behind me when I keeled over in February was Dr. Bob Bullington, a retired cardiologist. Behind that group were Cotton Fitzsimmons, former coach of the Phoenix Suns, and two of the Suns' current players, Joe Kleine and Dan Majerle. They called 911.

Bullington used chest compressions to revive me. I remember coming to, lying on the apron in front of the 3rd green and hearing another doctor tell Bullington he couldn't get a pulse.

"Isn't that nice?" I said.

I then suggested we let Cotton's group play through. I was too late. They already had skipped around me. I was lucky they didn't give me a two-stroke penalty for slow play.

In November, I holed a fifty-foot putt on the 5th hole. I was short of breath, possibly from the excitement of the putt, but made my way to the golf cart and passed out. My cartmate, Paul McCoy, immediately recognized my problem and raced to the group ahead of us, which, get this, included the same Dr. Bullington.

This episode was more serious. Bullington thought he had cracked a couple of ribs pounding on my chest. I didn't regain consciousness until reaching the intensive care ward. My problem apparently has been remedied by a new drug and a pacemaker.

One problem: Bullington won't play golf with me now. Says he wants to finish eighteen.

~Bob Hurt
Chicken Soup for the Golfer's Soul, The 2nd Round

Amanda

She looks like all the rest of them on the volleyball court with her gold number "12" on the purple jersey. Tall, blond, with incredible blue eyes and a slim athletic build, my fifteen-year-old daughter Amanda, the kid who gets good grades and works her tail off at everything she does, could easily be the cover girl for any teen magazine. My wife, Jackie, and I watch in amazement as she dives for another dig on the court, slides across the floor headfirst until she reaches the ball and sends it flying back over the net as the crowd claps its approval. As the coach calls time-out and the girls hurry to the sidelines, Amanda uses her jersey to wipe her face, like any other kid, but at that moment you can see the scar that runs down the right side of her abdomen and across her belly. She is not like all the rest of them. She has my kidney inside her.

As they huddle off-court, my mind drifts back to September 20, 1988, and the little girl who came into our lives. "Bubs" was her nickname, short for "Bubba Girl," a name tagged by Jackie's sister Kim when she first saw the ten-pound, two-ounce infant. At first everything was normal with Amanda, but a few months into her life she developed searing fevers, and every visit to the doctor left us more confused. Still, Amanda's toothless grin and shining blue eyes comforted us. Even after throwing up in the doctor's office, she would raise her head and smile as if to say, "Don't worry, be happy!" Her joy was contagious, but our fear was enormous.

Shortly after her first birthday, Amanda was diagnosed with

kidney reflux, a common condition that often reverses itself, but without treatment can be very harmful. Her doctors decided, with our approval, to perform a simple outpatient procedure to correct the problem. Surgery was scheduled just before Amanda's fifth birthday. Not long before we were to go to the hospital, the phone rang. It was Dr. Kevin Ghandi, Amanda's nephrologist, with some shocking news. "John, X-rays show that Amanda's right kidney is toxic and making her sick. It has to be removed." The news literally knocked us to our knees. How could this be?

The night before surgery, with Amanda between us in bed, we explained what would happen tomorrow. Amanda listened quietly and simply smiled, then whispered, "Do I get ice cream when it's all over?" Jackie and I looked at each other, wishing it could be that simple, and held her close.

We watched Amanda ride into the operating room, sitting up, with her trusted friend Teddy at her side. The gifted hands of "Dr. Kevin" removed Amanda's ailing organ and took care of the reimplantation of her ureter into the bladder. Everything looked good, but Amanda's optimistic prognosis came with a warning: Someday, she would need a transplant. "Someday" seemed very far away as Amanda held her own, leaving the doctors scratching their heads about how she was able to do so well with only 20 percent of one kidney functioning. We never told them our secret. Each night before Amanda went to bed and every morning when she woke up, I would ask her a very important question: "Bubs, what are we going to be today?"

She would answer, "Positive, and my kidney is getting better." This became a ritual for us, a powerful bridge between the mind and body. Soon "better" became "perfect" and "awesome" and "incredible." Her strength of spirit displayed itself in her physical condition.

Eight years passed. As Amanda's body changed, the little kidney grew tired and "someday" was fast approaching. Factors of age and relationship made me the best organ donor candidate, and the doctors ordered more tests. I held my breath, and a small voice inside reminded me of my grandfather's death from polycystic kidney disease—the same disease that would eventually lead to my father's death. My sister did not have it, and I had never been tested. I prayed and thought of Amanda's smiling face. Jackie and I sat with the ultrasound tech in the darkness as she slid the wand over my kidneys, searching for any cysts. She said, "I'm not really supposed to tell you guys, but I see two healthy kidneys in there." I knew then that a perfect plan was in place and that everything would be all right. It was the closest thing to a miracle I had ever known.

"Someday" turned out to be July 18, 2002. Amanda and I were wheeled into operating rooms at Children's Hospital at the University of Wisconsin in Madison. My healthy vital organ was removed, and a world-renowned surgeon, Dr. Hans Sollinger, delicately placed it in my daughter's body. It began making urine immediately! For the first time in her young life, Amanda had a healthy kidney!

When I awoke after surgery, the nurse placed her hand on my chest and said, "Amanda is down at the other end of the room and is doing great. Is there anything you want me to tell her?"

My throat raw from the breathing tube, I croaked two words, something she would understand, "Hubba-Bubba," my usual corny greeting to her. With tears in her eyes, the nurse delivered the unusual message, and Amanda, with eyes closed, did what she has always done: She smiled.

As fathers, we always hope to leave a piece of ourselves with our children. For Amanda and me, the bond goes far beyond the physical into a spiritual trust, a feeling for me that some agreement from long ago has been fulfilled. It is a rare thing to give life to your child not once, but twice. Two years have passed since the procedure, and as I watch her head back out onto the court, she glances my way and gives me a big smile and a "thumbs-up." I push back the tears and smile back. I am her father, but she is my hero.

~John St. Augustine
Chicken Soup for the Father & Daughter Soul

Lightning Strikes Twice

To be upset over what you don't have is to
waste what you do have.
~Ken S. Keyes, Jr.,
Handbook to Higher Consciousness

During a round with friends on March 18, 1990, seventy-four-year-old Margaret Waidron of Jacksonville, Florida, approached the par-3 seventh hole.

Legally blind, Waldron had lost her vision ten years earlier to an eye disease. Instead of giving up sports, though, she continued to be an active golfer, relying on her husband, Pete, to line her up and to describe the hole, distance and playing conditions.

Pete handed Margaret a 7-iron and pointed her toward the flag on Long Point's eighty-seven-yard seventh hole. "I hit the ball solidly," Margaret recalled. "One of my friends said, 'Good hit, Margaret... Wow! It's going for the green! It's going toward the hole!'"

"Another friend shouted, 'You've got a hole-in-one!' We all hugged and I felt a great sense of fulfillment. That night, Pete and I celebrated."

When Margaret arrived at the same hole the next day, she took the same 7-iron and once again hit the eighty-seven-yard shot perfectly. The ball rolled into the cup for another ace. "When we went back to the clubhouse, I was so proud," Margaret said. "I don't consider myself handicapped. I am challenged to do the best I can with what I have. What else should I do? Sit home and knit? Not me!"

Experts have computed the odds against an amateur scoring a hole-in-one at twelve thousand to one, and no one yet has attempted to establish the likelihood of a blind golfer recording an ace. "To do it twice on the same hole, two days in a row, using the same club and the same ball, makes the odds beyond comprehension," said Long Point golf pro Ed Tucker.

~Bruce Nash and Allan Zullo
Chicken Soup for the Golfer's Soul

Making Contact

51

Driving back to New Orleans with his cousin Bill Kyle after attending a wedding in Baton Rouge, Louisiana, Pat Browne's thoughts drifted to a round of golf he planned to play the next day. It was late afternoon on Saturday, February 26, 1966, and Kyle was driving, so the thirty-two-year-old Browne, who had played on the golf and basketball teams at Tulane University in his hometown of New Orleans, did not have to concentrate on the road.

Suddenly, though, he saw a car driving at a high rate of speed from the opposite direction. As it got closer, it swerved out of control, crossing a small median divider.

"Look out, Bill!" Pat Browne screamed. As he did, the other car slammed into the auto Bill Kyle was driving. The force of the impact drove the hood of Kyle's car through the windshield, sending shards of glass into Browne's eyes and severing his optic nerve.

The teenage driver of the speeding car, which had been stolen, was killed instantly. But both Browne and Kyle survived with serious injuries. "Seeing that car jump the divider was the last thing I ever saw," Browne recalled thirty-five years after the accident which left him blind along with a fractured collarbone, jaw and knee cap and cost him several front teeth.

"How in the world am I ever going to play golf again?" Browne thought to himself when doctors told him that he would never see again. "And how can I bear not seeing my three daughters again?"

At the time of the accident, Pat Browne was married with three young daughters, aged eleven, nine and seven, who were the joy of his life. He also was a lawyer with a large law firm in New Orleans and a well-known athlete. When he was able to find time, Browne also excelled on the golf course, shooting in the 70s and holding a 3 handicap, which was 2 less than the one he possessed while playing on the varsity golf team at Louisiana State University. Occasionally, the six-foot, four-inch 210-pound Browne also played some pickup basketball. As a player at Tulane, he had gone up against such Hall-of-Fame players as Bob Pettit of Louisiana State and Sam and K. C. Jones while they were winning back-to-back national championships at the University of San Francisco in the mid 1950s.

Indeed, Pat Browne had a lot going for him until, suddenly, the lights went out forever on that winter afternoon in 1966.

"Depressed? I guess I was for a while," said Browne, whose weight dropped from 210 pounds to 165 during his convalescence. "But I knew I had to get on with my life and was convinced that, even though I had lost my sight, I would still be able to do most of the things I did before the accident, including maybe even play golf."

Following months of hospitalization and a long convalescence, along with learning how to get along in a world that had suddenly gone dark, Browne returned to work with the law firm of Jones and Walker on a part time basis in June of 1966, four months after the accident. "In September, when I was back working fulltime, I tried my first case," he said, "and realized that I could still practice law effectively."

The following spring, two friends, Bobby Monsted and Doc Schneider, convinced Browne to try to hit a few golf balls at the New Orleans Country Club, to which the three men belonged.

"Come on, Pat, let's give it a try," Monsted said.

"Bobby, how in the world am I going to hit the ball when I can't see it?" Browne said.

"Don't worry, you'll do fine," Schneider said. "You're still going to be a good golfer."

At the club, after Browne had taken a few practice swings, Monsted placed a ball on a tee, set Browne in position, handed him a driver and set the club back on the ground directly back of the ball. "You're all set, Pat," he said. "Now all you've got to do is swing and hit it."

Browne, apprehensive and unsure of himself, swung easily and lofted a drive about 150 yards down the middle, about 100 yards shorter that he would normally hit his two shots before his accident. "That impact felt good," he told Monsted and Schneider. "Where did it go?"

"Right down the middle," Schneider responded. "Not bad for the first time out."

"Let's hit some more," an enthused Browne said.

For the next fifteen minutes or so, with Monsted and Schneider lining him up for every shot, Pat Browne struggled. Most of his wood shots went straight, some as far as 200 yards. But most of his iron shots sailed wide to the right—shanks, as they're known in golf.

As they left the driving range, Monsted said, "Pat, that was great for the first time. I think you ought to keep at it. After all, you were practically a scratch golfer before the accident, and you still have a great swing, good coordination and excellent reflexes."

"Maybe you're right, Bobby, and thanks a lot to you and Doe for your help today," Browne said to his friends as they walked towards the clubhouse. "Maybe if I really work at my game, I can still play reasonably well."

As it developed, Browne played more than reasonably well. Henry Sarpy, a member of the same law firm, volunteered to be Browne's coach, as the people who line up blind golfers for their shots and lead them around the golf course are known. Together, along with other friends, they played scores of rounds of golf together over the next two years. Then one day, Sarpy said, "Pat, I think you ought to consider playing in the national blind golfers tournament.

"A golf tournament for blind golfers?" Browne asked incredulously,

"Yes, they have it every year," Sarpy said. "Charlie Boswell is the head of the Blind Golfers Association, and the way you're playing, I'm sure you would do well."

Browne knew about Boswell. He had been an outstanding football and baseball player at the University of Alabama before losing his sight in World War II. After taking up golf following his blindness, Boswell had written a book entitled, *Now I See.*

With Sarpy as his coach, Browne played in his first blind tournament in Chattanooga, Tennessee, in 1969. At the time, the blind golfers' field was dominated by Boswell and Joe Lazaro, who, like Boswell, had been blinded during World War II, Browne finished fourth, shooting between 100 and 108, which is excellent in blind golf competition. "I know I can do better," he told Sarpy after the tournament ended. And he did, winning his first national tournament in 1975, and then, from 1978 through 1997, winning it a phenomenal twenty years in a row with Gerry Baraousse, a former All-America golfer at Washington & Lee, as his coach.

During that period, and into his sixties, Browne established himself as the best blind golfer in the world. Playing under U.S. Golf Association rules, he performed better than most sighted golfers, even very good ones. He carded an 80 at the very difficult Pinehurst course in North Carolina, a 76 at his home course, the New Orleans Country Club, and then, incredibly, put together four consecutive rounds in the 70s, including two in which he shot 74, in 1982 at the very challenging Mission Hills Country Club in California. By the 1990s, as the blind golf circuit expanded internationally, Browne was winning scores of other tournaments, both in the U.S. and abroad. At times during the mid-1990s, his "coach" often was his teenage son, Patrick, who had developed into one of the best junior golfers in Louisiana.

Numerous honors have been bestowed on Browne, who served as president of the U.S. Blind Golfers Association from 1976 to 1992, when he was succeeded by Bob Andrews, who lost his sight in Vietnam. Browne has received the Ben Hogan Award from the Golf Writers Association of America and been inducted into the Tulane Hall of Fame and the Louisiana Sports Hall of Fame.

"I think I've been blessed," said Browne, who for the last twenty-five years has been president and chief executive officer of a savings and loan association in New Orleans. "I've played at some of the world's greatest golf courses in England, Ireland, Scotland, Australia and New Zealand, which I may never have played if I hadn't lost my sight. And I've met some wonderful people along the way, particularly the other blinded golfers. I've also been to the Masters six or seven times since the accident and played the Augusta National Course. Now that's golfing heaven. And to think I've played it twice. I imagine that some people wonder why blind golfers play. But they don't understand that the thrill of hitting the golf ball is what counts. And you don't have to be able to see it to enjoy doing it."

~Jack Cavanaugh
Chicken Soup for the Golfer's Soul, The 2nd Round

52

If the Dream Is Big Enough, the Facts Don't Count

Some men see things as they are and ask why.
Others dream things that never were and ask why not.
~John F. Kennedy

I used to watch her from my kitchen window and laugh. She seemed so small as she muscled her way through the crowd of boys on the playground. The school was across the street from our home, and I often stood at my window, hands buried in dishwater or cookie dough, watching the kids as they played during recess. A sea of children, and yet to me, she stood out from them all.

I remember the first day I saw her playing basketball. I watched in wonder as she ran circles around the other kids. She managed to shoot jump-shots just over their heads and into the net. The boys always tried to stop her, but no one could.

I began to notice her at other times, on that same blacktop, basketball in hand, playing alone. She practiced dribbling and shooting over and over again, sometimes until dark. One day I asked her why she practiced so much. As she turned her head, her dark ponytail whipped quickly around, and she looked directly into my eyes. Without hesitating, she said, "I want to go to college. My dad wasn't able to go to college, and he has talked to me about going for as long as I can remember. The only way I can go is if I get a scholarship. I like basketball. I decided that if I were good enough, I would get a scholarship. I am going to play college basketball. I want to be the best. My daddy told me if the dream is big enough, the facts don't count." Then she smiled and ran toward the court to recap the routine I had seen over and over again.

Well, I had to give it to her — she was determined. I watched her through those junior high years and into high school. Every week, she led her varsity team to victory. It was always a thrill to watch her play.

One day in her senior year, I saw her sitting in the grass, head cradled in her arms. I walked across the street and sat down beside her. Quietly I asked what was wrong.

"Oh, nothing," came a soft reply. "I am just too short." The coach had told her that at five-feet, five-inches tall, she would probably never get to play for a top-ranked team — much less be offered a scholarship — so she should stop dreaming about college.

She was heartbroken, and I felt my own throat tighten as I sensed her disappointment. I asked her if she had talked to her dad about it yet.

She lifted her head from her hands and told me that her father said those coaches were wrong. They just did not understand the power of a dream. He told her that if she really wanted to play for a good college, if she truly wanted a scholarship, that nothing could stop her except one thing — her own attitude. He told her again, "If the dream is big enough, the facts don't count."

The next year, as she and her team went to the Northern California Championship game, she was seen by a college recruiter who was there to watch the opposing team. She was indeed offered a scholarship, a full ride, to an NCAA Division I women's basketball team. She accepted. She was going to get the college education that she had dreamed of and worked toward for all those years. And that little girl had more playing time as a freshman and sophomore than any other woman in the history of that university.

Late one night, during her junior year of college, her father called her. "I'm sick, Honey. I have cancer. No, don't quit school and come home. Everything will be okay. I love you."

He died six weeks later—her hero, her dad. She did leave school those last few days to support her mother and care for her father. Late one night, during the final hours before his death, he called for her in the darkness.

As she came to his side, he reached for her hand and struggled to speak. "Rachel, keep dreaming. Don't let your dream die with me. Promise me," he pleaded. "Promise me."

In those last few precious moments together, she replied, "I promise, Daddy."

Those years to follow were hard on her. She was torn between school and her family, knowing her mother was left alone with a new baby and three other children to raise. The grief she felt over the loss of her father was always there, hidden in that place she kept inside, waiting to raise its head at some unsuspecting moment and drop her again to her knees.

Everything seemed harder. She struggled daily with fear, doubt and frustration. A severe learning disability had forced her to go to school year-round for three years just to keep up with requirements. The testing facility on campus couldn't believe she had made it through even one semester. Every time she wanted to quit, she remembered her father's words: "Rachel, keep dreaming. Don't let your dream die. If the dream is big enough, you can do anything! I believe in you." And of course, she remembered the promise she made to him.

My daughter kept her promise and completed her degree. It took her six years, but she did not give up. She can still be found sometimes as the sun sets, bouncing a basketball. And often I hear her tell others, "If the dream is big enough, the facts don't count."

~Cynthia Stewart-Copier
Chicken Soup for the College Soul

The Lunar Golf Shot

What other people may find in poetry or art museums,
I find in the flight of a good drive.
~Arnold Palmer

Have you ever thought about hitting a driver 1500 yards or a 6-iron 900 yards? Or watching a white ball against a black sky with a time of flight of twenty-five to thirty seconds? What golfer even dares dream of these things?

I thought about these things during Apollo 14 in 1971. You see, the moon has one-sixth the gravity of Earth. That means with the same clubhead speed, the ball will go six times as far and stay in the air (or in this case the vacuum) six times as long!

Actually, Bob Hope gave me the idea of playing golf on the moon, although he didn't know about it until months after the flight. He was visiting NASA one day—Deke Slayton and I were showing him around—and he had an old driver that he was swinging as we walked around the campus. We hooked him up in a moon walker and as he was bouncing up and down on his toes, he used the driver for balance! That's when I said, only to myself, I had to find a way to hit a ball on the moon.

Perhaps people on Earth watching me on television thought it was spontaneous and unauthorized, but it was well-rehearsed and all approved before we launched.

I had planned to use a collapsible aluminum handle, which we normally used to scoop up dust samples, since we really couldn't bend over in a pressurized suit. And then I had a golf pro design a clubhead to snap on the handle, replacing the small scoop. It was a number 6-iron since the handle was about as long as a normal 6-iron shaft. I planned to take the clubhead and two ordinary golf balls in my suit pocket—at no expense to the taxpayers!

I practiced before the flight several times in the suit-training room to be sure I could swing safely. The pressurized suit is cumbersome and I couldn't get both hands on the club; still I could make a half swing with one hand. And, finally, I checked with the "boss" and told him my plan to hit two golf balls at the very end of the lunar stay, only if everything went perfectly up to that point. He agreed.

Fortunately, although we had some problems earlier, everything went just right while we were on the surface. Consequently, just before climbing up the ladder to come home, I prepared to tee off! When I dropped the first ball, it took about three seconds to land, and bounced a couple of times in the gray dust. Then, I improved my lie of course (winter rules in February) and made my best slow-motion, one-handed half-swing. Making a full swing in a space suit is impossible. I made good contact and the ball, which would have gone thirty to forty yards on Earth, went over 200 yards. The ball stayed up in the black sky almost thirty seconds. I was so excited I swung harder on the second one, which I shanked about forty yards into a nearby crater! I decided to call that a hole-in-one, even if the hole was several miles in diameter.

So I folded up the golf club and climbed up the ladder to take off. The two golf balls are still there and ready to be reclaimed and reused—after all, they were new. But the club resides in a place of honor at the U.S. Golf Association in Far Hills, New Jersey, where all who see it can imagine, as did I, what a 1500-yard tee shot would really be like!

~Alan Shepard as told to Carol Mann
Chicken Soup for the Golfer's Soul

54

The Man
with the Perfect Swing

On a warm morning at a country club near Orlando, a stocky gentleman with wispy gray hair makes his way past the crowd gathered for today's exhibition. To those who don't know better, the impish old fellow could be just another sunburned senior dreaming of bogey golf.

He wears a black turtleneck despite the heat. The left pocket of his neon-lime slacks bulges, as always, with two golf balls—never more, never fewer. All three watches on his left wrist are set to the same time.

Taking his position at the tee, he quickly lofts a few short wedge shots about 70 yards. At first the spectators seem unimpressed. Then they notice that the balls are landing on top of one another. "Every shot same as the last," chirps the golfer, as if to himself. "Same as the last."

Moving to a longer club, a 7-iron, he smoothly launches two dozen balls, which soar 150 yards and come to rest so close to each other you could cover them with a bedspread. He then pulls out his driver and sends a hail of balls 250 yards away—all clustered on a patch of grass the size of a two-car garage.

Astonished laughter erupts from the crowd. "Perfectly straight," says the golfer in a singsong voice. "There it goes. Perfectly straight."

People who have followed Moe Norman's career are no longer

surprised by his uncanny displays of accuracy. Many professionals and avid players consider the seventy-year-old Canadian a near-mythical figure. But few outside the sport have ever heard his name. Fewer still know the story of his struggle to find acceptance in the only world he understands.

One cold January morning in 1935, five-year-old Murray Norman was sledding double with a friend on an ice-packed hillside near his home in Kitchener, Ontario. Speeding downhill, the sled hurtled into the street and skidded under a passing car.

Both boys survived and ran home crying. But the car's right rear tire had rolled over Moe's head, pushing up the cheekbone on one side of his face. His parents, unable to afford medical care, could only pray he did not suffer serious brain injury.

As Moe grew older, he developed odd behavioral quirks and a repetitive, staccato speech pattern. His older brother Ron noticed that Moe seemed unusually frightened of unfamiliar situations. At night, Ron often heard his little brother sobbing in bed, devastated by some real or imagined slight.

At school, Moe felt glaringly out of place among other kids. Desperate for friends and acceptance, he tried to be playful, but his efforts often backfired — pinching people too hard or bear hugging them until they pushed him away. He heaped ridicule on himself and even coined his own nickname: Moe the Schmoe.

He became known as a slow student in every subject — except one. At math no one could touch Moe Norman. He astounded his classmates by memorizing complicated problems and multiplying two-digit numbers in his head almost instantly.

When he wasn't acting the clown, Moe walled himself off from others. Over time he plunged deeper into isolation, and yet, ironically, loneliness led him to his greatest happiness.

In the years following his accident, Moe spent hours atop that same winter sledding hill, hacking around an old golf ball with a rusty, wood-shafted 5-iron he found at home. Here in the solitary and magical world of golf, he found a reason to wake up each morning.

Kitchener, Ontario, in the 1940s was a gritty factory town where working-class teenagers had little desire or money to play the "sissy," upper-class game of golf. But Moe was spellbound, often skipping meals, school and chores to head off by himself in a field to hit balls—five hundred or more a day. He practiced until dark, sometimes until the blood from his hands made the club too slippery to hold.

In his early teens Moe landed a job as a caddie at a country club—only to be fired when he hurled the clubs of a low-tipping local mogul into some trees. Soon he gave up caddying to concentrate on playing, honing his skills at a nearby public golf course. He quit school in tenth grade, and by the time he was nineteen, he knew he was blessed with a rare talent: He could hit a golf ball wherever he wanted it to go.

Moe left home in his early twenties, hitching rides to compete in amateur golf tournaments all over Canada, supporting himself with a succession of low-paying jobs. At his first few tournaments in the late 1940s, fans didn't know what to make of the odd little fellow with the garish, mismatched outfits, straw-like red hair and crooked teeth.

His manner was playful, almost childlike, his self-taught technique wildly unorthodox. Legs spread wide, he stood over the ball like a slugger at the plate, clutching the club not with his fingers, as most golfers are taught to do, but tightly in his palms, wrists cocked, as if he were holding a sledgehammer.

Many spectators dismissed him as an amusing sideshow. Some giggled when he stepped up to the tee. Soon, though, Moe Norman was turning heads for reasons other than his personal style.

Recognized as a gifted player who could hit a golf ball with breathtaking precision, he quickly became a sensation on the amateur golf circuit. In one year alone he shot 61 four times, set nine course records and won seventeen out of twenty-six tournaments.

Even as his fame grew, Moe remained painfully shy and could not shake the sense that he was undeserving of the attention. Rather than bask in the spotlight, he avoided it. In 1955, after winning the Canadian Amateur Open in Calgary, Moe failed to show for the awards ceremony. Friends later found him by the nearby Elbow River, cooling his feet.

That victory qualified Moe for one of golf's most prestigious events: the Masters. When the invitation to the tournament arrived, he was only twenty-six and spending his winters setting pins in a Kitchener bowling alley. The Masters was his chance not only to represent his country but to show skeptics he wasn't just some freak on a run of beginner's luck.

But his old demons would give him no rest. Moe felt like an intruder among some of golf's bright lights. He played miserably in the first round and even worse on day two. So he fled to a nearby driving range to practice.

While hitting balls Moe noticed someone behind him. "Mind if I give you a little tip?" asked Sam Snead. The Hall-of-Famer merely suggested a slight change in his long-iron stroke.

But for Moe it was like Moses bringing the Eleventh Commandment down from the mountaintop.

Determined to put Snead's advice to good use, Moe stayed on the range until dark, hitting balls by the hundreds. His hands became raw and blistered. The next day, unable to hold a club, he withdrew from the Masters, humiliated.

But Moe climbed right back up the ladder to win the Canadian Amateur again a year later. A string of victories followed. In time, he had won so many tournaments and collected so many televisions, wristwatches and other prizes that he began selling off those he didn't want.

When the Royal Canadian Golf Association charged him with accepting donations for travel expenses, which was against regulations for amateurs, Moe decided to turn professional. His first move as a pro was to enter, and win, the Ontario Open.

As a newcomer to professional golf, Moe approached the game with the same impish lightheartedness of his amateur years. When people laughed, he played along by acting the clown. An extremely fast player, he'd set up and make his shot in about three seconds, then sometimes stretch out on the fairway and pretend to doze until the other players caught up.

Fans loved the show, but some of his fellow competitors on the

U.S. PGA Tour did not. At the Los Angeles Open in 1959, a small group of players cornered Moe in the locker room. "Stop goofing off," they told him, demanding that he improve his technique as well as his wardrobe.

Friends say a shadow fell across Moe that day. Some believe the episode shattered his self-confidence and persuaded him to back out of the American tour, never to return. More than anything, Moe had wanted to be accepted by the players he so admired. But he was unlike the others, and now he was being punished for it.

The laughter suddenly seemed barbed and personal. No longer could he shrug it off when some jerk in the galleries mimicked his high-pitched voice or hitched up his waistline to mock Moe's too-short trousers.

Because Moe never dueled the likes of Americans Jack Nicklaus or Arnold Palmer, he achieved little recognition beyond Canada. At home, though, his success was staggering. On the Canadian PGA Tour and in smaller events in Florida, Moe won fifty-four tournaments and set thirty-three course records. While most world-class golfers count their lifetime holes-in-one on a few fingers, Moe has scored at least seventeen.

Despite his fame and the passing years, Moe was continually buffeted by the mood swings that tormented him in childhood. Even among friends he could be curt, sometimes embarrassingly rude.

At other times he was charming, lovable Moe, bear hugging friends and tossing golf balls to children like candy—the happy-go-lucky clown from his amateur days.

Through the 1960s and '70s, Moe racked up one tournament victory after another. But in the early 1980s his enthusiasm for competition began to wane. His winnings dwindled, and he slipped into depression. Not being wealthy, he seemed to care very little for money, lending thousands to aspiring golfers and never bothering to collect.

Broke and all but forgotten, he drifted from shabby apartments and boardinghouses to cut-rate roadside motels, often sleeping in his car. Had it not been for the generosity of friends—and a stroke of good luck—he might have faded entirely into obscurity.

Moe has never had a telephone, a credit card or owned a house. Few people know where he might be living on any given day, and he seldom talks to strangers. Little wonder it took Jack Kuykendall two years to track him down.

Kuykendall, founder of a company called Natural Golf Corp., finally caught up with him in Titusville, Florida. He told Moe that, trained in physics, he had worked for years to develop the perfect golf swing—only to discover that an old-timer from Canada had been using the same technique for forty years. He had to meet this man.

Moe agreed to demonstrate his swing at clinics sponsored by Natural Golf Corp. Word spread quickly through the golfing grapevine, and before long, sports magazines were trumpeting the mysterious genius with the killer swing.

Among those following Moe's story was Wally Uihlein, president of the golf-ball company Titleist and FootJoy Worldwide. Hoping to preserve one of golf's treasures, Uihlein announced in 1995 that his company was awarding Norman five thousand dollars a month for the rest of his life. Stunned, Moe asked what he had to do to earn the money. "Nothing," said Uihlein. "You've already done it."

Two weeks later, Moe Norman was elected to the Canadian Golf Hall of Fame. Even today, however, he remains largely unknown outside his native country except among true disciples of the game. For them, Moe is golf's greatest unsung hero, the enigmatic loner once described by golfer Lee Trevino as "the best ball-striker I ever saw come down the pike." Many agree with Jack Kuykendall—had someone given Moe a hand forty years ago, "we would know his name like we know Babe Ruth's."

In the parking lot of a Florida country club, Moe Norman is leaning into his gray Cadillac, fumbling through a pile of motivational tapes. He seems nervous and rushed, but as he slides behind the wheel, he pauses to reflect on his life, his family and his obsession.

Moe never had a real mentor or a trusted advisor. "Today's kids," he says, "are driven right up to the country club. Nice golf shoes, twenty-dollar gloves, nice pants. 'Have a nice day, Son.' I cry when I hear that. Oooh, if I'd ever heard that when I was growing up..."

He squints into the sun and cocks his head. "Everyone wanted me to be happy their way," he says. "But I did it my way. Now, every night I sit in the corner of my room in the dark before I go to bed and say, 'My life belongs to me. My life belongs to me.'"

With that, he shuts the door and rolls down the window just a crack. Asked where he's going, Moe brightens instantly, and a look of delight spreads across his face.

"Gone to hit balls," he says, pulling away. "Hit balls."

It is, and forever will be, the highlight of his day.

~Bruce Selcraig
Chicken Soup for the Golfer's Soul, The 2nd Round

55

The Drive of a Champion

Having already accumulated a host of trophies since starting to play competitive golf at the age of ten, Larry Alford, at sixteen, had developed into one of the best young golf prospects in the country. Already shooting in the 70s, he was elected the most valuable player of the McCullough High School team during both his sophomore and junior years. Following his junior year, Alford matched against seventy-four of the nation's best junior golfers at the Mission Hills Desert Junior Tournament in Rancho Mirage, California. He was tied for the lead going into the final round after firing a 72 and a 71, but he dipped to a 78 in the final round, which tied him for second place, five strokes behind the winner—Tiger Woods.

Alford's performance drew the interest of coaches from some of the best college golf teams in the country, including Arizona, Arizona State, Stanford and Oklahoma State. Wanting to stay close to home, he accepted a scholarship at the University of Houston. "Just think, everything will be taken care of, and I'll be close to home, and it won't cost you anything while I'm going to college," Alford said to his mother, Missy, "and I'll be playing for one of the best college teams in the country."

Fighting back tears, Missy Alford hugged her son tightly, knowing that he had worked so hard to earn a scholarship to make it easier for her. "That's wonderful, Larry," she said. "I'm so happy for you."

That summer, Alford worked harder than ever on his golf game, hitting hundreds of balls daily while working at the golf cart barn at The Woodlands Country Club. At night, he and one of his best friends, Brendan, waded into water hazards at nearby golf courses to retrieve golf balls. Salvaging as many as 2,000 a night, they sold them for eighteen cents apiece, which enabled Larry to play more golf that summer. His paychecks from his golfing job went to his mother, an art teacher who also made and sold decorative wreaths and did wallpapering. "That's Larry," his father, Larry Alford Sr., said. "Finishing second in the biggest junior golf tournament of the year and then wading into water hazards to fish out golf balls. In no way was success going to change him."

Late that summer, a golf teammate asked if Larry could do him a favor and drive the teammate's father's Corvette to a relative's house. The teammate in turn would follow in his car and then drive Larry home. Larry said fine and off they went. Shortly after 6 P.M., while it was still broad daylight, Larry lost control of the Corvette on Interstate 45. The car flipped over three times, catapulting Alford through the open sun roof and onto the highway. Alford's friend braked his car to a halt and saw his teammate lying motionless and bleeding badly from the head, face and left arm.

In the emergency room at Hermann Hospital in Houston, a doctor emerged from behind a curtain and asked Larry's parents to come in. "Oh my God!" Mrs. Alford screamed to herself on seeing her son, who was the color of gray ice with a head as big as a basketball. Out of the corner of one eye, she saw what she perceived to be a look of horror on the face of one doctor.

"I got the feeling that they wanted us to see Larry once more, maybe for the last time," Missy recalled. Then, as she and Larry Sr. were led out, she pleaded to herself, "Dear God, please save him."

From the moment Larry Alford arrived at Hermann Hospital, Dr. James "Red" Duke, the hospital's chief trauma surgeon, knew that his severed left arm could not be saved. Far more important was a life-threatening head injury. Then there were the lesser injuries: a fractured eye orbital bone that had jarred Larry's eye partially out of its socket, a broken jaw, ankle and shoulder blade, a collapsed lung and a badly injured right arm. "I'm sorry, but we had to amputate your son's arm below the elbow," Dr. John Burns, an orthopedic surgeon, told Larry's parents.

"Is he going to be all right?" Missy Alford asked.

"We don't know," Dr. Burns answered.

Standing alongside Missy was Jay Hall, a friend of hers who could not help but wonder about Larry's reaction to the loss of his left arm if he were indeed going to survive. "How would Larry ever get along without golf?" Hall thought to himself. But then, catching himself in mid-thought, Hall also realized there was a far more pressing matter than a golf career at stake. They've got to save Larry's life, he said to himself. That's all that matters right now.

For almost ninety days Larry Alford remained unconscious and in critical condition. Then, gradually, his condition improved and he was no longer in danger. But his parents knew that difficult days lay ahead. For one thing, he would eventually learn that he had lost his left hand.

One night, Larry awakened and suddenly realized that his left hand was missing. He cried out for a nurse. One hurried into his room and said softly, "I'm sorry, Larry, but they had to amputate your hand." Meanwhile, his father, alerted, raced to the hospital.

"Dad, how am I ever going to play golf?" he asked.

"Don't worry, Larry," his father replied. "You'll play again, and you'll do fine."

Young Alford did not remain depressed for long. "Mom, I did it to myself," he said one day to his mother, "so I'm to blame. And God saved my life, so I'm lucky."

A few weeks later, while talking about golf, Larry turned to his father and asked, "Dad, do you have my clubs with you?"

"Yeah, I've got them in the trunk of the car, Larry."

"Good," Larry said excitedly. "Can you get my pitching wedge? Maybe we can chip some balls outside."

Within minutes Larry and his father were on the lawn outside the Del Oro Institute in Houston where Larry was recuperating. Although he had lost forty pounds and was weak, young Larry began to chip with his right arm. Ball after ball went soaring in beautiful arcs as both father and son looked on in delight.

"Dad, will you look at those shots," Larry said, ecstatic at swinging a golf club again.

"You're doing great, Son, just great," his father, replied heartened by Larry's joy.

A week later, at young Larry's suggestion, he and his father went out to play a round of golf at one of the four courses at The Woodlands Country Club. Understandably, Larry's father was both happy and apprehensive.

"God, I hope he does all right," Mr. Alford said to himself. "Don't let him be upset."

Larry Alford Sr. needn't have worried. Though still weak and lacking in stamina, his son hit his shots cleanly and accurately during his first outing as a one-handed golfer. His chipping and putting in particular were superb. "Boy, Dad this is great," he said at one point as he and his father walked down a fairway.

At the end of eighteen holes, Larry had shot an 86, about ten strokes above his average before his accident, but an extraordinary score for a one-handed golfer. As they headed for the clubhouse, Larry, obviously elated at how he had played, turned to his father and said, "Dad, do you think that I can still make the PGA Tour?"

Larry Sr. was prepared for the question. "Yes, I do," he replied. "But I think we're going to have to take this one day at a time."

After that, and unbeknownst to Larry, Jay Hall began calling prosthetic manufacturers to find out if there was such a thing as an artificial golf hand on the market that would enable Larry to play competitive golf. Finding none, Hall decided that he, himself, would try to design a golf hand for Larry on his own. "First, I had to ask myself just what does the left hand do on a golf swing for a right-handed golfer," said Hall, a professional psychologist and a good golfer himself. "And the answer is quite simple. It holds the club with three fingers and it hinges or cocks the club. Essentially, it provides those two functions, and that's about all."

Of paramount importance, Hall knew, was that the hand had to grip the club firmly enough so that the handle wouldn't be twisted by the force of the swing. To ensure that, Hall designed the palm of the hand with pumped-up air cells. For the wrist, he came up with a ball and socket mechanism which, Hall felt, could perform the function of a human joint.

Hall then took his design to Ted Muilenburg, the owner of a prosthetics company in Houston. "Jay knew nothing about prosthetics, and I knew nothing about golf," Muilenburg said.

"But I must say I was impressed with his design — so much so that we went ahead and made 'The Halford Grip,'" as it came to be known, blending Larry and Jay's last names. Muilenburg used an aluminum child's knee prosthesis for the wrist and some air cells, which when inflated, fit tightly around the grip on the golfing hand like human fingers. Then a silicone suction sleeve, which slides over the elbow to hold the hand in place, was attached.

Seeing the mold the first time, Missy's eyes brimmed with tears, as she envisioned her son's reaction to the hand, which she was going to give to him on Christmas morning. "It'll work," Hall said, after looking over what Muilenburg had wrought. "I know it's going to work."

Unwrapping the last Christmas gift of the day, Larry peeked inside the box and, a look of amazement on his face, cried out. "It's a hand — my golf hand."

"It was Jay's idea," Missy said to her son. "He even designed it."

Overwhelmed with emotion, Larry threw his arms around Jay. "Thanks so much."

The Halford Grip has been a rousing success, although a number of adjustments have been made over the years. "Some golfers, seeing how well my golf hand works, have said they'd like to trade arms with me, but I tell them, 'No way.'"

Since receiving his golf hand, Alford has shot his lowest score ever — a 69. He also recorded his first hole-in-one and played three years of varsity golf at Sam Houston University. Since his graduation in 1997, Alford has worked as an assistant golf pro at his home course, The Woodlands Country Club, and has helped raise money for a number of charities by challenging golfers to try to get closer to the pin than he has on par-3 holes. "Not many people have," said Alford, who shoots in the 70s and booms his tee-shots more than 250 yards.

"My accident has been a blessing for me," said Alford who delivers inspirational talks to young people in schools and churches in the Houston area. "It happened for a reason. I thank God for saving my life, for giving me such a positive attitude and then giving me a second chance as a golfer. As for having to play with only one real arm, I tell people that golf is hard enough with two hands, so it can't be that much harder with one."

~Jack Cavanaugh
Chicken Soup for the Golfer's Soul

Tales OF Golf AND Sport

Teammates and Sportsmanship

In basketball,
you can be the greatest player in the world and lose every game,
because a team will always beat an individual.
~Bill Walton

56

When Silence Is Golden

The idea is not to block every shot.
The idea is to make your opponent believe that you might block every shot.
~Bill Russell

All-American in basketball from Princeton; member (starting forward) of the 1964 U.S. Olympic team; Rhodes Scholar; member of two world-championship teams during his ten-year pro career with the Knicks; former senator from New Jersey; one-time candidate for president. That's Bill Bradley, or at least a little bit of the man.

As an NBA referee running up and down the court, I recognized his talent and skill when he was with the Knicks. He had a mighty finger-roll and was a leader—a champion whose work ethic was matched by his ability to handle victory and loss with equal class—but the incident that marked him as special for me happened in the 1964 Tokyo Olympic Games.

The U.S. team was matched in a hard-fought gold-medal game against the Soviet Union. At one point, Bradley was backed out of the key by a big, bulky Russian who threw him a sharp elbow to the solar plexus that sent the lanky six-foot, seven-inch Bradley to the floor. Bradley got up, stepped over to the guy and in perfect Russian said, "Please back off, big fella."

The Russian team had been calling their plays in Russian. After Bradley's fluent remark, they stopped communicating totally, afraid that Bradley could understand and would cue his teammates.

Bradley hadn't learned enough Russian to follow their crisp, shorthand calls across the floor. He'd learned just enough Russian to be courteous. When he said "back off," he included "please." That's Bradley's way. This time, though, his regular courtesy led to the Soviet team's unraveling. The U.S. won the gold.

~Joey Crawford
Chicken Soup for the Sports Fan's Soul

A Hole in "How Many?"

Golf is so popular simply because
it is the best game in the world at which to be bad. ~A.A. Milne

Two golfers were on the green of the 3rd hole at Bethpage Golf Course, when all of a sudden a golf ball came from nowhere and rolled right up to the cup. One of the golfers said, "Let's put the ball in the cup and give the guy a hole-in-one."

All of a sudden a golfer came out of the woods and said, "Did any of you see a golf ball around here?"

One of the golfers on the green said, "Yes, it landed right in the cup."

"Good," said the man who hit the "hole-in-one," "that gives me a 13 for this hole."

~Steven Schockett
Chicken Soup for the Golfer's Soul, The 2nd Round

Fair Play

One day while golfing with colleagues in the insurance industry, I discovered yet another example of honesty being the best policy. I knew two of the men in our foursome, and was just getting to know our fourth—I'll call him Ace. By the third hole, I had learned his story, an object lesson for all of us.

Ace and his business partner had owned a property-and-casualty insurance agency. They had put in the years and the sweat, and the agency grew into a respected midsize firm. It attracted the attention of one of the big conglomerates. After some negotiations back and forth, Ace and his partner decided to sell to the "big guns," agreeing to stay on as consultants and continue to do some selling. The paperwork was completed in a flash and everyone seemed pleased.

After a couple of years, Ace and his partner felt they weren't active enough and decided they wanted to go back to running a brisker business, like they had before. The "big guns" said they couldn't, claiming they had agreed to never again work in insurance outside the big firm.

Ace said, "Show me where we agreed to any such thing." The "big guns" claimed it had been an oral agreement.

Ace knew there had never been such a discussion, much less an agreement, so he said, in effect, "See ya in court."

In court, the judge agreed an oral contract is as good as a written one, if it could be established there was a contract. His issue was whom to believe. After two days of listening to both sides insist their memory was the truth of it, the judge said, in effect, "It's basically a question of who do I believe, and in the absence of any real evidence, I have to go with my gut. My gut tells me to trust experience. The experience that's relevant here is that a number of years ago Mr. Ace played in the golf state championship. On the eighteenth, he hooked a drive into the rough. He was up and out in one, made his putt and everyone thought he had won the tournament, except that Ace admitted he had grounded his club in the hazard and declared a two-shot penalty on himself. No one had seen him ground his club. He could have slinked through and taken the win, but he didn't. He told the truth when he didn't have to, and I believe he's telling the truth now." Case closed.

Fair play is the best policy, in sports, in business, in all relationships, for all the right reasons, and for ones you can't anticipate at the time you make your choices. I have seen this truth exposed time and time again, and never more tidily proving the old saw—virtue is its own reward—than here.

~Ed Marion
Chicken Soup for the Sports Fan's Soul

59

Your Cheatin' Heart

Golf gives you an insight into human nature,
your own as well as your opponent's.
~Grantland Rice

The one thing to be said about my Uncle Steve was that he never let a rule stand in his way of winning. I first witnessed this behavior when I challenged him to a game of Snakes and Ladders. I was only a mere child of five, but that didn't keep him from using his warped logic to win. He argued that since he was not afraid of snakes, he should be allowed to climb the beasts as well as the ladders. This comment, of course, begged the question: If my uncle would go to that much effort to win a child's game, how far would he go for something important?

By the time Steve was in his early thirties, he had become an adequate golfer whose handicap was that he still hated to lose. Because of his attitude and temper he was often forced to play alone, which did not keep him from playing as though his life depended on a victory. Rules became suggestions for people with limited imaginations. He would take a one-foot gimme and then whirl around to see if I was going to argue. I, of course, had long since learned that reminding my uncle of the rules meant a small tip.

I turned fifteen the summer Pine Greens Golf Club held its fiftieth annual championship. Pine Greens was the oldest business or club in the area and therefore was viewed with reverence. The Golf Trophy, a truly unimaginative name for the award, was the most prestigious prize in the county, and my uncle was geared up for the victory.

"Al, my boy," he said, "this year the Golf Trophy is mine and you'll be my caddie."

I hesitated to remind him of his promise to never play in the tournament again. This oath had been made after calling the tournament officials fascists for refusing to allow him his multi-mulligan rule.

"Are you sure you want to play?" I asked cautiously. "After all, you did offend quite a few people last year."

"Water under the bridge," he assured me. "I'm a changed man."

This appeared to be true. As the tournament wore on, my uncle demonstrated levels of self-control that would have put a Zen master to shame. He followed, without the slightest complaint, every rule he had ever dismissed as archaic. What made the situation even more unbelievable was that he managed to keep his anger in check.

At the 8th hole, he missed a three-foot putt and smiled. Everybody in the group, myself included, had fallen to the ground in preparation for the ritual tossing of the putter. "What gives?" I asked as I placed the putter back in the bag. "You're acting like a good sport. You should have lost your temper back at the 1st hole."

"I told you I was prepared this year," whispered Steve. "I went and got myself hypnotized last night. According to the Amazing Freddie, every time I would normally get angry, I focus the energy on the next shot. Considering the quality of my last drive, my tee shot should be a beaut."

It was. The hole was a dogleg left, 350 yards. Steve was on the green after his first shot and sunk a long putt for eagle. He smiled politely as the rest of his party bogeyed.

At the end of the day, Steve was tied with Angus Popovitch, a man whose reputation for cheating made Steve look like an amateur. According to club rules, they would face off the following day in an eighteen-hole match.

It was a lovely fall day as the two golfers prepared to tee off. Word had spread as to who was in the final, and a huge crowd had assembled. They had not come to see a great round of golf, but rather to witness what had the potential to be the first brawl in the history of Pine Greens.

The first sign of animosity occurred at the 2nd green. Angus's shot was within three feet of the cup, and he bent down to pick up his ball. Steve asked his opponent what he was doing, and Angus replied that anything under three feet was a gimme.

"Anything under three feet is a pygmy," snarled Steve. "Now putt the ball."

Thus the floodgates were thrust open, and those who had come to watch flagrant breaking of the rules were not disappointed. Angus drew first blood when he swore the wind from his practice swing had knocked the ball off his tee. It was not until Angus and his caddie were prepared to sign a sworn affidavit that Steve dropped his complaint.

At No. 3, Angus's second shot bounced into the rough among some daisies. It was not a difficult shot to recover from as the weeds offered a minimum of difficulty. Angus, however, was not one to take chances. He plucked a handful of daisies and dropped them in front of Steve's face.

"Wind appears to be from the west," he laughed.

There was a murmuring of displeasure from the gallery at what was generally considered poor decorum. Steve surprised everyone by not saying anything.

My uncle's second shot at the 6th hole saw his 5-iron take him into the rough. It was not a totally bad shot except that his ball landed behind a small boulder. Steve surveyed the ball from all angles, as did Angus. The shot was difficult, if not impossible, as the ball was less than an inch away from the rock. Angus showed his usual compassion. "Drop the ball and take a stroke. It's getting late."

Steve was ready to comply when he was struck with an epiphany. He reached down and grabbed the boulder with two hands and slowly lifted the rock off the ground. The boulder must have weighed about two hundred pounds, and Steve only managed to lift it waist-high. Before Angus could utter a protest, Steve tossed the rock away from his ball.

"You're right, Angus. The wind is westerly," Steve said, and he proceeded to hit his ball onto the green.

This time the gallery gave a polite round of applause at what it deemed to be poetic justice. Steve doffed his cap, leaving Angus to complain to his caddie.

At last the combatants arrived at the 18th. Angus had the lead by one stroke, and the par-3 offered little hope for my uncle to mount a comeback. Still, he did his best as his tee shot landed twenty yards from the green. We waited as Angus prepared for his tee shot and were rewarded by a drive that trailed left, toward the woods.

"Keep an eye on him, Al," warned Uncle Steve. "Angus will try to drop a ball in play if he can't find his."

We walked toward the green and watched as Angus and his caddie searched for the ball. I joined in the search, but Steve wouldn't move from where he was standing. It was not easy to look for the ball and watch Angus and his caddie. I was about to suggest that Steve help when I heard a shout of joy as Angus found his ball. It was a feat just short of a miracle, I thought, as I had searched the same piece of ground just moments earlier. I rushed back to Steve.

"We got him," I whispered. "That's not his ball."

The prestige of winning the tournament and the trophy disappeared with Steve's sharp retort. "I know," he answered. "I'm standing on it."

~Alan Broderick
Chicken Soup for the Golfer's Soul, The 2nd Round

Let's Keep a Date

If you have integrity, nothing else matters.
If you don't have integrity, nothing else matters.
~Alan Simpson

Just before Arnold Palmer won The Masters in 1960, he had committed to play in a country club exhibition shortly after The Masters. On the Monday after winning The Masters, I received a call (as Arnie's agent) from the organizers of the outing, saying they assumed that either Arnold wouldn't be available or that his fee would have significantly risen now that he had won The Masters.

I went to Arnold to find out what he wanted to do.

"Mark," Arnold said, "remind them that they wanted me long before I had won a major championship. I will honor my commitment, and, to show that I appreciate their faith in me, I'll do another outing for them next year at the same price."

People say that Arnold Palmer hasn't changed as a person despite his enormous wealth and popularity. This early story shows what a firm foundation he started from. It's easier to stay steady when you start steady.

~Mark H. McCormack
Chicken Soup for the Sports Fan's Soul

The Finest Gift

It makes a sweet and pure sound. Metallic, and yet at the same time, almost ceramic. And loud, oh yes, it's loud. Like a rifle shot, it'll snap your head around if you haven't heard it before.

Smack! I watched as my friend Carl lasered another golf ball to the back of the driving range. He held his follow through as the ball soared higher and higher against a fading afternoon sky.

"You know," he said, "buying this club has to be one of the best investments I've made all year." He turned and smiled, looking just a little too cocky.

Knowing Carl's penchant for tech stocks, I wasn't going to argue the point. And besides, I was becoming just faintly aware of jealousy's green tentacles beginning to tighten around my neck. I knew that somehow I had to get my hands on one of those drivers. Carl tried to explain what a scientific marvel it was.

"They call it elastic reticular venting, or ERV. It's the variable face thickness you know; it works sorta like a trampoline."

I nodded, but kept my eyes on the gleaming clubhead as Carl addressed another ball. Was this fair? Why should Carl have such a nice golf club, and I don't? Sensing my lower lip pushing up into a pout, I checked myself, threw back my shoulders and tried to appear indifferent as we both followed his next shot arching higher and higher until the ball nestled into the upper netting at the very back of the range.

"Yes sir, Jacky. You gotta get one of these little beauties."

"What did it set ya back?" The words sprang from my mouth before I could stop them. I felt my face redden. What did it matter, the cost of so fine an instrument? Would Perlman quibble about the price of a Stradivarius? Would Puck settle for cheap tomatoes? How could one place a price on perfection?

"Bout 290, with tax. I got it down at Reno Bob's. You know, at the mall."

Yes, of course I knew. Reno Bob's was the local discount golf shop where the teenage salesmen casually gossiped about their 220-yard 7-iron shots. I made a mental note to stop by the mall on my way home. But wait, did he say 290!? For one golf club!? My gosh! Hattie would kill me if I even thought about spending that kind of money on one golf club.

"So, you got any plans for the holidays?"

I didn't pick up on Carl's question right away. Two hundred and ninety, for just one club? The number echoed in my head.

"No, we're just planning a quiet Christmas at home this year."

Now, Carl's not a big guy. So maybe it was understandable how watching his next ball sail right over the top of the back fence made me feel just a little depressed.

I went straight home. Hattie was making meatloaf and my little five-year-old, Jennifer, was waiting by the back door, all ready to give her daddy the best hug she could.

Of course that lifted my spirits. She motioned me to bend down, then whispered in my ear.

"You know—it's only four more days."

I could see she was already giddy with excitement.

"Have you been a good girl? You know who's watching, don't you?"

Cupping her hands over her mouth, she looked up at me with those big green eyes and whispered, "Santa Claus."

Hattie saw us and frowned. I knew she was upset with me for stirring up such anticipation in the child. For a week we'd had the same conversation. "Christmas isn't just about Santa Claus, or receiving presents," she kept saying. And she was all business when I gave her a peck on the cheek. She just pointed me at the dining room table. Dinner was great, of course. My Hattie invented meatloaf. She waited until my cheeks were puffed out with food before speaking.

"I need to do some shopping tomorrow. So why don't you and Jennifer go with me to the mall? I understand there's going to be someone special there. While I'm busy, maybe you two can get a picture taken."

I took the hint and hoped that this year's Santa was a little more convincing. Last year, I spent nearly an hour trying to explain how the jolly old elf could have a Jamaican accent.

The next day, when we arrived at the mall, Hattie took off for parts unknown and I was left to stroll the rows of shops, Jennifer tugging anxiously on my hand. The stores were all decorated with twinkling lights, scarlet, silver and golden ribbons of streaming color. We followed the clatter of children, all laughing, running, skipping in the direction of an enormous snow-covered gingerbread house where occasional flashes told me that a photo opportunity lay just ahead. When we arrived, I was disappointed to see that the procession had stalled. A sign read, "Santa is out feeding the reindeer. Back in five minutes."

I suggested that we just walk around until Santa came back. But when we turned the corner, I felt my pulse jump. There it was. Right in the front window of Reno Bob's Discount Golf Shop. There was my ERV driver, glistening, beckoning, calling my name. I felt a sudden weakness in my knees.

"Let's walk over this way, Jenny."

My innocent little one obligingly followed. Could she feel the wave of excitement overwhelming me as we stood there in front of the golf shop? Could she imagine that her daddy might be so excited about some inanimate object? Something so silly as a golf club?

"So there you are!"

Hattie's voice made me jump.

"Have you seen Santa already?"

"No," I stammered. "He's feeding his reindeer." I smiled, feeling a little self-conscious.

"Well, I guessed that you'd eventually wind up here." There was a hint of insinuation in her voice. "It's your favorite store. Right?"

"Oh, yes—right—my favorite. I mean, it's one of my favorites. Of course I like the yarn shop, too."

"Oh yeah, the yarn shop. One of your favorites, too."

Clearly whatever I was selling, Hattie wasn't buying.

"Wow, look at that!" She pointed at the shop window. "Look at that golf club."

I nodded. "Yeah, she's a beauty, isn't she?" I was amazed. I never knew Hattie appreciated the finer lines of a good driver. And my ERV was just poised there, looking like a work of art.

"No, no. I mean, look at the price of that thing."

I realized that her finger was pointing at the bright red sales tag dangling from the grip of the club. Her mouth was gaping. She finally composed herself enough to say, "Can you imagine anyone spending that kind of money for a single golf club!? My lord!"

I smiled, but not showing my teeth. It occurred to me that it might be possible to marshal the facts—perhaps compile a list of the essential attributes of a highly advanced ball-striking device like this one. And, of course, I could argue that it's made out of titanium—the stuff of supersonic jet planes. But, I bit my lower lip instead and just stared at the shop window.

"Well," I finally said. "My friend Carl has one, and it's really quite a remarkable golf club, and several of the better players are getting them, and you know, if you really love golf it might almost be worth...."

I stopped. Hattie was giving me her "you must be nuts!" look. I could see that there was no point, so I suggested that we head back to the gingerbread house.

Hattie and I were always quite rational about Christmas. We agreed that neither of us would spend more than $150 on each other's present. She argued, and I agreed, that all the attention should be on Jennifer. It made perfect sense to me. Still, I remembered how as a child I persisted in imagining that my parents were going to give me that one gift I really wanted each Christmas. One year it was a bike. One year it was a BB gun. And when I was sixteen, I really thought my folks were going to give me a little red sports car. Christmas proved to be one disappointment after another. No bike, no BB gun and certainly no little red sports car.

"And I heard him exclaim as he rode out of sight, merry Christmas to all, and to all a good night." I snapped the book closed and looked at my beaming child. The embers in our fireplace cast a warm glow about the room, and the sparkling white lights on our tree reflected in my little girl's eyes. The kitchen door pushed open and Hattie emerged carrying a tray of cookies and two glasses of milk.

"Here's one for our girl, and one for Santa," she said. I feigned a frown of disapproval. I knew that at heart, Hattie loved Christmas—decorating the tree, making cookies, putting up the stockings. Like me, she was just a grown-up kid.

"Daddy, don't you think we should put out the fire so Santa doesn't burn his bum?"

I nodded thoughtfully, and snatched a cookie from the tray. Then I promised that I'd take care of everything and gathered her up in my arms.

"You know," I said. "Santa won't come until you're fast asleep."

Hattie and I tucked Jennifer in, and pulled her bedroom door closed. Standing in the hall I gave my wife a long kiss.

"You know, dear," I said. "Santa really won't come until we're fast asleep."

She looked at me enticingly.

"That's right, babe. So Santa better get to work on that bike. And don't forget the tassels and training wheels."

It was a chilly morning and I stepped spritely across our hardwood floor to the thermostat and cranked up the heat. I inspected the scab forming over my raw knuckle—a mark which I undoubtedly shared with thousands of bicycle-assembling fathers. Then I looked in on Jennifer. She was snoozing peacefully, so I brewed some coffee and roused Hattie. At last, when our little girl came careening dreamily into the living room, one hand brushing the sleepy-dust from her eyes, Hattie and I were sitting together on the sofa, spectators to the best show in town.

At that moment, seeing the teary eyes of my child as she pranced on tip-toes with delight, I was reminded of the real meaning of Christmas. In Christmas we find hope, coming first to us out of a mystical story about a babe born in a lowly manger, and then upon a gilded sleigh drawn by eight wondrous reindeer through a cold and quiet eve. And in that hope we hear an endless prayer that all the children of the world might share in the joy of a new and brighter age. A child was born, and after all, Christmas is really about the children.

It was a beautiful argyle vest, and I knew Hattie had paid more than our agreed-upon limit. I was very happy with it. In fact, I wore it to the club the next Saturday. And there on the driving range I saw my friend Carl. I guessed that he had an early tee-time because he was just finishing his warm-up session when I arrived. I watched as he hit a few 3-wood shots.

"Hey, Carl. How ya hittin' 'em?"

"Don't ask, Jacky. Don't ask."

I could see my friend was under a gray cloud. I watched quietly as he hit a few more shots. Then he tucked his 3-wood back in his bag.

"Hey, aren't you gonna hit that big stick?" I asked.

"What big stick?"

"Carl? You know, that ERV driver of yours. Your big stick."

"Oh that. I busted it."

"You what?"

"Yeah. On the 10th tee yesterday, I hit one right on the screws, but the face caved in. I guess they haven't perfected it yet. You can only hit it a few dozen times before it caves in. Wish I'd known that before I bought it."

I watched with an open mouth as Carl picked up his bag and started walking glumly off the practice tee. But then he turned and, looking me up and down, said, "Hey Jacky, that's a nice lookin' argyle."

~J. G. Nursall
Chicken Soup for the Golfer's Soul, The 2nd Round

Teammates Are for Life

If I had to sum up Friendship in one word,
it would be Comfort.
~Adabella Radici

One of the things many high school athletes don't realize until later in life is that the young men and young women they now call teammates will also be among the best friends they'll have throughout their lives.

I remain close with several teammates I had on the Macon (Missouri) High School football team back in the late 1970s, one of whom was a fellow named Greg Hyatt.

Hyatt, a linebacker, was one of those sorts who had to put a good lick on someone every play. If he couldn't get to the guy carrying the ball, then someone else had to go down. He and I were the only two players from our class to letter all four years in high school.

I remember a game during our senior season against one of our arch rivals. It was also a heated battle, filled with emotion and a lot of pads popping. Early in the game, on a punt, an opposing player attempted to block me on punt coverage. I sidestepped him, but as I went by he slugged me in the side of the head. I have to admit it dazed me somewhat, but not to the point where I didn't get his number.

It took about two more quarters, but opportunity finally arrived to provide a good, clean hit on him, and I did. He sprawled into a pile of players and came up quite irritated. Suddenly, I was nose to nose with not only that player, but about two or three of his teammates. That didn't last long though, as Hyatt was right next to me in about a second.

When you need a friend, you can always count on your teammates.

Ten years later, I found myself in a different kind of confrontation, a confrontation with adversity. My first wife, a lifetime asthma sufferer, had been hit with her worst attack ever. She died in my car as I was driving her to the hospital. Emergency room personnel were able to get her heart going again, but she was transferred to a trauma center in a deep coma.

I can remember standing there in a waiting room looking out the window at the city. Family members were there, but there are times when you just want to talk to a friend. About that time, I heard footsteps coming up the stairway. As I turned around, there stood my old friend Hyatt, tears filling his eyes.

Seeing him standing there, an eerie yet comforting and familiar feeling came over me. For a moment I was back on the football field in Macon. I was facing a tough situation, but I had backup.

Seeing him at the top of those steps meant the world to me that night, and still does today. That's something I tell high-school kids whenever I get the chance, that these guys you've gone to war with in high school will be some of the best friends you'll ever have.

There have been a lot of changes in my life since that October 1988 night, but one of the constants has been my friendship with Greg.

After all, we are teammates, and teammates are there for each other even after the noise of the crowd is gone.

~Jim Brown
Chicken Soup for the Sports Fan's Soul

All the Good Things Any Man Should Be

I have to tell you honestly that I never believed Squeek wouldn't be back carrying my bag. Not for one minute. Not until the very end, when he was so sick he couldn't even open his eyes to say goodbye. It's selfish, I guess, but that's what it's like when you lose a friend.

He was diligent and conscientious and humble and simple and honest and all the good things any man should be.

I remember often I would invite him in to share our success, to set the clubs down for a minute and drink a victory beer in the locker room. "Don't worry, Squeek, come on in," I'd tell him when he hesitated. "If there's a fine, I'll pay it."

We shared dinner often, but there were other times I would offer and he would decline politely, saying he had other plans. But I knew he really didn't. It was just his way of stepping back, never trying to take too much.

On the road, I think he was more content to babysit my kids and order a pizza. He loved to sit and play with them, and I know they loved him, too. They don't understand why he's gone now, anymore than I do.

For him, the rewards were more private. It was enough for him to get the flag from the eighteenth hole after a win and tack it up on his wall at home.

Doing the job well, doing it thoroughly, that was paramount for Squeek. In our six years together, I think I questioned a yardage only once. Once. That's unheard of.

He was no expert on the golf swing, but he learned what to look for in my swing. "Watch that right elbow," he would say when I was getting frustrated on the practice range.

In tournament play, he always had a knack for knowing the right thing to say, even when that meant saying nothing at all. And he understood the nuances of competition as well as anyone I'd ever met. He would always check the leader boards, and he could see a player struggling long before I would.

"He's feeling the pressure, Nick," he'd say as we headed down the last few holes, convincing me that a tournament still could be won.

He'd never let me get negative. At Turnberry in 1994, I had two terrible days of practice, but he never lost confidence in me. When I said, "Aww, I'm not swinging so well," immediately he pulled me up on it. "How can you expect me to be positive when you start talking like that?" he would demand.

When I asked Squeek at the end of 1990 to come work for me, he said Tom Watson had just asked him the same thing. A few days later, he came to me and said I was his choice. I sometimes wonder how different things might have been for me had that decision gone the other way.

We had one hell of a time together, I know that. I might have won without him, but it wouldn't have been nearly as often or nearly as fun.

The moment that stands out most for me was winning the Open at Turnberry. Squeek cheered me on through all the doubts of that final round. When I had to hit that last shot to clinch it, Squeek was never more positive, giving me the exact yardage and telling me to split the "D" in the big yellow sign behind the eighteenth green. When I had hit the shot and started up toward the green, the walk of a champion with the great crowd cheering, Squeek lingered behind humbly, typically, not wanting to intrude. I stopped for a moment and looked back at him.

"C'mon, Squeek," I said. "Let's enjoy this together. I don't know when we'll get the opportunity again."

If I never win again, I will always have the memory of that walk, shared with a friend.

~Nick Price
Chicken Soup for the Golfer's Soul

64

Golf Nuts

Let's talk about golf nuts.

I'll start with the runny little sixty-eight-year-old combatant who always insists on playing from the gold tees.

He says you can't really see a golf course unless you play it from the tips.

He finds something terribly intriguing, as opposed to insane, about a seventy-two-hundred-yard golf course, particularly if it's infested with water, waste, sand, bulkheads, trees, moguls, deep rough, violent wind, severe pins and slick greens.

He would never improve a lie. He is greatly offended at the mere suggestion of a mulligan.

He loves playing a par-5 hole with driver, 3-wood, 5-wood, 7-wood, sand blast, pitch, chip, and four putts.

He is enthralled by a long, brutal par-4 hole that he can attack with driver, lateral, spoon, unplayable, 5-iron, boundary, 9-iron, cart path, pitch, and three putts.

He is fascinated with a killer par-3 hole that he can bring to its knees with driver, water, 5-wood, bulkhead, wedge, chip, and three putts.

One day he hopes to break 126.

"How did you play today, dear?" his wife asks.

"Great. I had a putt for a par and three chips at birdies."

Next, I give you the tireless gentleman who calls me every year or so to bring me up to date on the progress he's making in trying to play all of America's famous courses.

He has been at this for about twenty-five years, I guess.

In all of the phone calls over the past quarter of a century, he has asked me the same question.

Can I suggest anything that will help him get on Pine Valley, Augusta National, Merion, Seminole, Cypress Point, Oakmont, Los Angeles Country Club, Bel Air, Shinnecock Hills, Colonial, Winged Foot, Chicago Golf, Brook Hollow or Olympic?

I used to say, "Crawl over the fence and don't play the 1st hole or the 18th."

Now I say, "Steal a hundred million dollars from your company and put a hyphen in your name."

I give you this retired fellow I've stumbled upon who plays six times a week and makes all of his own clubs. They are rather crude-looking things, but he makes them in his workshop.

Although golf is obviously his life, he has been pleased to inform me that he has never attended a tournament, doesn't watch golf on television, doesn't read golf books, doesn't read golf magazines and doesn't even read the sports pages of the newspapers.

One day he asked what I did for a living. I said I was a writer.

"What do you mean?" he said, looking at me as if he had just heard of the most bizarre profession imaginable.

I said, "Well, among other things, I write articles for a golf magazine."

He looked at me for a long moment, and then he said, "Why?"

I excused myself hurriedly and went home and reported to my wife that I thought I had just met the mysterious sniper who fires at motorists from a freeway overpass.

Also in my neighborhood is this elderly man who only plays on weekends but spends the rest of the time hunting golf balls.

He's always out there during the week, creeping through the trees or poking around at the edge of lagoons.

It is rumored that he has over ten thousand golf balls in his garage, where he keeps them neatly arranged on shelves.

More than one person has told me I must visit this man's garage — his collection of golf balls is astounding.

"It's on my list," I say nicely.

As amazing as anyone I've heard about lately is the dentist. He is said to be a lifelong fan of Arnold Palmer. He is said to be such a fan of Arnold's, it borders on mental illness.

I don't know if it's true — I can only hope — but the dentist is purported to carry in his pocket a ball marker made from the gold that was extracted from Arnold's teeth.

This might not make him the biggest Arnold Palmer fan in the world, however.

There was a journalist in Great Britain whose unbounding hero worship of Palmer became a legend. He was never satisfied, one hears, with autographs, scrapbooks, photos, paintings or articles about Arnold.

One day he got the inspired idea to begin collecting the divots Palmer would take out of fairways in England and Scotland. Eventually, the entire lawn of his home near London was made out of Arnold Palmer divots.

Actually, if I were to follow through on a thought I had the other day, I think I could be exempt on the Golf Nut Tour myself.

You see, I have this habit of knocking balls into the woods when they betray me. I might add that it doesn't take much for me to feel betrayed. A four-foot putt that curls out, a pulled 7-wood that winds up in a bunker, a chip shot that races across the green and into the frog hair, a tee shot that defies its stern warning and seeks out the forest.

I've been leaving these balls in the woods, but I've come up with a better idea. A small cemetery in my yard. It could be fenced in by a variety of broken shafts. Call me the Mortician.

In this cemetery I will bury all of the golf balls that betray me, because if they can betray me once, they will certainly betray me again. Planted into the earth, however, they will have nothing to do but rot in eternal hell forever.

Never again will they be able to bring unwarranted grief and anguish to some innocent golfer, like myself, who never meant them any harm whatsoever.

It's what they deserve, I say. All I've ever asked of them is a simple string of bogeys.

~Dan Jenkins
Chicken Soup for the Golfer's Soul, The 2nd Round

65

The Day I Cheated

Make yourself an honest man,
and then you may be sure there is one less rascal in the world.
~Thomas Carlyle

Golf has always been the game I love. The physical challenge. The mental challenge. The ability to summon a shot from the depths of my being when double bogey is staring me down. Golf is pure, and that's the way I play it. Except for that time a few years ago.

For the first time, for the only time, I cheated in a golf match. It haunts me to this day. It was against my best golfing buddy, Frank, and it changed me as a person and as a golfer. Forever.

Until that heated match one Sunday afternoon, I had never intentionally broken or even bent a single rule of golf. Never.

Like so many of our duels, our match that day was all square going into the eighteenth hole, a par-5 where anything worse than par meant losing the hole. At stake was the normal whopping three dollars. I hooked badly into the woods off the tee. Frank, aka Steady Eddie, split the middle of the fairway as usual.

After a short search alone amongst the trees, I found my ball wedged between two roots. It was quite unplayable.

Through the leaves, I could see Frank striding toward his tee shot. I dropped within two club lengths and smacked a 3-iron through an opening in the trees. Frank was applauding as I emerged from the woods, and for good reason. My ball laid 175 yards down the fairway in perfect position for my approach.

A few minutes later, Frank tapped in to match my "par."

"Nice match," he said, extending his hand. "No blood."

I shook his hand and kept my mouth shut. I don't know why. I have thought about that day often, and I have no answers.

I remember throwing cold water on my face in the clubhouse restroom after the round. I stared at myself in the mirror and let the water drip back into the sink.

Frank had obviously not seen me take the drop in the woods. He assumed my tap-in was for par, when I knew very well that it was for bogey. So I kept my three dollars that day.

The next morning I took a long hard look at myself. I wondered who this cheating person was and how long he would be around. It pained me to have cheated, and it pained me to have dishonored a game I consider so noble.

I can't help but think about that afternoon as each new golf season begins. I remember how badly I felt, but mostly I remind myself how good it feels to walk off a green after having ground out a par, a real par, or maybe even a hard-fought bogey, from a situation that looked like a sure double. I tell myself that the shots that feel the best — the ones you remember in the nineteenth hole and in the car on the ride home — are those you pull off from horrendous lies with a clump of mud stuck to the ball. I remind myself that my playing partners — my friends — should never, ever, have to question my integrity on the course, no matter how miraculous my recovery shot.

A trip to Ireland last year emphasized to me the importance of the relationship between golf and integrity. "Lad," said an Irishman I played a round with, "over here we touch the ball just twice each hole: when we tee it up and when we pluck it from the bottom of the cup."

Perhaps more than anything, it is precisely such memories of the men and women whom I have had the honor of walking a round with over in Ireland and Scotland that compel me to be true to myself on the course. It seems every player over there has been somehow imbued with the spirit of Old Tom Morris. Just as they cannot comprehend why Americans would choose to ride around in a "buggy" when it is abundantly clear that golf is walking, neither can they understand why anyone would ever do something as foolish and demeaning as cheating on the course.

In the British Isles, golf is played by the rules, and never by "winter rules."

The majority of players in this country break the rules—or choose to ignore them—every weekend, never understanding that they are diminishing themselves every time they roll it in the fairway. Is there a truer adage than the one that says we can tell everything we need to know about a person's character by playing a round of golf with him or her? If your playing partners witness you bumping your ball in the fairway, do you think this doesn't influence their opinion of you?

I only wonder what Frank thinks of me.

~John Meyers
Chicken Soup for the Golfer's Soul

66

Check Your Bag

A golfer's diet: live on greens as much as possible.
~Author Unknown

My brother Maurice and three of his buddies—Sam, Renwick and Earl—have a regular golf game every Friday during the summer. In order to make the game interesting and even, they use handicaps. As a result of this, Maurice and Earl are partners, and Sam and Renwick play together.

Maurice never walks the golf course and is always trying to get one of the other guys to ride with him. This particular Friday in July, it was very warm, and he asked Renwick to ride with him.

It just so happens that Renwick had been on a health kick for a couple of months, so he told Maurice that he would prefer to walk. Renwick had lost about twenty pounds and had just purchased a carry bag from the pro shop, deciding that toting, rather than using a pull cart as he walked the course, would help him stay in shape.

Maurice candidly cautioned Renwick, "Remember, you are fifty-eight years old. Walking the course is one thing; carrying your bag for eighteen holes is something else."

Nevertheless, Renwick insisted on walking, and off they went.

After nine holes, Renwick said to one of the other guys who was walking, "I think Maurice was right. Carrying this bag is wearing me out."

Naturally, the other guy suggested that Renwick ask Maurice

for a ride in the cart, to which Renwick stubbornly replied, "Not a chance. If you think I will admit this to Maurice, you are crazy."

They continued on. Renwick struggled but refused to give Maurice the satisfaction of giving up.

At about the 12th hole, Sam confided in Maurice, "Renwick realizes carrying the golf bag was a bad idea, but will not admit it to you because he knows he will be in for a real good ribbing."

Shortly after hearing this, Maurice called Renwick over and said, "Are you getting tired of carrying that golf bag? Why don't you take a load off and put the bag on the cart?"

Renwick grimaced but replied, "No thanks. It's not bad at all."

With a sly grin, Maurice continued, "Then why don't you unzip that side pocket and lighten your load?"

Knowing he'd been had, Renwick unzipped the side pocket, where he discovered two rocks—slightly smaller than a couple of footballs—that he had been carrying for twelve holes!

Needless to say, Renwick had some choice words for Maurice, while Sam and Earl were rolling on the tee, laughing until they were crying.

And rest assured, Renwick now checks his bag for foreign objects before every golf game... particularly on Fridays.

~Robert Lalonde
Chicken Soup for the Golfer's Soul, The 2nd Round

67

The Clutch Putt

I have a tip that can take five strokes off anyone's golf game:
it's called an eraser.
~Arnold Palmer

Pressure is part of golf. It shows up when a golfer fails to make a shot he would normally make because he tries too hard. A non-golfer doesn't understand this when he watches Freddie Couples nonchalantly knock in a fifteen-foot putt.

All golfers have experienced pressure, but what is perhaps more difficult to comprehend is the amount of additional pressure that is created when golf is played as a team sport, rather than an individual one. The fear of letting your teammates down is undoubtedly the big factor.

Whether golfers are playing in the Ryder Cup or the Border League, they have to contend with this extra pressure. In these parts, the Border League is a group of golf and country clubs along the New York State-Eastern Ontario border that play an annual team competition: eight-man teams from each club—total score to count—medal play.

One such competition was being played at the Prescott Golf Club, a nice course overlooking the St. Lawrence River in Ontario. I was a member of the Cornwall, Ontario, team. Most observers were saying if anybody was going to beat the home club, it would probably be us. As the day progressed, this analysis proved correct—Prescott and Cornwall well ahead of the other clubs. Seven of our eight players were in now, waiting and relaxing at the nineteenth hole, as golfers sometimes do, and our eighth man was now on the eighteenth tee. Our eighth man was Reggie Evans, an 8-handicapper, a school principal by profession, a keen but occasionally erratic golfer. We, of course, were tired, but anxious about the outcome. Somebody said, "Kenny, it's your turn—go over to the scoreboard and see how we stand." A quick trip over to the board revealed that all teams now had seven players finished and the scores were listed by teams. The scorekeeper, whoever he was, hadn't given us any subtotals, so I checked them out, did some quick mental additions and went back to where my teammates were sitting.

"Hey fellas, we got this thing in the bag—we are eleven shots up on Prescott and Reggie was one up on his man after nine; surely he can't blow a twelve-shot lead on the back nine."

The elation and excitement were rising; somebody suggested, "Hey, let's go over to the edge of the green and cheer Reggie in."

"Good idea."

By this time, Reggie had played his second shot onto the green—pin high about twenty feet to the right of the flag.

"Let's have some fun," I suggested. "Let's tell Reggie that he has to sink that putt."

"Wait," cautioned Alex. "Before you do that, you had better check out his lead—you wouldn't want to blow us out of first place."

"Okay."

We joined the small greenside gallery as the players approached the green. The Prescott player chipped up for what looked like a tap-in par, and the other two players had played onto the green when Reg came around to where I had strategically positioned myself.

"How are you doing, Reg?" I asked.

"Pretty good, Kenny, two putts here and I break 80."

"How is the Prescott player doing?"

"Well, let me see now, he'll get his par here and he will be one stroke ahead of me. How is the team doing?"

The stage was set and set perfectly.

"Look, Reg, listen now, we have a one-stroke lead over Prescott—you've got to sink that putt."

"A one-stroke lead?" Reg muttered, as he digested the situation. His facial muscles tightened. "That's not an easy putt."

"Give it a go, Reg. Knock it in and we win, but hell, don't three putt it."

Reg was on the green now, putter in hand, crouched behind the ball, studying the roll of the green.

"Don't be short, Reggie," chirped Joe from greenside.

"Shush, Joe, don't distract him," whispered Alex. But Reg wasn't going to be distracted; he was in full concentration like I have never seen him before. Things were working perfectly. He looked over the line from both directions, studied the surface to make sure there were no impediments, and now he was back behind the ball again.

My teammates were all watching intently, some with expectant grins on their faces. We were expecting anything, but inwardly hoping he might sink this putt.

Reggie took a couple of practice swings with his putter to ensure a smooth stroke and now took his position over the ball—pause—here it comes—the ball jumped off the putter face—bobbled a bit—lots of speed—a bit to the right of the cup—now a slowing down and breaking towards the cup.

"It's in!—way to go, Reggie—you did it! Boy!"

Loud cheers and high fives from the gang and then a sudden shushed silence to allow the others to putt out; then handshakes all around and back to the lounge to celebrate our victory.

When Reg sank into his chair, his face reflected both relief and excitement from his achievement. About this time, Joe decided to let the cat out of the bag. "Reggie, you really didn't have to sink the putt. We won by eleven strokes—we were just putting you on."

"Aw, you guys," groaned Reg, "you don't know the pressure you put on me out there."

"We just wanted to see how good you really are," I ventured. The chatter continued, only to be interrupted by the public address system: "Ladies and gentlemen, here are the results of today's tournament.

"In first place, Cornwall, with a total of..."

"Yeaaaa."

"In second place, one stroke behind, Prescott with a total of…"

"One stroke behind?"

"One stroke behind. Hey, Kenny, where did you learn to add?" exclaimed Alex.

"Aw come on, fellas," I said, "I was only telling Reggie the truth out there. You didn't expect me to lie to him, did you?"

~Ken Robertson
Chicken Soup for the Golfer's Soul

The Best Golfer Tantrum of All Time

Workers at the Riverside Golf and Country Club in Portland, Oregon, were taking down some of the golf course's towering poplars when they came upon evidence of what appeared to be the enraged-golfer tantrum of all time. Forty feet up in one tree was a 10-iron that looked as though it had been thrown right through a ten-inch branch.

Closer examination, however, revealed that the club, which is of the era when they first started making steel shafts, was probably thrown about forty years ago. It seems to have lodged in a high crotch in the tree, and since that terrible moment, the branch has grown around the club and the poplar itself has grown taller.

The cut section of tree—complete with club—will be kept on display at the pro shop.

~Rod Patterson
Chicken Soup for the Golfer's Soul, The 2nd Round

There Is No "I" in Team

Bob and Tina Andrews work together like a well-oiled machine. She sets him up on the tee box, steps back, looks down the fairway and says, "Okay." He takes a deep breath and swings, and the ball sails down the left side of the first fairway at Killearn Country Club near their Tallahassee, Florida, home.

They display impressive teamwork. Bob Andrews is totally blind. Tina, his wife, is his "coach," and together they make up one of the best teams in the United States Blind Golf Association.

"The first thing you learn is that blind golf is a team sport," says Bob, fifty-one, who was blinded by a grenade in Vietnam in 1967. "Until you have a coach, you're not a blind golfer. You're just a blind person with some golf clubs."

Bob and Tina were married not long after he returned from Vietnam. He took up golf first for the exercise. "I tried running," he says with a laugh, "but you get tired of taking those falls."

He had played golf as a kid, but he was never serious about it until he became blind. He joined the USBGA, and in 1995 he became president.

Tina is his third coach. Andrews's father did it at first, but it got to be too much for him. Then, Andrews's son took a turn. But he soon went off to college. That left Tina, who isn't a golfer, but Bob actually thinks that's a plus because she doesn't overload him with information. All she does is point him in the right direction.

After they play a couple of holes, it's understood how they do what they do. Or so you think. "Ready to try it?" asks Bob.

You stammer for a few moments, then answer weakly, "Sure."

Until you've "coached" a blind golfer, you can't appreciate how hard it is—and how wonderful it is when things go right. You find that you've never been so interested in someone else's golf game.

Bob holds the club out in front of him, and the first thing the coach does is place the club firmly on the ground, right behind the ball, square to the target. This serves as an anchor. Next is the position of his feet, also square to the target. Then the shoulders. When everything is right, a simple "okay" is all he needs.

Andrews swings, and the ball takes off. "Little fade down the right side?" he asks, judging the ball's path by its feel.

"Yep. Little fade down the right side."

Later, Andrews has about 160 yards, of which about 140 is a carry over water. "What do we got?" he asks.

"About 160 yards, over water," you say.

"Oh, boy," he says. "Let's try a 7-wood." After he's set up, Andrews spends a little more time standing over this shot. He hits it a little fat and it splashes in the water. Your heart sinks. That wouldn't have happened if Tina were coaching. "See, I wouldn't have even told him about the water," she says. "No point in giving him one more thing to worry about. Take advantage of his disadvantage, know what I mean?"

After dropping, Andrews hits a nice pitching wedge over the water and onto the green. You lead Andrews by the arm to the spot where his ball rests, then walk with him to the flagstick. "Fourteen feet," he says. "A little left-to-right, slightly uphill."

Andrews reads his own putts, feeling the contour of the green through his shoes. This seems amazing. But when you step behind him to take a look, you come to the same conclusion: left-to-right, slightly uphill.

You set him up with the putter's face aiming just outside the left edge of the cup.

"How's that look?" he asks.

"Perfect," you say. But you cross your fingers. His putting stroke is smooth and sure, a perfect pendulum. On its final rotation, the ball ducks into the left side of the cup. Andrews hears the hollow sound of a holed putt. It is a sweet sound indeed.

"Hey," you say as you head to the next tee, "that was a great bogey you made back there."

"No," he says, "that was a great bogey we made."

~Dave Sheinin
Chicken Soup for the Golfer's Soul

Chapter
7

Tales
OF Golf AND
Sport

The "Little" League

All kids need is a little help,
a little hope and somebody who believes in them.
~Earvin (Magic) Johnson

Life with Father

Children have more need of models than of critics.
~Carolyn Coats,
Things Your Dad Always Told You But You Didn't Want to Hear

One of my neighbors, a sincere young guy named Derek, recently approached me for advice on a specialized aspect of father-son relationships. That he should approach me about any aspect of parenting is remarkable, considering that Derek has actually met Graig, the nineteen-year-old product of my own efforts in this area. But Derek's options were limited: He was considering coaching his seven-year-old, Chad, in Little League. And given the decade-long record I compiled as a father-coach (I won a league title, came in second once and coached several All-Star teams) before hanging up my line-up card for good last season, he wondered if I might have any words of wisdom.

There was a lot I could have said, and maybe should have said, to Derek, but his request aroused mixed emotions. On the one hand, well, he did ask. On the other, he was just so bright-eyed and eager that I didn't want to make him feel unduly neurotic about something I knew he was going to undertake anyway. In the end, I merely whittled down the insights of my lengthy service as my son's coach to these points:

First, this was not a decision to be made on impulse. Anyone considering this step should spend a summer at the ball field, observing such relationships up close and personal.

Second, there should be a special plea available to fathers who do bodily harm to their sons as a consequence of coaching them in youth sports—something along the lines of "assault with an explanation."

Derek began to laugh and then, noting that my face remained set and unsmiling, thanked me and walked away. I don't know what he made of me, but he is careful not to leave me alone with his son these days.

In their attempts to shed light on the father-son coaching relationship, sports psychologists invest a lot of time in constructing intricate behavioral models, most of which reduce to the fact that both man and boy lug much more than the equipment with them when they travel from the home to ball field.

Sometimes the spillover from home is unmistakable: I think of the day my frowning nine-year-old folded his arms over his chest and plopped down in the outfield in protest over my refusal to buy him a Slurpee before the game. More often the link between cause and effect is foggy. On one occasion, when Graig, normally a hard thrower, was fourteen, I yelled out to the mound that he didn't seem to have much on the ball. "Come on, dammit!" I shouted. "Chow [the family mutt] could hit that crap." He glared at me, and his pitches began arcing toward the plate in a high, defiant softball lob. I yanked him at once, he stormed into the dugout and it was only when we talked about things days later that I recognized the depths of the emotional morass I had carelessly wandered into. "You say something about everything I do," Graig sniffed. "With my homework, if the answers are right, you complain about the penmanship. When I mow the lawn, you always tell me I missed a spot. Why can't you ever just accept that I'm doing the best I can?"

It's true that a coach's son struggles with his father's shifting identities. And that's sad. But it is equally true that kids can be world-class manipulators. Sensing that their fathers, too, are far from comfortable with the situation, they respond with the unerring, I've-got-you-over-a-barrel instincts of, say, a woman you love very much who knows she has caught you doing something you hoped never to be caught doing.

And that's infuriating.

Typically, a coach's kid wants all the special rewards of having a coach who is also his father but is reluctant to accept any of the special burdens of having a father who is also his coach. His advantage-seeking is expressed in countless ways large and small—from demanding "just one more pitch" during batting practice to lobbying to be penciled in at a glamour position such as shortstop regardless of whether he can actually stop, oh, one out of every four ground balls.

Coaches' kids reject the notion that this favoritism should come at the cost of any added responsibility. Graig despised my constant reminders to "set a good example." His chronic complaint was that he wanted to be "a member of the team just like everyone else." (Except expecting to pitch regularly, bat third or fourth, and have the green light to steal at will even though the backstop would have beaten him in a foot race.)

The successful management of such schizophrenia requires of father-coaches an even-temperedness bordering on the divine. Further complicating matters is that we fathers are not quite sure how "professional" we want the on-field relationship with our sons to be. The identification between man and boy, after all, is never so close as on the athletic field, where the kids become walking advertisements for the potency of the father's testosterone. Any other child strikes out with the bases jammed, and you pat him on the fanny and say, "Tough break."

The one time Graig watched a close pitch sail by for strike three in a championship game, stranding the tying run, I did not say, "Tough break." I meant to say it. Honest. I even formed the words. But something diabolical took hold of my larynx, and what I heard come out instead was, "How could you take a pitch that close with two strikes on you?" Then I kicked myself over it for the rest of the weekend.

Of course, my behavior toward Graig, like that of most father-coaches toward their sons, was marked by erratic cycles of indulgence and volatility. I would let him goad me, push me to the limit. I would look the other way as he cut up and did his best to undermine my authority over the team. All of this I would let slide until I would explode at him in a rage far out of proportion to the stimulus of the moment.

The worst of these eruptions came during the last year I coached Graig, when he was fifteen. We were having batting practice on a languorous afternoon in late May. Nobody felt like being there, yours truly included. It was too hot, too humid. But the team hadn't been hitting, and it struck me as a lousy time to be canceling a scheduled workout.

Wise guy that he is, Graig decided to liven things up. I would yell instructions to the batter, and from behind me I would hear my words repeated in this moronic voice that brought to mind Bullwinkle from *Rocky and His Friends*.

It took awhile, but I finally got so fed up with the lame echo from deep short that I whirled on the pitcher's mound and fired my best fastball in Graig's direction. It was an act I regretted at once, even before the ball had completely left my grip. But it was too late.

What happened next took a split second. And yet, amazingly, there was time enough for me to be aware of several things.

I was aware that around me, everything—everything—had ceased. There was no movement, no sound, no nothing.

I was aware of feeling more helpless than I had ever felt in my life.

And I was aware, in that terrifying instant before impact, that I could no longer see my son's mouth because it had been eclipsed by—and was about to merge with—the speeding ball in flight.

Graig was standing no more than thirty feet away. Had he not been looking directly at me and had he not been able to get his glove up in the nick of time, I might now be occupying the Bing Crosby chair at the College of Dubious Parenting.

As it developed, he made the catch cleanly and no damage was done. He just stood there for ten or fifteen seconds, holding the glove right where he had intercepted the ball, like a catcher giving the umpire a long look at a close pitch. His facial expression was a curious hybrid: half fear, half mirth. Several of the other kids, meanwhile, were staring at me with mouths agape, no doubt wondering what their psychotic coach might do for an encore.

I felt awful, ashamed. Above all, I was sickened by a thought that kept nagging at me for months afterward: What I had just done was not something you did to anybody's kid but your own. Graig had come within a whisker of being maimed, solely because he was the coach's kid.

Somehow we put that incident behind us and finished the season without trying to throttle one another. That winter Graig and I decided to go our separate ways. I would stay with our current team; he would graduate to "colt" ball, with a different coach. We both knew it was better this way.

I now ask myself whether I have a moral obligation to share these reminiscences with Derek. Should I tell him that when you are your son's coach, you are always your son's coach, even late at night and hours removed from the field? Should I tell Derek that as long as a son's coach remains his son's coach, the two of them will never be able to watch a ball game together in an unspoiled, purely recreational way? That the son's coach will find himself turning every play into an instructional video or an opportunity to critique the son's skills?

Maybe I should just tell Derek how much nicer it was for Graig and me after the breakup. In particular, I would tell him about the catch we had before the next season's tryouts. We threw freely, easily, without pressure. No longer were we coach and player. For the first time since Graig left kindergarten (kindergarten!), we were just a boy and his dad tossing a ball around in the sun.

Then I watched Graig go out and pound the horsehide, make graceful running catch after running catch and fire strikes to second base from the depths of the outfield. And you know what? Beaming on the sidelines, I thought, I wouldn't mind having that kid on my team.

~Steve Salerno
Chicken Soup for the Baseball Fan's Soul

71

Chicken Soup for the Soul

What Any Father Would Do

Each day of our lives we make deposits
in the memory banks of our children.
~Charles R. Swindoll,
The Strong Family

Jim Redmond did what any father would do. His child needed help. It was that simple. The Olympic Games have the kind of security that thousands of policemen and metal detectors can offer. But no venue is safe, when a father sees his son's dream drifting away.

"One minute I was running," Derek Redmond of Great Britain said. "The next thing there was a pop. I went down."

Derek, twenty-six, had waited for this four-hundred-meter semifinal for at least four years. In Seoul, he had an Achilles tendon problem. He waited until a minute-and-a-half before the race began before he would admit he couldn't run.

In November 1990, Derek underwent operations on both Achilles tendons. He has had five surgeries in all. But he came back. In the first two rounds, he had run 45.02 and 45.03, his fastest times in five years.

"I really wanted to compete in my first Olympics," Redmond said. "I was feeling great. It just came out of the blue."

Halfway around the track, Redmond lay sprawled across lane five, his right hamstring gone bad.

Redmond struggled to his feet and began hobbling around the track. The winner of the heat, defending Olympic champion Steve Lewis, had finished and headed toward the tunnel. So had the other six runners. But the last runner in the heat hadn't finished. He continued to run.

Jim Redmond (Derek's dad), sitting high in the stands at Olympic Stadium, saw Derek collapse.

"You don't need accreditation in an emergency," Redmond said.

So Redmond, a forty-nine-year-old machine-shop owner in Northampton, ran down the steps and onto the track.

"I was thinking," Jim Redmond said, "I had to get him there so he could say he finished the semifinal."

The crowd realized that Derek Redmond was running the race of his life. Around the stands, from around the world, the fans stood and honored him with cheers.

At the final turn, Jim Redmond caught up to his son and put his arm around him. Derek leaned on his dad's right shoulder and sobbed. But they kept going. An usher attempted to intercede and escort Jim Redmond off the track. If ever a futile mission had been undertaken...

They crossed the finish line, father and son, arm in arm.

~Ivan Maisel
Chicken Soup for the Father's Soul

72

Three Strikes of Life

The Organic Produce Little League team was taking pregame batting practice. The stars were smacking the ball hard. Everyone else was missing. After a bit, an old man in brown suit pants put his fingers through the chain links of the backstop. He looked eighty, though his shoes looked only half that.

"You kids want to hit the ball better?" he asked. The better players laughed. What did an old man know about hitting? But a handful of the lesser players tentatively put their hands up. They were willing to try anything.

"Listen up," the old man said. His hands trembled until they fastened around an aluminum bat. Then they seemed strong. His eyes were red and his complexion was mottled, with a stubble of white whisker on his cheek.

"You get three strikes," he said. "Each one's different. Each strike, you change who you are."

The kids squinted.

"The first pitch is your rookie pitch. The pitcher doesn't know you. Anything can happen. Maybe you close your eyes, you get lucky and beat one back up the middle.

"But usually you don't. You miss, and all the weaknesses of the rookie come down on you. You're thinking about failing, and getting ready to fail. You're scared of the pitcher, scared of the ball. You get revved up. You forget what your coaches say and swing crazy, hoping to get lucky. Or you stand like a statue while the umpire calls a strike.

"Most young hitters give up now. They swing at the next two just to get it over. They don't grow in the at bat. The bat's a white flag, and they're waving it to surrender.

"To have a good rookie pitch, you have to be good inside. Good rookies go up to the plate respecting the pitcher and humble about their odds. They respect the ball, and they shut out everything else.

"You need courage on the first strike pitch, because you're a stranger in a strange land. You put yourself in harm's way, close to the ball, close to the plate.

"Maybe you'll get drilled. It'll hurt. But only a bit. You stand close anyway, because good things happen when you put yourself in a little danger.

"You need faith that if you do it in the right spirit, things will work out.

"That's the rookie pitch.

"By the second pitch, you're in your prime. Now you know what the at bat is about. You've seen the pitch. You know what you have to do to turn on it. The first strike filled you with adrenaline. Now you're strong. You feel electrified. You feel good. You grip the bat tight.

"The prime pitch is when good things usually happen. You're ahead of the pitcher, even with the first strike. Because you know what he's got, and you feel good. If you fail on the prime pitch, it's because maybe you felt too good. People in their prime get overconfident. They swing too hard. They miss.

"That's the prime pitch." The old man spat but the spit dripped out at about five points, and he had to wipe some off his lip.

"Third pitch. Now you're a veteran. You're at the end of your rope. If you fail now, there won't be another pitch. It's life or death. You're like an old prizefighter, and you stand almost perfectly still, waiting for your moment. The bat's loose and tight at the same time.

"You're not relying on luck, like the first pitch. Or talent, like the second pitch. Now you're calling on your guts, and everything you've learned.

"You mess up on the veteran pitch when you're angry at the pitcher for making you miss the other two pitches. The bad veteran is always making excuses. He's making up excuses for missing before he misses.

"But the good veteran welcomes the battle. It's serious, but it gives him joy, too. He knows that baseball means pain, and he welcomes the suffering. He may go down, but he's grateful he ever got up. If he goes down, it will be swinging."

"Sir, what if you strike out?" asked one kid, shielding the sun from his eyes with his glove.

"You just hope there's another game, and you're in it." The old man scanned the horizon to the west. "I gotta go, kids. Good luck out there." And he turned and was gone.

The kids mumbled as they got their equipment together. Did anyone know who that guy was? Maybe a retired sportswriter, someone suggested. Or an ex-player. Maybe even a Hall of Famer, one wishful thinker said.

"No, it's just my dad," said a slender infielder. "He was in the sixties."

The players nodded sagely and they took the field. In the game, the Organic Produce team skunked the Subway Sandwich team 14-3. And every one of the kids who listened got a hit.

~Michael Finley
Chicken Soup for the Baseball Fan's Soul

73

Wake Up Call

While we try to teach our children all about life,
Our children teach us what life is all about.
~Angela Schwindt

I was sitting in a bathtub full of moldy sheetrock when my thirteen-year-old son asked the question. "Can you take me golfing sometime?" he said.

I had a bathroom to remodel. It was fall, and the forecast for the next week was for a one hundred percent chance of Oregon's liquid sunshine. I wanted to say no. "Sure," I said, "what did you have in mind?"

"Well, maybe you could, like, pick up Jared and me after school on Friday and take us out to Oakway."

"Sounds good."

Friday came. The showers continued. Looking out the window, moldy sheetrock seemed the saner choice. But at the appointed hour, I changed from home-improvement garb to rain-protection garb and loaded the boys' clubs and mine in the back of the car. In front of the school, Ryan and Jared piled in. Ryan looked at me with a perplexed expression.

"What's with the golf hat, Dad?" he said.

It was, I thought, a silly question, like asking a scuba diver what's with the swim fins.

"Well, I thought we were going to play some golf."

A peculiar pause ensued, like a phone line temporarily gone dead.

"Uh, you're going, too?" he asked.

Suddenly, it struck me like a three-iron to my gut: I hadn't been invited.

Thirteen years of parenting flashed before my eyes. The birth. The diapers. The late-night feedings. Helping with homework. Building forts. Fixing bikes. Going to games. Going camping. Going everywhere together—my son and I.

Now I hadn't been invited. This was it. This was the end of our relationship as I had always known it. This was "Adios, Old Man, thanks for the memories but I'm old enough to swing my own clubs now, so go back to your rocking chair and crossword puzzles and—oh yeah—here's a half-off coupon for your next bottle of Geritol."

All these memories sped by in about two seconds, leaving me about three seconds to respond before Ryan would get suspicious and think I had actually expected to be playing golf with him and his friend.

I had to say something. I wanted to say this: "How could you do this to me? Throw me overboard like unused crab bait?" We had always been a team. But this was abandonment. Adult abuse.

This was Lewis turning to Clark in 1805 and saying: "Later, Bill. I can make it the rest of the way to Oregon without you." John Glenn radioing Mission Control to say thanks, but he could take it from here. Simon bailing out on Garfunkel during "Bridge over Troubled Water."

Why did it all have to change?

Enough of this mind-wandering. I needed to level with him. I needed to express how hurt I was. Share my gut-level feelings. Muster all the courage I could find, bite the bullet and spill my soul.

So I said, "Me? Play? Naw. You know I'm up to my ears in the remodel project."

We drove on in silence for a few moments. "So, how are you planning to pay for this?" I asked, my wounded ego reaching for the dagger.

"Uh, could you loan me seven dollars?"

Oh, I get it. He doesn't want me, but he'll gladly take my money.

"No problem," I said.

I dropped Ryan and Jared off, wished them luck and headed for home. My son was on his own now. Nobody there to tell him how to fade a five-iron, how to play that tricky downhiller, how to hit the sand shot. And what if there's lightning? What about hypothermia? A runaway golf cart? A band of militant gophers? He's so small. Who would take care of him?

There I was, alone, driving away from him. Not just for now. Forever. This was it. The bond was broken. Life would never be the same.

I walked in the door. "What are you doing home?" my wife asked.

I knew it would sound like some thirteen-year-old who was the only one in the gang not invited to the slumber party, but maintaining my immature demur, I said it anyway.

"I wasn't invited," I replied, with a trace of snottiness.

Another one of those peculiar pauses ensued. Then my wife laughed. Out loud. At first I was hurt. Then I, too, laughed, the situation suddenly becoming much clearer.

I went back to the bathroom remodel and began realizing that this is what life is all about: Fathers and sons must ultimately change. I've been preparing him for this moment since he first looked at me and screamed in terror: not to play golf without me, but to take on the world without me. With his own set of clubs. His own game plan. His own faith.

God was remodeling my son. Adding some space here. Putting in a new feature there. In short, allowing him to become more than he could ever be if I continued to hover over him. Just like when I was a kid and, at Ryan's age, I would sling my plaid golf bag over my shoulder and ride my bike five miles across town to play golf at a small public course called Marysville that I imagined as Augusta National.

I remember how grown up I felt, walking into that dark club-house, the smoke rising from the poker game off to the left, and proudly plunking down my two dollars for nine holes. Would I have wanted my father there with me that day? Naw. A boy's gotta do what a boy's gotta do: Grow up.

I went back to the bathroom remodel project. A few hours later, I heard Ryan walk in the front door. I heard him complain to his mother that his putts wouldn't drop, that his drives were slicing and that the course was like a lake. He sounded like someone I knew. His tennis shoes squeaked with water as I heard him walk back to where I was working on the bathroom.

"Dad," he said, dripping on the floor, "my game stinks. Can you take me golfing sometime? I need some help."

I wanted to hug him, rev my radial-arm saw in celebration and shout, "I'm still needed!" I wanted to tell God, "Thanks for letting me be part of this kid's remodel job."

Instead, I plastered one of those serious-Dad looks on my face and stoically said, "Sure, Ry, anytime."

~Bob Welch
Chicken Soup for the Father's Soul

74

T-Ball and the Beaver

Don't forget to swing hard, in case you hit the ball.
~Woodie Held

"Just call me Beaver. Everyone does. See why?"

With that he wrinkled up his face, displayed two extra large upper front teeth over his lower lip, flapped his arms, chirped like a bird and moved his posterior up and down.

So we called him "Beaver."

He was the least athletic member of our T-ball team—quite a distinction, for T-ball is populated by kids who are probably never going to be varsity players because they lack speed, coordination, strength or skill—or maybe all four, like Beaver. But no one was more lovable than the Beaver.

One of the goals of each season is to somehow help each kid—eight- and nine-year-old boys—have a moment when he is the hero, when his teammates mob him and praise his great feat on the diamond. It was going to be very hard to help the Beaver have his moment of glory.

Try as he would, the Beaver could not hit the ball off the tee very often, and when he did, the ball would dribble out to the pitcher, who would run and touch first base while an amazed Beaver stood and watched. Often the umpire—one of the dads recruited for the job—would give Beaver six strikes, usually in a futile attempt to help the Beaver hit the ball.

It bothered me to see the Beaver fail so often, and it hurt the whole team to watch. But it did not bother the Beaver. He always smiled and laughed after each disaster at the plate.

Beaver was no better in the outfield. Usually he and the closest outfielder teammate would be talking and laughing about who knows what. The Beaver was having a good time. Just being on the team was good enough.

The season was almost over. It was one of the last games. Then the miracle I prayed for happened. The Beaver accidentally hit the ball hard and just right after five strikes. The ball sailed over the heads of the shortstop and the left fielder, who were standing side by side, discussing which was worse—little brothers or sisters—and rolled out into left field.

Beaver just stood there in awe and utter amazement. All his coaches, teammates and fans, including me, yelled, "Run, Beaver. Go to first base. Yea, Beaver! Go, go, go!"

Beaver, totally overcome and utterly perplexed, stood motionless for a moment. Then he ran over to me and sat on the bench at my side.

"What are you doing here?" I asked. Beaver replied, "Everyone was yelling and screaming at me. I figured I was doing something wrong, so I ran over to be by you."

"Beaver, you did great. Now run over to first base where Mr. Johnson [one of the dads] is coaching."

Beaver got up and, with a gentle push from me, ran to first base. (The complexities of staying in the base path were for a future time.) The ball was still out in left field as a result of a badly executed relay.

When Beaver reached first base, Mr. Johnson told him to run to second base and gave him a gentle push in the right direction. He hollered at the Beaver as he ran toward second base, "Watch Mr. Andrews [the dad coaching third base] when you get to second base."

The throw to second base was wild and went out into right field. Mr. Andrews yelled to Beaver, "Come here, Beaver." Beaver ran to third base and stopped. The right fielder now had the ball. Another shout of encouragement and a gentle push from Mr. Andrews had

Beaver running home. He beat the last wild throw of the play and scored! He just stood there, standing on home plate. He was smiling now.

His teammates, coaches, mothers and dads, and I ran to him and congratulated Beaver with unrestrained enthusiasm and utter joy. It was the kind of moment every kid should have at least once.

After the game, Beaver taught us another lesson, in addition to facing adversity with a smile.

I said to him, "From now on we will call you Home-Run Ted."

"No," he said with a smile, "just call me Beaver." With that he wrinkled up his face, displayed two extra large upper front teeth over his lower lip, flapped his arms, chirped like a bird and moved his posterior up and down.

Beaver taught us that modesty in victory was a virtue as great as a happy disposition in adversity.

Amazing what we can learn from an eight-year-old in T-ball. In some thirty seasons of coaching kids' sports, T-ball and the Beaver was the greatest moment of all.

~Judge Keith J. Leenhouts
Chicken Soup for the Baseball Fan's Soul

75

A Place in the Sun

Don't tell me about the world. Not today.
It's springtime and they're knocking baseballs around fields
where the grass is damp and green in the morning
and the kids are trying to hit the curve ball.
~Pete Hamill

It's been years since my sons were in Little League baseball. I get a bit nostalgic as I see the neighborhood children going off to their games, looking sharp and proud in their uniforms with a number on their backs they will never forget.

In 1963, Colin, my eldest son, played centerfield for the Tigers, a Little League team in Hampton, Virginia. In his first year, his father told him that keeping a ball firmly gripped in his baseball glove would help form a good pocket in his new glove. We'd often find him sleeping with the glove still on his hand, baseball gripped tightly.

I made sure I was at all of our sons' games, even when I was pregnant with number-four child (another future Little Leaguer) and pushing my youngest daughter around in a stroller. The older daughter was already old enough to help whenever I had concession-stand duty. It was our family entertainment every night of the week during baseball season.

The most unforgettable game came at the conclusion of the '63 season and Colin's last year of Little League baseball. He was on the all-star team, and this game would determine who went on to compete in the regional playoffs. Our all-stars needed to clinch this one.

It meant traveling out of town to an unfamiliar field, but we went in hopes of watching our boys beat the socks off the opposing team.

Tied, the game went into extra innings. It was a hard-fought game and a toss-up right to the final hit deep into midfield. In some ballfields, it might have been considered a homerun, but standing tall and ready to save the day far out in center field stood my son with his eye on that fly ball all the way. He seemed to hesitate as he stood there, anticipating the trajectory, and then he began his dash for the landing zone. I sat in the stands praying this wasn't going to be one of those days that Colin got ahead of his size-thirteen feet as he watched the ball heading into no-man's land, a weedy patch of knee-high grass and low trailing vines. It arched high, stalled and became lost to us in the lowering five o'clock sun. From the stands, the players were silhouetted against the glare, their mouths gaping open as they followed the ball into the raw afternoon light. Collectively, we held our breath, frantically squinting against the sun for a glimpse of Colin and the ball as it dropped toward the outfield where maintenance had long since been abandoned.

Parents sat mute, resisting their usual sideline coaching. It was the quiet of a golf tournament. Colin took off, feet following his steady concentration on the baseball; first attempting to run, then leaping through the thick and tangled weeds and vines until he appeared to be right under the descending ball. He had his glove stuck out before him. It looked as though he was attempting to correct his position, but then he stumbled backward, vanishing from view.

The crowd in our bleachers groaned as one.

The other team jumped up and down in their dugout, and their parents cheered and whistled.

We fixed smiles on our faces for the sake of our team's spirit, which would soon be congratulating the other team as victors and league champs. At the same time, we strained our eyes to see if Colin was going to get up to chase the ball.

Then above the weeds, we saw an arm with a mitt raised high. Someone yelled, "He caught it!" The umpire nodded.

The crowd went wild. I thought our bleachers would fall apart with the pounding of feet.

Such a game fulfills the dreams of heroics for little boys and their parents there to witness it. It may be the best day they remember, when they had their place in the sun... and a pocket in their glove!

~Rosalie Griffin
Chicken Soup for the Mother and Son Soul

76

Letting Go

The orange-clad monk smiled at our blond hair.

"From where you come?" he asked.

I wondered if he could understand how far away the Rocky Mountains actually were from this Buddhist temple in southern Thailand, and yet how much at home I really felt.

"America?" he beamed, and pointed at himself: "I student of English!"

He handed me a book in English on Buddha's four noble truths. As I opened it, my eyes came to rest on a page dealing with the origin of suffering. Buddha says that the root of all suffering stems from attachment—attachment to ourselves, to our possessions, to our activities, to our opinions.

I looked at my teenage son, Eri. Here we were on our father-and-son journey to new places and new ideas, exploring the world with all our senses, finding real sights and sounds, smells and tastes—things you can't get through textbooks and television. We were taking a year off from what we thought was our life, to discover what else it could be.

Two boys, one in his forties and the other fourteen, both celebrating a rite of passage of sorts, wandering in Southeast Asia—our backpacks filled with camera, clothing and assorted "necessities."

Reading the wisdom of Buddha's words, Eri and I nodded in agreement with the principle of nonattachment. I stared at the radiant, shaven-headed monk who owned nothing, and reflected on attachment. Life does seem to get easier when I let go a bit. There are the little things like giving away old clothes or tossing out old files after years of pack-ratting. Then there are the big things, like letting go of an unworkable relationship, or a job that makes dollars, but no sense.

Driving away, we thought about the monk's smile, Buddha's words and an old mindfulness prayer:

Breathing in, I calm body and mind.
Breathing out, I smile.
Dwelling in the present moment,
I know this is the only moment.

The test for letting go was just beginning. Somehow I think God knew we were just novices and that more training was needed. Each day it was something else—misplaced keys, passports, scuba mask and more. It kept the pressure on to really let go. After a couple of arduous weeks, we thought we had it made, the principle of letting go now firmly established. We purchased a new Nikon camera, to replace the one we had accidentally ruined.

It was late afternoon some days later on the tenth hole of a jungle golf course. Eri and I are both avid golfers, and the one constant in life (besides change) is that golf can be played anywhere, even in the jungles of Southeast Asia. I was about to nail my approach shot to the green when a monkey came out of the jungle and began to cross the fairway. We had never seen a monkey in the wild before—and certainly never one on a golf course—so Eri immediately took out our new camera. As he approached, the animal growled, bared his teeth and made an ugly swipe with its hand. Eri backed up and froze. Four baby monkeys appeared out of the forest behind the monkey. The threatening gesture must have been to protect the babies. We smiled at this unique sight, something never seen on the Pebble Beach links.

Suddenly, a large male with a full beard, jagged teeth and a Clint Eastwood squint emerged and slowly began to knuckle his way toward us. Despite all my years of martial-art training, I was devoid of aikido techniques for large, hostile simians. One look at the size of his arms made me thankful I was holding a five-iron. With each step he took toward us, we backed away. He kept coming.

"What do we do, Dad?" Eri asked nervously.

I said, "Judging the lie the monkey has, and the distance to the pin, a five-iron is the club of choice."

He grabbed a three-wood. Eri rarely takes my golf tips.

Laughing, we calmed ourselves and relaxed, and the monkey seemed to relax too, and turned away from us as he developed an interest in my recently abandoned golf bag. He began touching the clubs, and picking up my ball and tossing it, as if to say, I don't play Top-Flites. Do you have any Titleists here?

Just as I said to Eri, "This will make some great photos," all three of us noticed the camera on the ground near the bag where Eri had left it when he had hurriedly picked up his three-wood. The monkey eyed it carefully and approached it... my camera. So much for my attitude of detachment.

I stepped forward to claim what was rightfully mine and said to the macho primate, "Hey, don't even think about it, you big..." But I was frozen in my tracks by one fixed make-my-day glare. The monkey reached down and swooped up the camera... my brand-new camera!

I tried mental telepathy. No response. He deftly removed the case, took the camera and held it up to one eye.

I know this sounds like too much artistic license, and I'm sure if I didn't have a witness to corroborate the story, I couldn't trust myself to repeat it. But I swear that this hairy primate with the beady eyes began to mimic a professional fashion photographer, as if working on the proper angles and lighting. I imagined him muttering to himself: Beautiful, beautiful. You two look great! After a couple of minutes, he wrapped the camera strap around his wrist and ambled off into the jungle.

In the approaching darkness, father and son, golf clubs in hand, followed nervously, looking for a monkey who had stolen their camera. To what strange karmic past did I owe such a teaching?

Exposing our human inadequacy, the monkey gracefully and swiftly ascended sixty feet up a tree. We agonized as he swung happily from branch to branch, banging our camera along with him. Mercifully, an idea surfaced. "Remember the book *Caps for Sale?*" I asked Eri.

It's a children's story about a cap peddler who has all but one stolen by monkeys, who each put on a cap, climb into a tree and mimic the peddler as he rages below. Finally, the peddler throws his remaining cap on the ground, and voilà! The rest of the caps come flying out of the tree as they mimic him again. Our solution was obvious.

We began to throw clubs, coconuts, rocks, golf balls and sunglasses to the ground, all with one eye on our hairy friend as he studied our antics below and fingered our camera. Then, in the honored lineage of all the great masters, he opened the battery compartment, removed the two batteries, and in a frivolous gesture, tossed them at our feet.

The sun had now set. Two boys, one in his forties and the other fourteen, lay laughing on the jungle floor, looking up at a bemused, long-armed relative. The boys had been forced to let go of a killer case of the clings. Let go, let God. Relax. Release attachments. Everything is unfolding perfectly. And, after all, we did get the batteries back.

As soon as we were ready to go, what do you think happened? Did the monkey toss our camera down? No. But the principle of letting go is that it is not a manipulative technique to control the universe. As Buckminster Fuller once said, "You did not create this universe, and you do not control it."

However, if you ever stumble across a monkey somewhere in Southeast Asia carrying a Nikon camera, follow him. It was a good camera.

~Thomas F. Crum
Chicken Soup to Inspire the Body & Soul

77

Hero for the Day

When I was ten, I wanted to play on my grammar school baseball team so badly I'd go to bed every night and dream about it. Those were the days long before Little League, and there were no tryouts. Team members were selected mostly on a clique basis by class buddies who had played together since the first grade, and they naturally assumed there was no one else in the class who could catch or bat as well as they.

The times when the team was short of players due to chickenpox or measles, I'd beg to substitute, but the team captain—his name was Buzzy Bennett—always picked someone else.

Undaunted, I went home and attacked the problem as if it were a war. I began by coaxing my dad into being my trainer. We lived on a hill, and Dad would stand at the top and hit balls while I waited at the bottom to catch them. This gave the illusion that the balls were coming from a far distance at a staggering height.

I couldn't afford a mitt. This was the Depression, and every cent counted. I learned to catch with my bare hands. I soon built up calluses, but not before I bent fingers, sprained a wrist and tore off fingernails. But before long, very few lofted balls got past me.

Then I had a stroke of luck. A college student who lived just up the block from me played baseball at a nearby city college. He caught fly balls with me and showed me how to hit. His name was Ralph Kiner, a guy who later had an outstanding major-league career and became a broadcaster.

The day finally came when our class team was scheduled to play the team from the class above us. When you're ten, a kid who is eleven looks as big as a mountain and twice as athletic. The whole school turned out, and everybody expected our guys to lose in a rout. I begged to play, but was totally ignored. There was a little blond girl I wanted to impress, but since I wasn't on the team she didn't give me the time of day.

Then, in the middle of the third with the score nothing to nothing, our team's first baseman was knocked flat by a runner and cracked a rib. Buzzy brought in his right fielder to play first. He then looked around the crowd. Finding no one who looked like he could throw a ball, he stared a long minute at me.

"Okay, Cussler," he finally said. "Go play right field. You should be all right. Nobody ever hits 'em out there."

I ran to the position, still without a glove.

The fourth inning looked like the start of a massacre. We got two outs, but the big guys loaded the bases. The next batter looked like a cross between Babe Ruth and Roger Maris. The impact with the bat sounded like a cannon shot and the ball lifted high in the air. Like a movie in slow motion, every eye on every face was on the ball. I began running back. I stole a glance at the kid in center field. He was just standing there. Now that I recall, he was eating a candy bar.

I ran. Oh, God, how I ran. Out of the corner of one eye I saw the chain-link fence coming closer. I ran two more steps and then jumped. I felt the fence become one with my right hip and shoulder. The ball smacked into my open hand. I had made a one-handed catch of a ball that should have been a home run. And without the help of a mitt.

There was stunned silence on the school ground. Plays like that just didn't happen in grammar school. The months of perseverance with the able assistance of Dad and Ralph Kiner had paid off. The force was now mine. I walked from right field to the bench, slowly tossing the ball up and down, trying to look cool. Only when I passed near home plate did I nonchalantly flip the ball to the opposing pitcher.

Nor did it stop there. I went on that day to hit a single and a triple. Sure, we lost, 6-3, but I was still the hero of the hour. And the little blond girl who ignored me before the game? Her name was Joy, and she became the first girl I ever kissed.

~Clive Cussler
Chicken Soup for the Baseball Fan's Soul

78

The Big Slip

I was getting ready to walk out the door after my usual morning routine when my mother yelled for me to get out to the car—as she often had to do just to get me moving. I grabbed my book bag, threw on some shoes, and walked through the door to the garage with no idea what was going to happen that day.

The morning went off without a hitch: math class, English, social studies. Finally it was 11:30, time for lunch.

I went to my locker, grabbed my lunch, and walked to our gym/cafeteria with the rest of my friends. The lunchroom was always a mess when it was our turn, because we were the last ones in the school to eat—after the kindergarten through fifth-grade kids were done. We had a very small school and it was used as both a cafeteria and a gym. Dust and dirt often collected on the floor from students' shoes—not to mention spilled milk, drinks and dropped food.

I sat down at a table with my friends, ate my lunch and sat back to talk with them for the remainder of the lunch period. We got up when it was finally time for recess. During recess there was never anyone eating in the gym, so we had the option of using it. We started playing a game of half-court basketball.

The game was about halfway through, and my team had the lead. I was outside of the key, guarding an opponent, when he shot the ball over my head. I jumped to block but missed. Michael, a teammate, got the rebound and was immediately covered by Andrew. Seeing that I was open and that he had a clear passing lane, he threw the ball to the ground for a bounce pass. I remember the ball hitting the floor only to come back up and hit me in the chest. Then my memory just goes blank. Just like when you fall asleep. You never see it coming — it just happens and there is a gap of memory between that instant and when you wake up.

It turns out that I caught the ball, slipped and bounced on my head. Maybe it was the wet floor or the shoes I was wearing. But either way, I was headed to the hospital.

The next part of this story is a little sketchy because I don't remember it at all. What you are reading now is what I've heard from various sources. I was lying on the ground with blood coming out of my nose, and Jarred asked me, "Are you all right?" There was no reply. The lunch aides ran to my side as I suddenly sat up and began hitting away or waving my arms at anyone who came close to me. I said that I had a really bad headache and the aides suggested that I lie down on the couch in the teachers' lounge. Our principal came into the gym and started to ask me questions. When I hit her with my fist, she realized I wasn't myself and yelled for someone to call an ambulance.

The paramedics arrived and took me to St. Luke's. The doctors, noticing I was going to need an emergency CAT scan, called and told them to rush the person out to make it available for me. Such a call is uncommon. Usually they simply rush the patient up there, hoping it's open. They rushed me to the CAT scan and took the pictures of my brain. The doctors found that I had ruptured a blood vessel inside my skull. I was bleeding inside my head, and the growing amount of blood was applying a lot of pressure to my brain.

The doctors had to surgically relieve the pressure, so I was rushed to surgery where Dr. Shinko would operate. He told my mother that there was a 75 percent chance he could relieve the pressure. My father, who was away in Chicago on business, was frantically awaiting a flight home after hearing about what had happened to me. As I headed into surgery, I have a vague memory of saying to my mother, "Tell everyone that I love them."

Inside the operating room, I have another vague memory of

about six people around me, very busy doing things. I remember yelling, "My head hurts like heck, my head hurts like heck!" Then a female nurse kindly said to me, "We're doing everything we can." That's where the memory ceases.

Dr. Shinko had to shave the side of my head to make a clean incision, which begins at the front side of my ear and ends about a centimeter away from my left eye. He cut through a lot of nerves, but he knew they would grow back. He was able to relieve the pressure and close the incision using staples instead of stitches. Then I was taken to a hospital room where the doctors and my parents awaited my awakening.

I remember slowly raising my eyelids. My eyes half open, I heard someone whispering, "He's awake." Then another person saying the same thing. I remember thinking, "What is going on?" There was a machine to my right displaying my heart rate and other information. To my left was an IV bag hanging on a rack. Sitting on a chair to my left was my mother and standing behind her was my father. I asked in a soft voice, "What happened?"

They explained what had happened, and they asked me if I remembered the basketball game. I remembered every detail of it—even who was on my team and who was on the opposing one—everything, that is, except the accident. I stayed in the hospital for about a week, really groggy most of the time. I did more sleeping than anything else.

I woke up one day to find my room showered with cards. A few of my friends visited me to tell me how all the girls cried after it happened. And they asked if I could play in our upcoming tournament basketball game. I knew I wouldn't be able to, no matter how much I wanted to.

After some more tests, I finally left the hospital in a wheelchair, all the while insisting I didn't need one. But I didn't get my way.

It was weird going to church the following Sunday and hearing my name on the sick list to be prayed for. My punishment, as I call it, was that I couldn't run for two months and worse, couldn't play contact sports for six months. It stunk having to be tied down like that, but I got through it.

Dr. Shinko say he fixxxed everythiiing but for ssomme eason me dont realllly belive himm.

~Scott Allen, 11
Chicken Soup for the Preteen Soul 2

Tales OF Golf AND Sport

Defining Moments

*You hear that winning breeds winning. But no winners are bred from
losing. They learn they don't like it.*
~Tom Watson

79

Early Retirement

Forgiveness is a funny thing.
It warms the heart and cools the sting.
~William Arthur Ward

My fiancée, Lauren, and I were in her hometown of Philadelphia, where her aunt was hosting Lauren's bridal shower. The plans for the day largely entailed my staying out of everyone's way until the end of the shower, when I would then be introduced to several of her parents' friends and family.

My prospective father-in-law, Milt, who had only recently taken up golf, naturally thought the best form of introduction would be a golf outing involving me, him and a family friend whose wife would be attending the shower.

Now I hadn't picked up a club in months, but not wanting to disappoint Milt (and not wanting to play a larger role in the bridal shower than absolutely necessary), I agreed.

As it turned out, we were running a little late in making our tee time and I didn't have any opportunity to warm up with a bucket of balls before the round, as I had hoped. There was also a slight backup on the first tee. To make room for the influx of golfers, Milt had pulled our cart a little farther forward than safety would normally dictate. I thought about saying something to him but as he was to the left of the tee box, and I normally hit the ball so far right that golfers in the next fairway are occasionally sent ducking for cover, I assumed he would be in no danger. I was wrong.

I caught the ball off the heel of my driver, sending it directly into my future father-in-law's right hand. Now, my relationship with Milt had always been friendly, but formal. At this point, not only was I confident that was going to change, but I wasn't certain Milt was going to lend his blessing to my marrying his youngest daughter.

I was also convinced that I had, with that one blow, sent my future father-in-law heading toward an early retirement. Milt is an ear-nose-and-throat doctor and is required to perform certain types of surgery in order to continue his practice.

Horrified at what I had just done, I began to shake so badly that I couldn't even think about finishing out the hole. So I picked up my ball, got an ice pack for Milt, and took the wheel of the cart while Milt bravely attempted to continue playing. By the time we got to the second hole, Milt somehow had me laughing about the whole incident.

"Todd, you didn't hit me hard enough," he told me. He explained that if I'd done more significant damage, he'd have been able to retire (something it turned out he'd been contemplating anyway), while collecting on a nice insurance policy he'd taken out just in case of golfing accidents involving future sons-in-law.

I chuckled, then replied, "Well, we've got seventeen more holes. I'll see what I can do."

It was the first time I'd felt completely at ease with my future father-in-law, and perhaps more than anything else that took place during Lauren's and my engagement period, his gentle, good nature during the incident made me feel like a part of her family. After all, who else but a family member could have forgiven such an act?

Milt finished the round and made it to the bridal shower before heading to the emergency room. It was determined that I had, indeed, broken a bone in his hand—a fact he kept hidden from me until well after the wedding as he didn't want me to feel any worse than I already did.

But now that I know, I feel even better.

~Todd Behrendt
Chicken Soup for the Golfer's Soul

Give Me a Break!

One day at a local course, the first tee was loaded with players and spectators. Over the PA system we heard, "Would the man in the green slacks and white hat respect the tee markers? Please get behind them."

The player stopped his address and looked around in disgust, and then stepped up to the ball again. Again the PA system announcer said, "Would the man in the green slacks and white hat please respect the markers!"

The player stopped his address, turned around and shouted, "Will someone please tell the jerk on the PA system that this is my second shot!"

~Gene Doherty
Chicken Soup for the Sports Fan's Soul

Plimpton to the Fore

A passion, an obsession, a romance,
a nice acquaintanceship with trees, sand, and water.
~Bob Ryan

I should have known that the week of the Crosby Pro-Am tournament was going to be taxing when I checked in for the flight to California. The clerk had been very helpful tying the clubs together and encasing them in a plastic bag. It was when he tipped the bag over to see if the clubs were secure that the mouse nest fell out.

We stared at the small heap of shavings and string lying on the floor. "I see that you're ticketed through Monterey," he said. "Going to the Crosby?"

"That's right," I said. "I played it once, fourteen years ago. I'm going to take another crack at it."

"You've really been spending the years getting ready," he said, looking at the mouse nest.

In the first Bing Crosby National Pro-Am I played, in 1966, my golf bag was carried by a diminutive furniture mover named Abe — a somewhat elderly local who occasionally worked as a caddie at Pebble Beach, one of the Monterey Peninsula courses used for the tournament. To my astonishment Abe was waiting for me this time when I arrived to register. He had heard I was coming and hoped I would have him back to "pack" my bag. I was delighted.

Abe felt it would be a good idea if we walked the course, "to refresh our minds" on what the holes looked like.

We started off by following a foursome that included Jack Lemmon. Duffers hold Lemmon in particular affection for his difficulties on the final holes of Pebble Beach, all graphically caught by the television cameras the first time he played the Crosby more than a decade ago. I recalled with relish Lemmon's attempts to make a recovery shot up a steep slope. The ball bounced jauntily up the slope and, as if appalled by what it discovered at the top, turned and hurried back down. We could see the top of Lemmon's head as he shifted about to address the ball a second time. Exactly the same thing happened. The ball bobbed up to the top of the slope, then curled back down. We never saw much of Lemmon himself, just a great deal of his errant golf ball—it seemed to fill the screen with its antic behavior.

As we walked along, Lemmon reminisced about the experience. "The whole mess started when our foursome came into view of the television cameras for the first time. You'd think I'd be used to cameras by now, but when it comes to golf, I'm not. I think I averaged ten shots on each of these last five holes."

Lemmon said that on the eighteenth, as he lay 12 with his ball still thirty-five feet from the cup. He had an elderly caddie whose sense of dignity seemed overtaxed by what was going on. He kept sidling away. Lemmon, down on one knee on the green trying to sight his putt, had to call him out of the crowd for advice. The caddie moved reluctantly until, finally, Lemmon could hear him breathing behind him. "Which way does it break?" Lemmon had asked, over his shoulder. "Who cares?" the caddie muttered.

Now, on the same eighteenth, the famous ocean hole, Lemmon hooked his drive down onto the smooth, wave-worn boulders at the foot of the seawall that curves along the length of the fairways. The ball remained in sight for an astonishing length of time, skipping and ricocheting hysterically from one rock to another. "Life is an irreplaceable divot," Lemmon said to me mysteriously as he stepped off the tee.

In the Crosby, one professional and one amateur play together as partners from start to finish. This means that even a rank amateur can play in front of the TV cameras on the final day, assuming he and his pro partner make the cut.

Not many golfers go through the stress of the first drive of a tournament in front of a large crowd. It is one thing to start off a country club Labor Day tournament before two witnesses jiggling Bloody Marys in plastic cups, and quite another to bend down to set the ball on its tee, acutely aware that five hundred people are watching you. The blood rushes to the head. The ball falls off the tee. To start the swing takes almost a physical command of "Now!"

My first drive surprised me, a high slice down the fairway that managed to stay in bounds. I hurried after it, feeling almost palpable relief in getting away from the first tee and its witnesses. After the first round I went with Abe to the practice range to try to do something about my miserable showing. I had not scored a par and had not helped my professional partner, Jack Ferenz.

My second round, on the nearby Cypress Point course, was no better than the first. I spent a great deal of time searching with Abe for errant shots. I had played thirty-six holes without scoring a par. The next day we would be playing Spyglass Hill—one of the most difficult courses in the world. The thought was very much in my mind that I, not a bad athlete, with a golf swing worked on through the years by a bevy of pros, might not achieve even one par.

The round at Spyglass did not start propitiously. My drive moved out onto the fairway, hopping along nicely, but the second shot went off at a sharp angle, hit a pine, then another, and rolled back toward me, ending not more than eight yards away after a flight that might have totaled almost two hundred yards. I stared at the ball as if it were a smoking grenade.

On the next drive I tried to slow things down. The great golf writer, Bernard Darwin, said of Bobby Jones's swing that it had a "certain drowsy beauty." I thought of that on the tee, and slowly, too slowly, I brought the club back. Imperceptibly, like an ocean liner inching away from the pier, the club head slowly moved away from the ball, gradually lifting to the top of the swing. But at the summit everything went out of control. The club head faltered like a paper airplane stalling on the wind, and then it dashed earthward in a cruel whistling swipe. A cry erupted from my throat as the club pounded into the earth a foot behind the tee, bounced, and sent the ball perfectly straight down the fairway for about ninety yards.

"Straight as an arrow," Ferenz's caddie said helpfully.

On the twelfth, Matt Mitchell, the other amateur in our foursome, threw his ball into the water hazard. Of all the indignities that man tries to heap on inanimate objects, throwing a golf ball into the water is perhaps the most hapless. The lake accepts the ball with a slight ripple that disappears almost immediately, leaving the surface smooth, almost smug. "I suppose the thing to do is to think of the ball bloating down there," I said comfortingly to Matt. He stared at me furiously.

As if to make him feel better, on the last par-3 hole, my 8-iron shot described a high parabola and dropped into the water edging the green, stitching it with a little geyser.

"It'll be bloating any minute now," Mitchell said.

The par-4 eighteenth would be my last chance in the tournament to make a par. I hit an enormous hook into a grove of pines. "It's gone," Abe said gloomily.

I told Abe that we had to find the ball. It was my last chance. If we found it, I told him, I would take a tremendous swing and catch it to perfection, whatever its lie. The ball would rocket into the clear open air above the fairway and float gently toward the green. From where it landed, I would hit a delicate wedge onto the green, and then sink a long, curling putt for a par. I would tip my hat gracefully to the spectators. But there was no sign of the ball. My last chance was gone.

When I got back home, I called a place outside New York City called Golf-O-Rama. It has indoor driving ranges that simulate actual golf courses by flashing a picture of each hole on a screen while computers track the flight of the ball. The man said they had the Pebble Beach course. I made a reservation.

Norman Schaut, president of Golf-O-Rama, showed me around. One side of the hangar-like room was taken up with the "golf courses," lined up side to side, each with an elevated tee. The golfer hits the ball twenty feet or so into a nine-foot square screen on which can be seen a color-slide reproduction of the golf hole.

We stepped up on the Pebble Beach tee. "If the computer says you've driven the ball into a water hazard," Schaut said, "there'll be the sound of splash."

I said, "You should have the sound of the waves breaking and the seals barking out there in the Pacific."

Schaut switched on the course. The picture of the par-4, 482-yard first hole at Pebble Beach flashed on. "That's it!" I said. "The dogleg to the right." I remembered the names of the contestants being called out by the starting marshal, the patter of applause from the crowds by the tee and the dryness of my throat when I had bent down to set the tee into the grass—and even here, with the Muzak playing Deep Purple, I felt my nerves tighten.

I teed up and swung. My drive, according to the computer, was an excellent one for me, 205 yards out. My second shot stopped fifty yards from the pin, and then I hit a lovely, easy wedge, which left me with a six-foot putt for my par. I stepped onto the Astroturf green with my putter. I stared down, brought the putter back, then forward, and watched the ball ease down the line and drop into the hole.

I had the urge to throw my putter into the air. Instead I turned and tried to look suave. Schaut came hurrying over. "Have you got something to say?" he asked, looking at my face, which had broken into a broad grin.

"Piece of cake," I said.

~George Plimpton
Chicken Soup for the Golfer's Soul

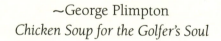

82

My Favorite Injury

I've always believed that life provides a series of experiences that serve our growth, insight and wisdom. That philosophy was tested—and ultimately deepened—during a series of surprising and challenging incidents at the age of twenty-six in the year 1979.

The previous year I had run my first under-three-hour marathon and, armed with the goal of improving that time, I intensified my training. By midsummer I was running seventy miles per week and keeping up with much faster runners for the first time in my racing career. My training partners included elite-level runners whose presence and encouragement contributed to my progress. They told me I could run a 2:40 marathon (two hours and forty minutes), with the potential to reach 2:20, given the progress in our training. Running had become both a physical and spiritual passion in my life, and I was riding a wave of rising excitement and bliss.

That all came to a grinding halt when I developed a painful injury in my knee. From running an effortless twenty miles at a fast tempo in the mountains, I could now barely run one mile. The pain increased until I couldn't even run a few steps without sharp pain. I decided to rest a few weeks, expecting to return to my training. As the weeks passed, however, my body experienced no improvement and my spirits sank. The doctors were unable to predict when I might recover. With each passing day, I could see the benefits of my hard, progressive work of the last six months ebbing away, and I grew increasingly disheartened.

I had to find some way to sustain my fitness as my knee healed. My body had grown accustomed to the rigors of training for two or more hours a day. It felt imperative that I keep my cardiovascular system strong and not lose the gains of the last half-year. I bought some swimming goggles, joined the local YMCA and set about duplicating my training regimen, assuming I'd soon be able to swim for several hours a day. I was about to receive my second difficult lesson in dealing with challenges and setbacks.

I had a smattering of swim lessons as a kid and believed that, as a marathoner, I would have no problems with a transition to the pool. But the first day I plunged into the water, it was painfully apparent that my expectations far exceeded my ability. After swimming only one length of the pool, I stopped and clung to the edge, gasping and winded. I tried a second lap with the same result. This continued for about twenty minutes, one lap at a time. I was exhausted.

I recalled that while growing up in New York I had little exposure to swimming. I didn't really like being in the water. In fact, the ocean frightened me. I remembered when a camp counselor forced us to stay out in the ocean for "our full thirty minutes," despite the chilling water temperature. A poor swimmer, I found the waves intimidating. Even as an adult I had rarely ventured into the sea.

In early July, determined to solve my dilemma, I befriended the lifeguard who spent many hours a day by the dimly lit, indoor pool in the YMCA basement. He patiently guided me seven days a week. I worked hard, determined to improve, but progress was slow. I would swim every day until exhausted; then I'd wait a few minutes and try a few more laps. Week by week, my effort and his coaching and encouragement began to pay off.

By August I was swimming nearly forty laps a day. In September I swam a mile a day, learned the breaststroke, backstroke and crawl, and even started lifesaving lessons. Feeling more competent, my confidence grew and I pushed onward. By December I could swim two miles a day and felt as comfortable in the water as I had running on land.

By the Christmas holidays, my knee had improved, but it was not yet ready for running. So I decided to travel to Hawaii, hitchhike around the islands and camp on the beaches. This seemed an idyllic break in my past routine — and besides, my budget didn't allow for much else.

I learned soon after my arrival, however, that during this period in the islands, tensions between locals and tourists had reached a peak. Recently, newspapers and radio reports had related several incidents of campers being burned out of their tents and visitors being assaulted at night by locals. As I made my way around Maui, I was repeatedly warned to be cautious when hitchhiking and especially careful if sleeping on the beach.

Hearing this news, I remember standing on Makena Beach late that afternoon, feeling vulnerable, depressed and alone, when a distant scream pulled me out of my dark reverie. It was a voice crying "Help!" from the ocean. I looked out to see several figures bobbing in the ocean beyond large, crashing waves. Without thinking, I threw off my shirt and shoes and raced into the water. Swimming through the rough surf, I found two men in their twenties holding up a terrified, much older man. They said they were exhausted from the riptide and had no strength left to bring him in. They asked me to take over so they could swim to the beach and get help.

The older man started panicking, grabbing my neck and pulling me under as huge waves thrashed us. I grabbed him firmly, looked directly into his terrified eyes and said, "Do what I tell you and I promise I won't let you die." He nodded and stopped struggling. I turned him on his back, held him with my left arm and, using all the strength of my right arm, started to swim against the riptide. The surf was terrible. A fierce storm two days earlier had shifted the sand and left behind enormous waves and an even more ferocious undertow. Sharp coral to the east precluded swimming at an angle to the beach. I would have to overcome the waves and swim straight in, against the riptide, towing the weight of an exhausted elderly man.

At first I swam with all my strength, thinking my fitness would be enough. I quickly tired, however, in the strong surf and undertow, which repeatedly pulled us out back into the sea as if we were weightless corks. I realized I had to conserve my energy—not only to make it back in with this man, but to save my own life as well.

Little by little, I neared the beach, trying to ride each wave and swim when propelled forward. A group of rescuers had locked arms and formed a human chain in the shallow water, reaching out toward the crashing waves. After an eternity, I pulled the man within thirty feet of the beach and placed him into the arms of the other rescuers.

I staggered out of the water and collapsed onto the beach, breathing hard. Then I stumbled away from the rescue group and the elderly man, to sit alone with my thoughts, which were rushing back in like the tide. Only minutes earlier I had been standing on the beach consumed by my own problems. Now, a few paces down the beach lay a man whose life I had saved. My past concerns disappeared. His cry for help had pushed me to a place far beyond my inward troubles and personal predicaments—past my fear of the ocean into an act of courage and strength.

I never again spoke to the man I saved. I never even learned his name. It wasn't necessary. He was safe now, surrounded by the group. I was consumed by a revelation... free and liberated. Life's incredible lessons and opportunities had again worked their magic.

The same knee injury that seemed to end my marathon dreams had catapulted me into choices and events that had a profound effect in my life—and had saved the life of another human being. It struck me then how the interconnected threads of our destiny are profoundly tied to one another. I used to wonder if things happen for a reason. Now I believe I understand: When things happen, it's our job to make the best use of the events. Everything that happens is a chance to grow, to create something positive out of a negative. When one door closes, another always opens. It's our job to pay attention.

I work as a sports chiropractor now, and when my patients struggle with an injury, I sometimes share the story of my favorite injury—one that saved a life, and maybe two.

~Leonard Stein
Chicken Soup to Inspire the Body & Soul

83

Beat the Pro

A hole in one is amazing when you think of the
different universes this white mass of molecules has to pass through
on its way to the hole.
~Mac O'Grady

S am Snead tells the story of a charity golf challenge he played years ago.

A pro was stationed at each hole, and threesomes would come up and bet against the pro individually. Sam was positioned at a par-3 hole and, with one shot to the green, whoever's ball was closest to the pin on the tee-off was the winner.

A threesome approached and the first man said, "Hello, Mr. Snead. I'd like to bet you five hundred dollars that I'll get closer to the pin than you do." Snead accepted the challenge. The golfer hit a good shot to the green. Snead hit it past the green and lost the bet.

The second golfer approached, saying, "It's great to meet you, Mr. Snead. I'm going to make the same bet as my friend. Five hundred dollars says that I'll hit the ball closer to the pin than you will." This time, Sam hit the ball twenty yards past the hole and lost the bet again. He just laughed. It was, after all, a charity event and the object was to raise money and have fun.

The last one of the threesome strolled up to Snead and, with a brash New Jersey accent, said, "You washed-up old man! You just don't have it anymore, do you? I'll bet thirty-five hundred dollars that I can beat you." Sam just smiled and quietly accepted the bet.

The cocky golfer hit the ball four inches from the pin. "Now beat that, old man," he said. "You should have put down those clubs years ago." Again, Sam just smiled. He leaned over and positioned the ball, drew back, took a swing and made a hole-in-one. "Better luck next time," said Slammin' Sammy Snead.

~Susan D. Brandenburg
Chicken Soup for the Golfer's Soul

A Heart of Compassion

Be kind and show compassion.
Everyone you meet is fighting a hard battle.
~T.H. Thompson

"Mom, he's picking on me again!"

I cringed at the shrill sound of seven-year-old Austin's voice rising above the rap music on the radio. Between the radio, the rumble of the truck's diesel engine, the whirl of the air conditioning and the snickering coming from the back seat, my nerves were stretched taut.

"Devin! Didn't I tell you to stop it?" I glanced into the rearview mirror, making eye contact with my middle son, freezing him in some act of mischief.

"He started it!" came the disgruntled reply.

"How many times do I have to tell you? If you don't want him to do to you what you're doing to him, then don't do it in the first place!"

Under the brim of the red baseball cap, a strange, confused look crossed Devin's face. I cringed at what I had just said. No wonder he was confused. I backtracked and rephrased it before his attention wandered onto ideas of more turmoil he could put his younger brother through.

"If you don't want him to tease you, then don't tease him. I mean it! Leave him alone!"

When I looked back into the mirror, clear understanding showed on his nine-year-old face.

"Let's see if we can make it to the baseball field without any more fighting, okay?" My two younger sons pretended to listen while my sixteen-year-old ignored us all.

Austin's game was scheduled to start in fifteen minutes, and I was, as usual, running late. Dealing with work, kids in school and now baseball games caused my husband and me to rearrange and adjust our schedules to fit the kids'.

I sign up my three sons to play baseball every year to give them a chance to learn an athletic skill and, hopefully, good sportsmanship. I wonder at times if the morals I am trying to instill in them are filtering through. There are usually no outward signs that they have absorbed these things. This worry weighs on me at times, like that day.

Steering the extended-cab pickup into an empty spot near the field, I cut the engine, then issued instructions to the boys. My sixteen-year-old, John, nodded, his CD headphone wires swaying, and jumped out. He sauntered off in the direction of the Majors field without a word, while Austin and Devin tripped and shoved each other on the way out the truck door.

"Mom, can I get something to drink?" Devin was the first to ask.

"I want something, too!"

"All right. Austin, go on and meet your coach. Devin and I will bring you something."

I heard Austin's coach call out to him. "Hey, buddy, you gonna hit us some home runs tonight?"

"Yep!" came Austin's excited answer. With two older brothers honing his skills, Austin was one of the best players on the team. They expected him to hit home runs, and he did, two to three a game.

Smiling, I crossed over to the concession stand and waited at the end of the line. A friend of Devin's ran to him, and they were off to play ball. "Stay where I can see you." The words were barely out of my mouth when he ran to a grassy triangle section between two of the fenced-in fields.

Alone, I walked the rest of the way to the dugout and gave Austin his bottle of water and sunflower seeds. Standing there watching the kids, I listened to seven-year-old girls tease the other players on their team, as long as the coach didn't hear them. My son, of course, was exempted from this teasing because he played a little better than the other kids.

"Hey, guys, maybe you should try helping each other instead of cutting each other down." I spoke to no one of the kids in particular, hoping that at least one would pay attention. They all froze and looked up at me with wide, innocent eyes. Guilt, I have found with my sons, is a taught emotion. I was satisfied they would stop for the time being, and I took a seat at the top of the bleachers.

The game started and excitement built. Family members cheered and hollered advice to the little ones as they played. Midway through, I felt a tap on my arm. Kevin, my husband, had arrived.

"How's the game?"

"Good, it's running about even," I told him, my eyes riveted on a little boy named Justin coming up to bat. I felt empathy for the dark-haired child. He tried so hard, but didn't seem to catch on. Standing as rigid as a soldier, he reared back and swung, completely missing the ball. The third swing produced a short, low ball, easily caught by the pitcher and thrown to first base. Justin made his first out for the night.

"Aw, poor baby!" I spoke softly to Kevin as I watched the boy half-walk, half-run off the field. "Justin tries so hard. I think he's the only one who hasn't made a base hit all season. The kids were giving him a hard time earlier. He has the heart, but he hasn't developed the skills yet."

"He'll get there," Kevin muttered. His voice grew louder when Austin stepped up to the batter's box. "Hey, Austin, keep your eye on the ball. You can do it, buddy."

Sure enough, our son made his first home run for the night. His fellow players cheered him and clapped him on the back when he jogged into the dugout. This scenario continued throughout the game—Justin got put out, and Austin had home runs. Kudos were handed to Austin, and Justin got nothing from his fellow players except groans when he came up to bat.

In the last inning, Justin's hit was repeated. As he stumbled, defeated, into the dugout, head down, shoulders slumped, I noticed Austin standing by the gate watching him. When Justin stepped inside the dugout, Austin wrapped his arm around his shoulders and patted him as he walked him back to the bench. His head lowered to the boy's ear. They sat side-by-side, Austin talking and Justin nodding every now and then.

My heart swelled. I silently thanked God for showing me our son had a heart of compassion. I don't know what Austin said to Justin, I didn't ask him, but the fact was, he saw a person in need and reached out to him.

On the way home, in the dark, the interior of the truck was quiet and still for about five minutes. During this peaceful time, I basked in the knowledge of my son's kindness, feeling we had succeeded as parents. Soon, whispers and commotion started from the back seat. Before I could ask what was going on back there, Devin's voice piped up.

"Mom, Austin said I was adopted!"

~Judy L. Leger
Chicken Soup for the Mother and Son Soul

Golf and the Caddie at Royal Troon

My wife and I had planned our first trip to Scotland for more than a year. Working through Scottish Golfing Holidays, we started our week at Royal Troon. I was to play the course in the morning, then my wife would join me in the afternoon across the street on the Portland Course.

This was the first morning of the first day of my first golf in Scotland.

Two things happened that will remain with me forever.

First, we were delayed more than fifteen minutes waiting for Payne Stewart and his group to show up. Clad in uncustomary slacks and regular golf-style cap, Stewart and his group finally appeared and were escorted to the back, or "medal" tees, where they all teed off. Playing with Stewart were three others, the best of whom probably was no more than a 10 handicap. Having already been rebuffed from playing the back tees, I decided to give it another go. The starter, with whom I had been enjoying a long conversation waiting for Stewart's group to appear, said it was impossible — unless, of course, the club secretary gave his approval. He then volunteered to speak with the secretary on my behalf. Taking my letter of introduction, which said I was an honorable fellow from Nebraska who had played in several

USGA events, including Amateurs and Mid-Amateurs (I have never qualified, but that didn't stop me from trying) and currently holding a 2.4 index, he disappeared into the clubhouse.

A few minutes later, a tall, respectable gentleman wearing a coat and tie came to the tee box. Colin Montgomery's father looked down at my five-feet-six-inches, from somewhere high above six feet, fixed me with a Scottish stare I would get to know over the coming week, and asked me directly, "Have you one to waste?" Being fully loaded with far too many golf balls to fit comfortably into my carry bag, I responded affirmatively.

He then said, "Hit your driver o'er that hillock," pointing to a tall mound between the first tee and the ocean. With slightly sweaty palms, and a crowd of twenty-five or so golfers watching, I managed to make a good swing and sent a fine drive directly over the hillock. Mr. Montgomery then turned to the starter and said, in a voice that carried clearly to the surrounding crowd, "Mr. Kahler is a fine amateur from the States and will be allowed to play the medal tees. Everyone else will play the regular tees." With that statement he turned and strode directly into the clubhouse. And I played Royal Troon from the medal tees.

The second event that day involved Payne Stewart. As we were teeing off on the seventh hole, a dogleg-right slightly downhill, the rain and wind simultaneously picked up. Stewart's group had moved off the fairway into two rain shelters on the left side of the hole. We hit our drives, then agreed to also seek shelter to allow the storm to pass. I had hit a great drive and was just a few yards behind another ball from the group in front of us. As we reached the shelter, our twosome was huddled in one shelter and Stewart's group in another.

A few minutes later, Stewart's local caddie ran over to our shelter and said a few words to my caddie. My caddie then said to me, "Mr. Stewart would like to know if you would like a small wager: closest to the pin for a pound." I agreed. Not because I thought I could hit it closer than Payne Stewart, but I would have a great story to tell and it would only cost me a pound. Because we were a twosome, and more willing to brave the elements than Stewart's foursome, they invited us to play through as the rain and wind lessened. I hit a career shot, holding it into the wind, coming to rest within ten feet of the hole. As we walked to the green, Stewart's caddie came running out and handed my caddie a pound coin, which he, in turn, passed on to me.

I don't know whether Payne Stewart actually made the bet or provided the pound. The more I have learned about caddies in Scotland, the more likely it was the caddie himself who made and paid the bet. And I don't know how close Payne Stewart hit the ball to the hole; we went on to the famous Postage Stamp eighth hole before they resumed play. But I did leave a ball marker in the green where my ball had been on No. 7. And no one asked me for the pound back later. I use it to this day as my ball marker.

~Jeff Kahler
Chicken Soup for the Golfer's Soul

86

A Chance to Say Thank You

One can pay back the loan of gold,
but one dies forever in debt to those who are kind.
~Malayan Proverb

I played for Vince Lombardi for nine of my sixteen years in pro football. I know well his coaching accomplishments with the Green Bay Packers and his skill at teaching and motivating players. There are more stories about Coach's methods and results than any other person associated with the National Football League, in that era or any time.

One sign of the respect and affection Lombardi inspired is that everyone called him simply "Coach"—all the players, the trainers, the grounds crew, everyone associated with the Packers organization; the sportswriters and media; avid Green Bay fans. Even people on the street who had never attended a game at Lambeau Field called Lombardi simply "Coach," with pride and thanks in their voice.

His reputation is deserved, even today, nearly three decades after his death, for he was a true original—a colorful, always passionate man who loved the game and those who loved it. He did not abide loose play and nonchalance. He expected and respected commitment. However, my most cherished memory of Coach is far more personal.

Coach left the Packers in 1969 to become head coach and general manager of the Washington Redskins. In May 1970, he returned to

Green Bay for a visit and some time with his golfing buddies. My wife Cherry and I were surprised to receive a call from him on Saturday morning, asking if he could stop by to see our new home, which had recently been completed. Of course!

He greeted us warmly upon arriving and asked for a "walk-through" of the house. Afterward, we sat in the family room trading quips and reflecting on our great years together. Cherry and I were obviously pleased we could spend some time with him. Coach seemed relaxed, complimenting Cherry on details of how she had furnished the house and saying how happy he was for us.

"Coach," she said, "none of this would have been possible if you had not believed in Bart; if you had not given him the opportunity you did. We are very grateful to you."

I was surprised to see Coach's eyes fill with tears. He rose immediately, announcing he had to leave. He embraced both of us and walked out.

A short time later we learned Coach had been diagnosed with the cancer that would quickly take his life less than four months later, on September 3, 1970.

Cherry and I will always cherish that visit with Coach. We were blessed with a rare and timely opportunity to say "Thank you," to express our appreciation for what a truly great man had done to change our lives.

~Bart Starr
Chicken Soup for the Sports Fan's Soul

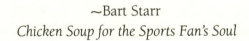

87

Putter Devotion

Perseverance is not a long race;
it is many short races one after another.
~Walter Elliott,
The Spiritual Life

When I was working for General Electric in Ithaca, New York in the early 1950s, I began to notice an interesting phenomenon on Mondays and Fridays during fair weather. Several of my fellow engineers seemed to be in high spirits those days. When I listened in on their conversations, I figured out why. Fridays they were planning their weekend golf outings; Mondays they were ribbing one another about what went on in them. It all seemed such a good time that I asked if I could join in.

I was forty-two years old and had never so much as picked up a golf club. "How hard can it be?" I asked myself. That Saturday, after borrowing some clubs and meeting up with my friends, I found out: harder than I could ever have imagined.

On the first tee, I watched my friends and took a few practice swings, imitating them as closely as I could. It felt pretty good. Then it was my turn. I teed up a ball, waggled the driver as my friends had and took a good cut. Whoosh! A clean miss. Then another. "Take it easy," my companions said. "Just keep your eye on the ball and swing evenly."

I did, and caught a huge clod of dirt, but not the ball. Soon dirt and grass were flying everywhere, but my ball just sat. I was still swinging away when my friends gave up and told me to catch up to them on the second tee. Grimly, I hacked my way to the first green, only to discover that putting was even more frustrating. As an engineer I was confident that I could figure the slope of the green and anticipate the correct trajectory for my ball. Not so. I couldn't get my putter to send the ball where I wanted it to go. There's no reason putting should be this hard, I thought.

My score for the round would have been a good one if I'd been bowling. I was frustrated, but I liked spending Saturdays outdoors. Being with the fellows was fun too, so I kept practicing. I was determined to find out why a seemingly simple game was so difficult.

After playing several times more, I felt confident I could make some improvements in the clubs, and I shared my ideas with my wife, Louise.

"It seems to me that if a fellow can putt well he can certainly improve his game," I said. "And I've got some ideas about this putter...."

"I was wondering when you would get around to the nuts and bolts of it!" she said with a laugh.

"Well," I said, showing her my borrowed club, "it's no wonder I have a hard time putting, the way this thing is made."

She nodded and smiled knowingly. "No doubt you'll have it fixed up to your liking soon."

She was right about that. In time I bought my own clubs and began working on the improvements I had in mind. I loved working with my hands, fixing things. It's something I had discovered back in my dad's cobbler shop, where he taught me the basics of shoemaking. Before I was out of grammar school I was helping him resole shoes. It was a good place for a curious and handy kid to get his start.

Later, I started college with high hopes of becoming an engineer, but the Depression put an end to that after only one year. So I ran one of my father's two shoe-repair shops. Soon after, I met Louise, just out of high school, at church, and I asked her father's permission to marry her. He said no. Louise and I were disappointed, but I told her I was sure our marriage was meant to be and God would direct our path to it if we could be patient and trust him. When her father saw how determined we were to marry, he accepted it.

I resumed my engineering studies, but soon World War II intervened. I went to work in the defense industry, designing radar and missile systems, then moved to GE, where I worked on improving existing products and developed a new portable television set with an attachable rabbit ears antenna.

It was all this engineering experience that I put to work fashioning a new putter. I made myself a simple blade putter by shaping a block of aluminum and inserting weights in the heel and toe. The effect was to keep the putter from twisting in my hands. Finally the putting motion began to feel right to me.

I started haunting the practice green at our local golf club, and my handicap began going down. Even some of the pros were asking me to play with them.

One afternoon a club pro stopped me as I was coming off the practice green. "You really putt well," he said.

I laughed. "Thanks, but you should have seen me before I made this."

"You made the putter?" he asked. "Well you should make more and sell them, because it sure does work."

That afternoon I determined to make my putter even better. I took my design to a nearby toolmaker, who soon returned to me a putter head. I took it home and inserted a shaft, then struck a ball. Ping! So that's what I called my putters, PINGs, and I began trying to sell one at local golf shops. That's exactly what I did. I sold one — in six months of trying.

I started traveling to golf tournaments and asking pros to try my club and give me their opinions. I took their suggestions back to my garage workshop and made improvements. My youngest son, John, then in junior high, helped me with a jerry-rigged drill press to bore out the club heads; then I heated the heads on the kitchen stove to insert the shafts.

That may sound funny, but back in the beginning I had to make the best use of the equipment I had. Besides, some people say I've always had a mad scientist side. Like the time I was working on a more aerodynamic wood club head, only to be stymied by how to test my different models. Riding along in a car one day, I got an idea. I persuaded my son Allan to take me to a deserted secondary highway in our 1959 Citroen. When there were no cars in sight I told him to step on it, then I held each of my drivers out the window at different angles to test their wind resistance. We had a good laugh over that, but the test worked and I got the answer I was looking for.

Still, none of my improvements made my PING putters any better looking. One pro told me, "That thing looks like a hot dog on a stick." I didn't care much about its appearance, just its performance.

I was having so much fun with my fledgling enterprise that I wanted more than anything to devote myself full-time to it. But the advice of the first pro-shop owner to stock my club haunted me. "These putters of yours are great, but whatever you do, don't give up your job. This is a fickle business." Even so, sales began to pick up when a few professionals started using the PING putter on tour. Then a well-known professional, Julius Boros, used one in winning the 1967 Phoenix Open.

But by then Louise and I were mulling over a big decision. The previous fall, my boss had told me that General Electric wanted to transfer me to a plant in Oklahoma City. I was torn. My job was solid and safe, and more than anything, I wanted my family to be secure. Yet we had invested a lot of time and money in my putter business, and my latest one was selling so fast we couldn't keep up with the orders.

"What do you think?" I asked Louise one morning at breakfast.

"I think back to that confident young man who courted me," she said. "Remember what you told me? You said, 'God will direct our path. He will lead us where he wants us to go.' Besides," she said, her brown eyes twinkling, "I'm keeping the books. I know we can make it."

So in early 1967 I retired from GE, and we began manufacturing clubs full-time in a small building we had bought in northwest Phoenix. More and more golf professionals were winning with PING putters, so I turned my attention to building a better iron, then to woods and other golf products. Karsten Manufacturing Corporation, as we've called it since 1967, became a storybook success.

It's hard to believe a golf outing more than forty years ago, when I couldn't sink a putt no matter how hard I tried, has resulted in a company that ships clubs to seventy countries worldwide and employs fifteen hundred people. Yet in a way I'm not surprised. As Louise and I learned so long ago, if you trust completely in God's goodness and follow where he leads, things have a way of turning out nicely.

Now I'm proud to say that our son John is president of our company. These days I'm taking it a little easier. But who knows, one day I might even figure a way to make that putter of ours a little prettier. Meantime, even I can sink a putt with it.

~Karsten Solheim as told to Gina Bridgeman
Chicken Soup for the Golfer's Soul

Nuts to Par

It was a beautiful autumn day, and I decided to play a round of golf. When I called a friend to see if he wanted to join me, his wife answered the phone. "Pat's enjoying himself cleaning the yard," she said. "Right now he's pitching walnuts from under a tree into the vacant lot next door."

"That's enjoyable?" I asked.

"He's using an 8-iron," she replied.

~Jerry P. Lightner
Chicken Soup for the Golfer's Soul, The 2nd Round

An Important Phone Call

S peedy Morris, men's basketball coach for La Salle University, tells this story: "When I first got the job at La Salle, the phone rang and my wife told me it was *Sports Illustrated*. I cut myself shaving and fell down the steps in my rush to get to the phone. When I got there, a voice on the other end said, 'For just seventy-five cents an issue....'"

~M. G. Misanelli
Chicken Soup for the Sports Fan's Soul

My Quest for a Baseball

The difference between try and triumph is a little umph.
~Author Unknown

While attending the hundred or so major league baseball games that make up the better parts of my childhood memory bank, souvenirs of all kinds were gathered in earnest. Pennants and programs and tickets stubs and autograph after autograph—including one of Philadelphia Phillies star Mike Schmidt that was corralled after a parking lot sprint and is little more than an indecipherable wiggle, wave and dash of a pen.

But there was never a baseball—not a real live baseball. And a foul ball or home-run ball or batting-practice ball—any kind of ball from a major league baseball game was all I wanted.

As the years passed, near-misses accumulated along with my ticket stubs. At a sparsely attended minor-league game, I watched each pitch with eagle eyes, figuring nearly empty stands quadrupled my chances. I turned my back for one sip of a Coke and only heard—never even saw—the ball that thwacked the seat next to mine and was gobbled up by a more nimble adversary.

Lower deck seats and an uninteresting game at one Phillies contest emptied the stands and again increased my chances. But when a high pop foul was lofted my way, I froze in fear of its height and in awe at my dream coming true. It hit a few rows over and hopped over my head. My uncle called me "Gluefoot."

Friends of my parents finagled third-base line seats for one game, and invited me to join them and borrow their fishing net in an attempt to snag batting practice grounders. Instead, stadium security snagged the net.

As time went by, and I grew from chubby ten-year-old to a chubby and awkward thirteen-year-old, my foul ball lust only increased. But so did my knowledge that I was no longer cute, and no player or kindly nearby fan was going to toss me a free ball at this point. That was reserved for gap-toothed eight-year-olds waiting for the tooth fairy—and high school girls who were anything but awkward.

This was reinforced on a family trip to California the summer after my eighth-grade year. An unplanned trip to a California Angels game left my typically upper-deck family with front-row seats, again down third base. My glove was home in Pennsylvania. So when a batting practice grounder caromed toward me, I had only my hat with which to snag it. The cap gathered the ball in—and the force ripped them both out of my hand. A Milwaukee Brewers outfielder came over, picked up the ball and tossed it to me in the stands.

I nearly fainted in my moment of ecstasy—until the player pointed at me.

"No," he said. "For him."

He then pointed to the adorable six-year-old next to me. I looked down and handed over my ball. I went home to deface the player's baseball card—which I then carried in my wallet until college.

At Northwestern University outside Chicago, I planned my spring class schedule around the afternoon games at Wrigley Field. Not just Chicago Cubs games, but Chicago Cubs batting practices. I'd hop the subway with my glove, knowing that this day in the left-field bleachers would reward me with my first real baseball. But for two and a half years, it was nothing but misjudgments and missed opportunities.

Until one series when the Phillies were in town. Over time, I had grown loyal to the Cubs, turning my attention from catching baseballs to taunting the opposing left fielder once the game started. And of course, there was the time-honored ritual of chanting "Throw it back" whenever an opposing player hit a home-run ball into the bleachers. Whoever grabbed the ball had little choice but to fire it back onto the field.

But when the Phillies were in town, I didn't taunt the opponents. I cheered for them. I wore my Phillies jersey and Phillies cap and rooted against the Cubs.

And for a ball.

The Cubs were ahead by several runs in the third inning. I sat in my usual seat in the second row, the girlfriend who would later become my wife beside me.

Darren Daulton, the Phillies catcher and best hitter, was at the plate. His left-handed swing produced a slicing opposite-field line drive that looked to be headed for the left field wall.

But it cleared the wall, smacking into the crowd just to my left. Bodies flew as fans dove for the home-run ball, hands grasping at air. I reached my hand into a teeming mass of flesh and grabbed.

All ball.

I pulled Daulton's homer from the chaos and raised my arm triumphantly in the air. I finally had my real live baseball.

And I was wearing a Phillies jersey in the Wrigley Field bleachers, the enemy's home run in my hand.

I did the only thing I could: ducked and covered.

I pulled down my arm and curled up in the fetal position as the hands suddenly started reaching for me. As the "Throw it back" chant started, the hands became more aggressive in their efforts to pry the ball from me.

I stayed curled, the strength from twenty years of futility keeping my fingers firmly clasped around my ball.

Finally, the hands stopped and the negotiations began. As the chant died, the bleacher leader that night began to reason with me.

"It's a Phillie homer, you have to throw it back."

But I would not be reasoned with. Soon a compromise was reached—rather, thrust on me. The Bleacher Bum pulled the Phillies cap off my head and offered a choice.

Something was going on the field—the hat or the ball.

Away went my hat.

It didn't end. The crowd started a new chant that would continue between every half-inning for the next six innings—a chant that can't be printed here. I took off my Phillies jersey and shoved it in my backpack, hoping to eventually fade into the crowd.

It didn't work.

As other fans continued to harass me, two strangers in front of me told the others to leave me alone. A minor scuffle ensued and my defenders were kicked out of the game.

Then from behind me, a fan dumped half a cup of water on my back and was also ejected. All the while, the Phillies were rallying to take the lead, causing the between-innings chant to grow more intense. Finally, as random fans decided to make more diving grabs for my baseball, a security guard came by and suggested that he take the ball and stash it in a security room under the stands.

I readily agreed, and was left to smile as I endured the chants for the rest of game, knowing the Phillies were winning and my ball was safe. Even the fact that my girlfriend was pretending not to know me didn't deter my joy.

When the game ended in a Phillies win and she and I stood to leave, a Wrigley regular stopped us.

"You took everything we did and handled it okay," he said, shaking my hand. "You're alright."

Of course I was. I had my baseball.

That's all I cared about as my girlfriend and I walked back to the subway—escorted by a security guard, just in case a Cubs fan still wanted to kill me.

~Doug Lesmerises
Chicken Soup for the Baseball Fan's Soul

91

Chicken Soup for the Soul®

Reach for the Stars

When it is dark enough,
you can see the stars.
~Ralph Waldo Emerson

When striving for the extraordinary, life often delivers gifts that transform us. One such immeasurable gift came to me at the end of the 1985 season.

It was a "Cinderella" season for the New England Patriots. We had started miserably, with four straight losses in which we managed to average less than one yard per rushing attempt. This pitiful showing earned us the unceremonious distinction of the worst rushing offense in the NFL.

We turned it around, though, thanks to spectacular plays by first one team member, then another, and the steady hands of quarterbacks Steve Grogan and Tony Eason. Thanks to teamwork, we pulled together a 10-4 record going into the next-to-last game of the season against Miami. Beat the Dolphins and we would lock a spot in the playoffs and make a try for the AFC championship for the first time in the twenty-five-year history of the Patriots. The sportswriters and broadcast analysts gave us no chance.

Since the game was scheduled for *Monday Night Football*, the pre-game hype was as wild and ready as we were. On game day, the fans in the stands and on their couches at home were not disappointed. We gave 'em a dramatic, back-and-forth, feisty game punctuated with long bombs of desperate hope, and when it counted most, pinpoint accuracy from the Dolphins' Dan Marino. We proved the sportswriters right: we lost.

The season was down to one last chance. We had to pack our hopes and head home for a cold winter game against the Cincinnati Bengals. If we won that one, we could still make the playoffs in a wild-card spot.

That game was almost surreal. We felt like we could not be stopped. Most would have thought we were crazy, but we knew the offense, the defense and how the special teams were going to score. Even when we fumbled the ball, we had an intuitive sense that now our defense would get its chance to score. We were in the zone as a team, when everything seems effortless and time doesn't exist. The extraordinary seemed to unfold, always in our favor. Our home crowd was standing, cheering, roaring the entire game. You could literally feel the Bengals' will to win being drained out of them. We won that game 34-23 and claimed our team's greatest moment.

The atmosphere in the locker room afterward was giddy. Players, coaches, trainers, the media. Hugs, tears, laughter and flying champagne everywhere. A few players were so stunned they could only sit on benches and silently hug the moment. John Hannah sat with Pete Brock, Andre Tippet with Don Blackmon. Head coach Raymond Berry smiled, but I could tell he was already past this game, preparing his mind for the first round of the playoffs. We were contenders!

And then it happened. As I had done so many times after home games, I left the locker room, walked upstairs past the group of special guests and family members being held back by security. A woman reached through the ring of security and the clamor of celebration seemed to pause as I heard her ask, quietly but enthusiastically, for an autograph for her two boys. As I looked into her face I realized she was Christa McAuliffe, the woman who as America's Teacher-in-Space was about to head into space on the Challenger.

"Absolutely," I said. I was surprised to notice my hand trembling as I signed the paper she had presented. She smiled with a brightness and clarity I had noticed on television interviews. Without hesitation, I said, "And would you be so kind as to give me your autograph?"

She smiled even wider and her sons looked up at her in awe. "Mom," one of them whispered, "he wants your autograph!" I grabbed a piece of paper off a desk nearby and she signed it.

I knew what we had just done as a team was a triumphant life moment. We were making a run for the Super Bowl, the top prize for every professional football player. Yet, this accomplishment was eclipsed in my mind by a schoolteacher with a million-dollar smile and the courage, commitment and driving passion to inspire schoolchildren, teachers, national leaders, all of America and most of the world by living her dream.

I gave her a hug and said, "All the best for your flight. I admire you."

A few weeks later, I was in Hawaii for Pro Bowl Week. On Tuesday morning, January 28, 1986, I was in my hotel room watching the run-up to the Challenger liftoff, remembering Christa McAuliffe's easy friendliness and marveling at her grit, which was greater, surely, than any football player's, no matter how big, how willing to hit and be hit, how determined to do the best he can on the field. Off into space! This is in a whole different league. And then, my God, no! Plumes of white smoke. Just seventy-three seconds of excitement, and then tragedy.

I sat on the end of the bed, head in my hands, and cried. After a long time, I opened my briefcase, pulled out the piece of paper she had signed, taped it to the dresser mirror and left the room, closing the door quietly. I walked down the beach, thinking of her smile and her courage, trying to understand fate or at least accept it.

I walked for hours. When I stopped I didn't know where I was. I only knew where Christa was. I looked across the Pacific Ocean and repeated the words she had written to me:

"To Brian, Reach for the Stars. I'll be there."

~Brian Holloway
Chicken Soup for the Sports Fan's Soul

92

The One Hundred Greatest Golf Courses

I am an optimist.
It does not seem too much use being anything else.
~Winston Churchill

A golfer called the Chicago Golf Club and explained that he was playing the "One Hundred Greatest Courses" and desperately needed to add the club to his list. The club was very private but reluctantly agreed to allow him to play under these special circumstances.

After the round, a member asked the man, "By the way, how many do you have left to complete the One Hundred Greatest?"

"Ninety-nine," he replied.

~Bruce Nash and Allan Zullo
Chicken Soup for the Golfer's Soul, The 2nd Round

Tales OF Golf AND Sport

From the Heart

*What lies before us and what lies behind us are tiny matters to what
lies within us.*
~Author Unknown

93

Walter Won the Honors

The guardian angels of life fly so high as to be beyond our sight, but they are always looking down upon us.
~Jean Paul Richter

If you ever felt that there is a wee touch of the spiritual in golf, like the famous book *Golf in the Kingdom* says, let me tell you a true story that may further the notion.

Last autumn, Walter Donoughe, one of my closest friends, was told by his doctors they couldn't cure his pancreatic cancer, but they thought treatments could extend his life and, yes, he could play a lot more golf. He and I were talking all about it a couple of days after he got his prognosis while we were playing the front nine as a twosome. As we sat in the cart waiting for the eighth green to clear, I asked Walter which he would prefer, three more years of golf, or a guarantee of eternity in heaven. He answered immediately that he would take the guarantee of heaven, but he smiled and said he hoped he could play golf there instead of harps. From other things Walter told me over the winter and last spring I knew he had a lock on membership in heaven's best golf club.

We also talked a lot about golf, and how a really sweet swing starts effortlessly, like somebody else takes it back, then brings it down on plane and you hear more than feel the click as the ball jumps off the club. We spent some great hours hitting 5-irons into the net in the bag room as we forgot the winter cold outside and tried for the sweet swing feeling.

Walter kept hanging in there fighting the cancer and was still swinging pretty well early in the spring when the golf committee decided to initiate for July a two-day tournament that each year would honor some member who has meant a lot to the club. They selected Walter as the first honoree. A great choice. He had worked many, many years as a board member and on every committee the club ever had. He won the handicap championship twice, numerous flight and senior championships, and he even won the annual gin tournament twice. A fine man, a good competitor and a great friend.

In the July 5-6 tournament honoring him, Walter and I would have been partners, as we usually were in team events, but he died on June 5. I was invited by, and played with, our club champion, Scott Arthur, who played well enough for us to win it all. But I made sure we didn't as I rolled the ball off the tee, heeled and toed fairway woods, scraped irons right and left, bladed and chili-dipped chips and pitches, and three- and four-putted my way to an agony of double and triple bogeys.

With only two holes left to play, as we headed to the par-3 thirteenth, I told Scott there had to be some lesson for me to learn from these humiliating two rounds, but I didn't think the lesson could be worth it. When we got on the thirteenth tee a hawk was circling high above the green. Scott said it was our last chance for a hole-in-one and he would like one because it was his fortieth birthday. For all the years he had been playing golf he said he had seen only one ace — hit by Walter Donoughe years ago when Scott caddied for him.

With zero enthusiasm I teed up the ball to hit and get it over with, then something strange happened. My 5-iron started back effortlessly like somebody else was swinging it back then bringing it down on plane, and I heard the click more than I felt it as the ball jumped off the club. My myopic eyes couldn't follow the ball but I knew it was hit by that sweet swing Walter always talked about, a swing that I felt only a few times before, at the practice net when he coached me.

Bill Kelley, Chris Vasiliades and Scott started to holler things like

"Great swing... Great shot... Go in the hole!" There was a sudden hush, then, "It did! It did! It went in the hole!" Chris grabbed my hat, threw it towards the green, then picked me up and swung me around like a rag. I was thinking, "Please Chris, don't throw me after my hat."

The screams kept up and were truly sky-splitting, but that hawk was undisturbed. Like the steady pilot Walter was when he earned his wings with the Air Force years ago, that hawk just kept calmly circling the green and was not surprised at all by the miracle that happened down below him.

Now, I don't know how Walter petitioned the Almighty for me, but I know he did. Perhaps he said his buddy down there was getting close to giving up the game, breaking the commandment, Thou Shalt Not Quit. So he took over during his tournament, and before it was too late he arranged to send his pal Frank a message about hanging in there—a hole-in-one. Thanks, Walter, for swinging it for me. Go in peace.

~Frank J. Haller
Chicken Soup for the Golfer's Soul

Lyle's Second Go

Excellence is not a skill.
It is an attitude.
~Ralph Marston

In 1982, when I was coaching the Raiders, we were approached by Cleveland on a possible trade for Lyle Alzado. After watching him on tape, I was not very impressed, but Raiders owner Al Davis felt we could pump some life into Lyle by surrounding him with the right atmosphere. We made the deal.

That summer at training camp, preparing for our first year in Los Angeles, Lyle was having a tough time mentally. He had that look in his eyes that many rookies and some old veterans get when things aren't going well. It's a scared, glazed look that isn't pretty to a coach.

One morning Lyle came into my office and closed the door. He looked like he hadn't slept. Here was a huge hulk of a man, with his head about as low as it could go. We talked, or rather, I listened. The bottom line was that Lyle felt his career was over and it would be best for him and for the team if he retired. He apologized for disappointing us since we had just traded for him.

Lyle was always an emotional guy. This is one of the reasons he was a good defensive end. He carried all that emotional energy with him constantly, ready to fire out at the snap of the ball. Now he was in front of me, on the verge of tears.

I thought for a moment, realizing we had to stoke that fire. Then, calmly, I went through my reasons why he should not retire. He was running with the second defensive line. I assured him that would change if he stepped it up, but that he couldn't reach that level in his present mental state. At the end of our talk, I said, "You go out and play like hell, and let us decide if you still have it. Personally, I think you do."

Jump now to January 1984. Tampa Bay Stadium. Super Bowl XVIII. I'm pacing the sidelines. With less than two minutes remaining, we're leading 38-9. It's over! We're the world champions of professional football. My second Super Bowl win as a head coach. As I paced, I saw coaches and players ready to burst with joy, just trying to hold themselves on the sideline until the game was officially over. Then I saw Lyle, standing by the bench, crying like a baby. I had to turn away quickly or I would have joined him in tears.

I remembered that morning in my office, and what Lyle, and what the Raiders, had accomplished since he came to us: 8-1 in the 1982 strike year, and 12-4 in 1983, straight through the playoffs to the AFC title over Seattle, and now a win over Washington in Super Bowl XVIII to make us world champions. If Lyle hadn't kicked into gear and given his career another shot, he wouldn't have had this victory. Maybe the Raiders wouldn't have had this victory. During that moment, amid the almost-hysterical joy of the whole team organization, I felt one of the greatest satisfactions of my coaching career.

Lyle is gone now, the victim of an aggressive brain cancer that took him early, but not before he became a world champion.

~Tom Flores
Chicken Soup for the Sports Fan's Soul

The Price of Success

Don't aim for success if you want it;
just do what you love and believe in, and it will come naturally.
~David Frost

uccess came late for golf pro Harvey Penick. His first golf book, *Harvey Penick's Little Red Book*, has sold more than a million copies, which makes it one of the biggest things in the history of sports books. His second book, *And If You Play Golf, You're My Friend*, has already sold nearly three-quarters of a million copies. But anyone who imagines that Penick wrote the books to make money didn't know the man.

In the 1920s, Penick bought a red spiral notebook and began jotting down observations about golf. He never showed the book to anyone except his son until 1991, when he shared it with a local writer, Bud Shrake, and asked if he thought it was worth publishing. Shrake read it and told him yes. He left word with Penick's wife the next evening that Simon & Schuster had agreed to an advance of ninety thousand dollars.

When Shrake saw Penick later, the old man seemed troubled. Finally Penick came clean. With all his medical bills, he said, there was just no way he could advance Simon & Schuster that much money. The writer had to explain that Penick would be the one to receive the ninety thousand dollars.

~Terry Todd
Chicken Soup for the Golfer's Soul

Humor at Its Best

Hartman was a big man. Physically, he was a solid 280 pounds and stood around six-foot-two. He had a presence about him that demanded attention when he entered a room, and he had a twinkle in his eye. Oh that twinkle! Hartman was the kind of man who could talk a half dozen men into walking outside in the snow in their bare feet, and still be in position to close the door and lock it, before he actually had to go out himself.

Hartman was the person who introduced me to golf. He loved the game. On one occasion, when we were younger, a group of us rented a farmhouse for the summer. It was a place where we could go at the end of the week and just do whatever comes to mind. Hartman suggested one evening that we go to the local golf course the following day and play a round. Eight of us agreed immediately and went off to bed at a reasonable hour, which at the time was not the norm, so we could get an early start.

The next morning, we arrived at the golf course early enough to be the first two groups off. Being a small "farmers field" type of golf course we fit right in. The skill level of all the participants varied from just above beginner to really struggling for a bogey round. Hartman was one of the more accomplished players out that day, but it was obvious that he was struggling along with the rest of us.

Finally, after the increasing frustration seemed to win out,

Hartman snapped! He stood up on the tee of the par-3, 157-yard 8th hole and pulled his driver from his bag. With a great deal of drama, for which Hartman was known, he pulled back on that club and pasted that poor ball with every ounce of his 280 pounds. The ball took off as if it knew it was no longer wanted and headed straight for the trees and the river just to the left of the hole. By this time the other group had already joined us on the tee and the seven of us were howling with laughter. No one really tracked the ball except Hartman, who cringed as we all heard the ball hit a tree to the left of the green. What none of us were ready for was the look on his face as he excitedly asked us, "Did you see that?"

"See what?" was the common reply.

"My ball. It came off that tree, bounced off that rock in front of the green and rolled towards the pin. I think I'm close!"

"Yeah, right. That ball was so far gone you'll never find it," I said with a note of finality.

Fully convinced that there was no way in the world Hartman's ball was even on the golf course any more, let alone anywhere near the hole, we watched as Hartman teed up what we considered to be his serious ball. He hit it fat with his 8-iron, and we all started to walk toward the green disregarding everything he had to say about it being a provisional ball.

As we approached the green we were giving Hartman a pretty hard time. It was becoming more and more obvious his ball wasn't on the green. Hartman couldn't believe it.

"I know I saw it head in this direction." he said with absolute conviction.

"Maybe it's in the hole!" suggested Pete in a sarcastic tone.

Pete walked up to the hole, looked down and yelled back to Hartman.

"What are you hitting?"

"Top Flite number 4" was Hartman's reply.

You could have knocked Pete over with a feather as he leaned over and picked the ball out of the hole.

"It's in the hole," was all he was able to stammer.

Hartman was the last one of us to arrive at the hole to authenticate the ball.

"That's it. I don't believe it! A hole-in-one!" he exclaimed excitedly.

The rest of us just stood there with our mouths open and looks of utter disbelief on our faces. It wasn't possible, yet seven of us witnessed it. The most incredible shot in history.

We finished our round in a state of excited numbness, anxiously waiting to tell someone, anyone, what we had witnessed.

Back at the clubhouse we were indulging in a few beers and regaling the story among ourselves and anyone else who would listen. That's when someone suggested we call the local newspaper and maybe get our pictures taken and enjoy our fifteen minutes of fame. While we were planning all the TV appearances and endorsement contracts, Hartman sat at the end of the table with that twinkle in his eye. Oh that twinkle! It was the unmistakable tone of his laugh at that point that removed all doubt. We had been duped!

Being the first group off that morning put us in the unique position of being the first to each hole. Hartman took advantage of that fact when playing the 6th hole, which paralleled the 8th.

Having hit his ball in the narrow stretch of woods between the two holes, no one thought anything of his activities while he was looking for his ball. While wandering around in this no-man's-land he meandered over to the 8th green, casually dropped his ball in the hole and then wandered back to the 6th fairway as if he had just played his ball out of the rough. The rest of that hole and the next one leading up to the 8th was a display of acting on a Shakespearean level, to bring his apparent frustration level to a peak on the 8th tee.

The number of people with the imagination and savvy to pull off a prank of this magnitude and make all his victims feel good about being had are few and far between. This was the case with most of his pranks, the ones who laughed hardest were the ones at the center of the prank. We lost Hartman to cancer at the young age of forty-three, but he left behind a legacy of good-natured humor, a zest for life and a true appreciation of the good friends he had.

I miss the big man.

~John Spielbergs
Chicken Soup for the Golfer's Soul, The 2nd Round

97

A Little Further Down the Road

Shared joy is a double joy;
shared sorrow is half a sorrow.
~Swedish Proverb

U p until the time that I was eight or nine years old, I thought everyone's father had a race car. I didn't know that anybody did anything else. I never thought of what my father did as being different from what anybody else's father did. We just went to races on the weekends and traveled around and saw a lot of the country from the time I was in the first or second grade. We went to California, New York, Florida and a little bit of everywhere.

We used to go up and down the highway in station wagons or regular passenger cars. This was long before the minivans or big vans were around. It was nothing for us to leave on a Thursday afternoon and drive straight through to Michigan, which could take fifteen or sixteen hours. If you say, "Okay, how can families be close together?" I say, "Just lock them in a car and make them ride around for sixteen hours, and they'll be close." My sisters Sharon and Lisa had their own little world, playing with Barbies; I'd be in the back with a baseball glove, and we'd all be talking together. I think that's why we are such a close family now. We talk almost every day.

When anything new came along on a car, like electric windows or lights in the back, we'd run the battery down. There's nothing my father hated worse than to come out after a race and the battery be dead in the car. On one of our trips to Michigan, a fuse blew, and we got locked in the car because we couldn't get the automatic door locks to open. My mother pulled up at a Chrysler dealership, and the salesman came out to find this woman with three kids in a car screaming through the window because the window wouldn't roll down, either.

We grew up next door to my grandfather in a small farming community called Level Cross where everybody knew you. The guy down the road was a dairy farmer and in the other direction was a tobacco farmer. To them my father wasn't Richard Petty; he was just Richard, and my grandfather was just Lee.

The family farms around here have been here for seventy-five or a hundred years. I always compare our racing business to a family farm. For us, our farm was the race cars; we have cars instead of crops. This has always been a family endeavor. When my grandfather started, it wasn't about going out and winning the trophies; it was about putting food on the table for your family. It was about survival when they started, but this is all we know, and it is all we do.

There are times when the family connection hasn't been the best thing, and we've suffered tragedy because of it. From the time my father started dating my mother, her only brother, Randy, helped in the business. Uncle Randy thought Richard Petty hung the moon. He was only five years older than me and was more like a brother than an uncle. To my father, he was like a son. Randy always wanted to work on race cars and helped Dad during the summers of his junior high and high school years, then full-time after high school. He had been working for a couple of years when a pit-road accident happened in Talladega. An air tank or water tank blew up and killed him. After the accident, Dad had to come back and be with my mother and my grandparents, and that was very hard for the family to get through.

I started hanging out around the business when I was twelve. From the time I was in the third grade, I went all summer long with the race team. As soon as baseball season was over, right after school was out, I would travel with my father. In my senior year of high school I told my father I wanted to drive and race. He told me I had to wait until I was twenty-one. He said, "Well, you know your mother and I really want you to go off to college." I told him, "Just let me try it and if I don't like it, then I'll go to college." That was the kicker because I think he knew I was going to like it, and he knew I'd never go to college. My mother wanted me to be a pharmacist. I can't imagine myself being a pharmacist.

I ran my first race when I was only eighteen years old. It was the ARCA race at Daytona. I had no experience, just really good people working with me, and I don't remember a lot about it. They gave me a car and said, "Go run 195 miles an hour." I was fortunate and won the race. When I look back on it, it was just a lot of fun, but it wasn't my job. My job was still working on the pit crew and working for my father. I drove his car one weekend and won a race, and then as soon as Monday came around, I was back at the racetrack working on his car and doing other things with him.

I met my wife, Patty, through my sister, Sharon, and their horse shows. Patty worked for Winston, and she was one of the R. J. Reynolds girls. We dated for a couple of years and then married in '79. She didn't grow up around racing. Her father worked a regular nine-to-five job and had weekends off and took normal vacations. I think it was hard on her in the beginning, but gradually she's gotten used to the racing lifestyle. That was twenty-two years ago, and we still have horses. Now I have a daughter, Montgomery Lee, who shares Patty's love of horses.

Our son Austin has always loved kids, even when he was still a kid. As he got a little older, he started spending time at camps and doing things with church organizations. When he was sixteen, he joined a mission group that went to Romania to build playgrounds and orphanages. For the past four years, he has been a camp counselor for critically ill children with AIDS, cancer or hemophilia.

I did with Adam what my father did with me—I neither encouraged nor discouraged him from pursuing racing as a career. I have steered Austin and Montgomery Lee in the same way. I tell them, "One day, you're going to wake up and decide what you want to do and what you want to be. When you're sure in your heart of hearts that's what you want to do, I'll help you any way I can."

Adam started by running go-carts, then he wanted a late-model stock car. So we bought it and I told him, "You put it together, we'll work on it, and we'll go racin'." We worked on it for about three weeks, and then he didn't show up anymore. About six or seven months went by, and one day he came back and said, "I think I'm ready to put that thing together now." We went back and worked. He was ready.

After Adam's death, our family sat down and talked about who would drive the #45 car. It has been a healing process for me to drive it, to get back in the car and feel that connection, that closeness. Going to the shop and seeing those guys working on the car has been a part of the healing process for our family.

Patty and I have always spent a lot of time with our children. One important thing we've done from the beginning is to live in small houses. We never had a big house. Everybody's room was right there together. Even today, Montgomery Lee and Austin's rooms are right above us so that when they get out of bed in the middle of the night, you can hear them and you know where they are and they know where you are.

Every night before we go to bed, we all gather in our room and say prayers, and we always have. From the time that Adam was born, and from the time that each one was old enough to walk and talk and understand what prayer was, we have prayed together. Even with the recent tragedy of Adam's death, Montgomery Lee and Austin still come in, and we all get together and say prayers before we all divide up and go to our own rooms. Austin may be gone to a movie until eleven-thirty or twelve o'clock at night, but when he comes in we get together, even if it's only for five or six minutes.

I've always wanted to be a part of everything my kids did. During the years my grandfather was raising a family, his main focus was keeping his family alive. He was molded and shaped by being born in the early 1900s and coming through the depression and two world wars. Society taught men that you go off to war, you fight, you come back and you don't talk about what you saw. There was no such thing as being "shell-shocked" and having "syndromes." Guys just came back and picked up and were basically expected to carry on from where they left off.

My father came along and was molded, to some degree, by the changes in America during the '50s and '60s during the time of Vietnam and the civil unrest. His focus, too, was on putting food on the table for his family. When I was born, Vietnam went on, but as a nine-year-old, I paid no attention to the war. I had the luxury of being able to relate to my family in a different way than my grandfather or father could.

It's easier for fathers to show emotions to their little girls than to their sons. I can't imagine not kissing Montgomery Lee or telling her I love her every time she walks out the door. At the same time, I think that's what you should do with your sons, too. Austin never leaves on a date, never goes to bed, never hangs up the phone without me telling him I love him. Adam never got into a race car that I didn't kiss him and say a prayer and tell him I loved him. He never walked out the door or hung up the phone that I didn't tell him.

The last time I talked to Adam, Montgomery Lee and I were on an airplane flying to England, and we called him from the air. We both told him we loved him. There's not a doubt in my mind he knew that when the accident happened. I think that the most important thing in life is to tell your kids because they know they are loved, and then they'll pass that love along to somebody else.

When I look back on the forty years I've been alive and the things that have happened in my life, there are only really two or three defining moments that changed the course of my life. The first one was when my Uncle Randy was killed when I was only fourteen. I realized that you couldn't just take the hands of the clock and click it back and rearrange events to make it not happen. At the same time, in the same hour, I realized that I needed Christ as a personal Savior because there was more than just being here on Earth and doing what we do.

Adam's accident was another defining moment. You begin to

question what is important. Winning races and all the other stuff isn't important. Montgomery Lee's important, Patty's important, Austin's important, and my relationship with Christ is important. Helping other people and making people's lives better or happier is important. We refocused on that sort of thing after the accident, supporting the Starbright Foundation that Adam had been a part of and several other children's charities.

It has definitely refocused me and my Christianity. To say that God gave his only son, you can't imagine how hard that was. I've got two sons; I had Adam, and I've got Austin. One of my sons is gone. I can't imagine how hard it was that his only son was sent to save all of us. It would be an incredible sacrifice for a human, much less for a God.

We are blessed that God gave us life, and we should go through life loving it, enjoying it and making the most out of every day. We should try to help somebody along the way, too. There is a great saying I've heard that goes, "You never help somebody climb the hill without getting a little bit closer to the top yourself." I think that's the way it is. As we go through life, if we can help somebody along, the first thing you know, we're a little further down that road, too.

~Kyle Petty
Chicken Soup for the NASCAR Soul

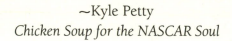

98

Big Men, Big Hearts

How beautiful a day can be
When kindness touches it!
~George Elliston

On the weekends I work in a coffee store in an old cigar factory in the historic area of Tampa. Sometimes kids from the projects stop by for candy sticks, and if I'm not too busy, I let them weigh out coffee and grind it, fill the jars with candy and even run the cash register.

A few weeks ago on a big football weekend, Omar, a bright little ten-year-old, came by to visit, and I gave him some chores to help pass a rainy day. In mid-afternoon, a giant of a man appeared in the doorway, and Omar was goggle-eyed at his size.

"I bet he's a famous football player," I whispered to him.

Omar giggled.

The big man approached the counter with a wide grin on his ebony face.

"What you gigglin' at?"

"I told him you were probably a famous football player," I explained with some embarrassment.

He held out a hand as big as a ham hock with a gold ring on his middle finger.

"Can you read that?" he asked Omar.

Omar twisted the ring so he could see it better.

"Pitts-burgh Steel-ers," he read slowly.

"That's right," said the man and turned his finger sideways. "Can you read this?"

Omar squinted. "Super Bowl Champion!"

A light clicked in my less-than-athletic brain. "You know who this is?" I nudged Omar, hardly able to contain my excitement. "This is Mean Joe Green!"

Omar looked at him quizzically. Then his face lit up. "Do you know Franco Harris?"

I glared at Omar. "I bet you'd like Joe Green's autograph, wouldn't you?" I prodded.

"Yeah, sure," said Omar while I rummaged for paper and pen. "How could I get in touch with Franco Harris?"

Joe grinned. "He's staying at the downtown Hyatt. Call his room and say you're a friend of mine."

Joe signed his autograph and handed it to Omar.

While nudging Omar a reminder to say thank you, I said, "Give me that autograph, and I'll put it in a candy bag so you don't get it all crumpled up." I laid it on the shelf for safekeeping and turned to thank Mr. Green myself before he moved on to another store.

"Why in the world would you ask about another player when you had Joe Green right here?" I snapped. "That was downright insulting!"

Omar shrugged and said innocently, "I like Franco Harris."

"I'm surprised he even bothered to give you an autograph!" I glared at him.

I returned to helping customers. The day ended with a flurry of business, and Omar, thoroughly chastened, departed abruptly, leaving his autograph behind.

The next Saturday he appeared again. "I forgot my autograph."

"I know," I said, pointing to the shelf. "It's still up here where I put it for safekeeping."

I reached for the bag thinking, He is only ten after all. Maybe Joe was big enough not to have been offended.

Omar reached into the bag to look at his trophy once more.

"There's something else in the bag," he said, puzzled, handing me a second piece of paper. Because I'd been off-duty since the prior weekend myself, I, too, was surprised to see something other than what I had personally placed in the bag for Omar.

I opened it and read out loud:

"Omar... sorry I missed you. Franco Harris!"

Omar's eyes lit up with both disbelief and excitement as he took the paper to see for himself.

These two big men—with equally big hearts—apparently came back into the store after my shift to leave a special surprise for a young boy. Mean Joe Green isn't so "mean" after all—quite the contrary!

~Phyllis W. Zeno
Chicken Soup for the African American Soul

99

Winnie's Barn

I was raking my yard on a warm autumn afternoon when Arnold Palmer phoned to say Winnie had passed away that morning (November 20, 1999). He said he wanted me to know before I heard the news on television or from someone else. I thanked him and asked if he was okay. He sighed, and his voice cracked. "I don't know," he said. "I feel like I just took 12 on the opening hole."

Golf, to say nothing of life, would never be the same for anyone who knew Winnie Palmer, least of all her husband, Arnold.

Being invited to help Arnold Palmer craft his memoirs was a dream come true for me, because like millions of you, decades before I actually met the man, Palmer was my sports hero, my personal god in golf shoes. As the mortals of Greek mythology learned the hard way, though, mingling with gods and heroes comes with certain perils. The private great man is seldom as engaging as the public one and, at least in my professional experience, rarely as nice. The good news in Arnold's case was that he turned out to be everything he appears to be and then some—as warm, thoughtful, open and honest as I dared to hope he might be, an autobiographer's ace. The best thing I can say about my golf hero is that I liked him even better after I got to know him.

The unexpected bonus of the three-year project, however, was Winnie Palmer.

Almost from the moment we met, we became good friends and devoted allies in the task of putting Arnold's oversized life on paper.

It was really Winnie's book, as I came to think of it, something she understood the golf world needed but Arnold would never seriously undertake on his own, and I quickly learned that the best way to convince Arnold Palmer to do anything was to get Winnie Palmer behind the idea.

A marriage, someone said, is like a medieval morality play. There are things you see on one level, currents you feel on another. After spending nearly eight hundred days slipping in and out of Arnold's and Winnie's lives, being granted poignant proximity to the ordinary ups and downs of the extraordinary Palmer family life, I began to understand what a unique and powerful partnership Arnold and Winnie really were. Their marriage had been tested in almost unfathomable ways, and perhaps because they'd been through so much together—the trials of fame and the dangers of fortune—they often appeared to cling together like shipwreck survivors on a beach.

You could see it in the way they instinctively clasped hands while moving through large crowds or relaxing with intimate groups of friends, you could feel its currency when Arnold affectionately called her "Lover" and teased her about running his life and bossing him about. Whatever else was true, when Winnie spoke about a subject that mattered, Arnold truly listened. The truth is, he relied on her opinions on just about everything for the simple reason that he would have been crazy not to. She was a crack judge of character, a no-nonsense advisor with an Ivy League brain, an unfaltering follower of the heart.

Besides Arnold's memoir, the other great project Winnie had in mind, well over a year and a half before being diagnosed with cancer of the intestinal lining, was the restoration of an old barn adjacent to the golf course in Latrobe. She jokingly referred to it as her "mink coat" while Arnold simply called it "Winnie's barn."

One gorgeously flaring summer afternoon she drove me to the high hill above the barn, overlooking the golf course, and explained that someday she hoped to convince Arnie—that's what she called him—to build a cozy "retirement" cottage up there for just the two of them, if and when he ever agreed to retire. The night before at dinner, out of the blue, Arnold had revealed his latest brainstorm: He was thinking of planting a vineyard and starting a winery on the hill adjacent to the barn. This was news to Winnie. She had looked at me and rolled her eyes with deep amusement as if to say, "Arnold the Dreamer at work again."

Now, Arnold, who happened to be playing the par-5 14th with a group of visiting corporate bigwigs, spotted us and sped up the hill in a golf cart, grinning suspiciously. He asked what the devil we were doing up there, and she replied cheekily, "Why, just checking out the view from the living room of our retirement house."

"Winifred, I'm going to build that house for you," he bellowed good-naturedly at her. "Just you wait and see!"

"Right, Lover," she teased gently. "Will that be before or after the winery?"

With that, she laughed that great laugh of hers, sounding every bit like the smoky, polished, dark-haired, underage beauty who kept her father Shube Walzer's accounting books. She was studying to become an interior designer and dreamed of traveling the world when a handsome, smooth-talking, largely unsuccessful paint sales-man from Cleveland, who happened to be the new National Amateur golf champion, reached beneath the dinner table at Shawnee-on-Delaware. He impulsively took her hand and audaciously suggested that she marry him, three days after their introduction.

Strong-willed as a spring colt, she said yes in a matter of hours, beginning golf's most durable love story, and spent the next four decades shaping the views and interior life of the modern game's most commanding figure.

By her own design, Winnie Palmer was one of golf's most private people. Even at the height of Arnold's fame, she walked outside the ropes and a few steps behind, never asking nor tolerating any special privilege, as comfortable among the caddies as the VIPs, often invisible but always watching. "Arnie's the people person," she would say. "I'm a person person."

That was true. One-on-one, Winnie had a way of making everyone feel unique and deeply valued in her sphere. Her home was simple and unpretentious but as gorgeously made and richly hued as an Amish quilt, always dressed immaculately for the season.

There were private times with Winnie I will cherish most. Sometimes, after Arnold and I finished up one of our productive early-morning research sessions, he would jet away to fulfill an obligation, to film a commercial or appear at a function or charity tournament, at which point Winnie would take me under her wing for the balance of the day.

Several times after lunch we slipped out and took long drives with Prince, their retriever, through the countryside. One afternoon she drove me to see Unity Chapel, a two-hundred-year-old Presbyterian chapel sitting on a hill outside Latrobe. She told me its history and explained how the chapel had once fallen into disrepair but thanks to a number of people who loved the place, Unity Chapel had been restored to its simple grandeur.

I realized later that Winnie was one of those special people, but she wouldn't have told me that in a million years. The fact is, she loved going to church—almost any church—and sometimes she took me with her. She enjoyed old hymns and a sermon that made you think. She worried about the world her grandchildren and yours and mine will inherit. She took her quiet faith very seriously but never herself overly so.

I took professional insight and personal wisdom from these moments of easy companionship when we roamed around, went to church, talked about everything—God, books, children, art, dogs, music, history, the passing scene or the passing landscape. Occasionally, we even talked about golf and Arnold. I learned she loved the paintings of Andrew Wyeth and David Armstrong, the piano of Doug Montgomery, Andy Rooney commentaries and a well-made Fitzgerald old-fashioned. The rest of the short list included her daughters and seven grandchildren, icebox cake, good manners, peonies, her brother Marty, London's West End, Augusta galleries, cozy hotels, museums of any kind, early suppers, British golf writers and phone conversations with her partner-in-crime, Barbara Nicklaus.

Speaking of crime, the woman seemed to have read every other book published in the English language, especially mysteries. She was keen for a foggy night, a door left ajar, a crime unsolved. Somehow, she also found time to read half a dozen or so magazines and regularly corresponded with friends by way of handwritten notes packed with clipped articles she thought they should read. I used to kid her that if golf failed to pan out for Arnie, she could support them both by starting a journalism clipping service.

I loved her Moravian sense of economy and value. After my children and I lost our retrievers to old age, Winnie set out to help me find the right replacement. She introduced me to a woman she'd heard about who bred champion goldens. A month or so later the woman rang me up to say she had the "perfect" dog for us: a three-year-old spayed female, beautiful disposition, papers, the whole nine yards, and a real bargain at just eighteen hundred dollars. When I reported this news to Winnie, she thundered, "Don't you dare buy that dog or I'll reach into this phone and break your arm!"

Her funeral service at Unity Chapel, on a stunning Indian summer day, was a simple and beautiful affair. The music was Bach and Beethoven. A few prayers of thanksgiving were read, the Navy hymn sung. Her granddaughter Emily read a few passages from Proverbs. There was no eulogy under Winnie's strict orders—but none was necessary because each of us sat there writing our own eulogies in our heads for the new patron saint of golf wives.

After a little while—Winnie hated services that went on too long—we all filed out and drove to Latrobe Country Club for lunch. In the din of conversation, I was pleased to see Arnold laughing again, gently needling Jack when he pulled out a cellular phone to see how Gary was doing at the PGA Tour Q School. A few minutes later, I saw him lead George and Barbara Bush out the grillroom door, and I knew exactly where he was taking them—to see Winnie's barn, now fully restored, sitting in the autumnal sunlight like a David Armstrong original.

The truth is, some of us stood there worrying about how Arnold Palmer will fare without his Pennsylvania original, Winnie. I was lost in these thoughts, I confess, selfishly thinking how I was going to miss Arnold and Latrobe and most of all, my weekly phone conversations with Winnie, when a large, strong pair of hands suddenly settled on my shoulders. I turned around and it was Arnold, looking at me with what Winnie once called his "Deacon look."

We hadn't really spoken up to this point. Perhaps I'd even consciously evaded him a bit—and maybe him, me. He knew what I thought of his wife, how we were all a bit in awe and in love with pretty Winnie Walzer. He thanked me for coming, and I asked him for the second time in two days if he was okay. Arnold's look softened. His eyes began to glisten.

"I'm okay for now," golf's most public man said softly of his most private loss. We both knew it would be the early mornings and evenings to come that would be toughest for him to get through, when Winnie's presence filled their house with such warm abundance.

He cleared his throat and managed a smile. "The good news is, she left me good instructions on how to live the rest of my life," he said, still squeezing my arm with those huge blacksmith hands of his, perhaps picturing Winnie that gorgeous summer day on the hill above the barn. Remembering her as I always will.

"Very firm instructions," he said.

~James Dodson
Chicken Soup for the Golfer's Soul, The 2nd Round

More Than a Friend

You are my sonshine.
~Author Unknown

Louisville, Kentucky, is a place where basketball is an important part of life, and taking my son to an NBA exhibition game is very special. Little did I realize how special the evening was going to be! It was a biting winter cold that was blowing some mean wind, as Josh held my hand as we crossed the Kentucky Fairgrounds parking lot headed for famous Freedom Hall. Being eight years old, he still felt it was okay to hold his father's hand, and I felt grateful, knowing that these kind of moments would pass all too soon.

The arena holds nineteen-thousand-plus fans, and it definitely looked like a sellout as the masses gathered. We had been to many a University of Louisville basketball game and even a few University of Kentucky games in this hallowed hall, but the anticipation of seeing Michael Jordan and the Chicago Bulls against the Washington Bullets (with ex-University of Louisville star Felton Spencer) made our pace across the massive parking lot seem like a quick one, with lots of speculation about how the game was going to go.

The turnstile clicked and Josh hung on to his souvenir ticket stub like he had just won the lottery! Climbing the ramps to the upper elevation seemed more an adventure than a chore, as we got to the upper-level seats of the "true" fans. Before we knew it, the game was underway and the battle had begun. During a time out, we dashed for the mandatory hot dog and Coke and trotted back so that we wouldn't miss a single layup or jump shot. Things were going as expected until halftime. I started to talk to some friends nearby when there was a tug on my sleeve, my arm was pulled over by a determined young Josh Frager, and he began putting a multicolored, woven yarn bracelet around my wrist. It fit really well, and he was really focused intently as he carefully made a double square knot to keep it secure (those Scouting skills really are handy). Being a Scoutmaster with a lot of teenage Scouts, I recognized the significance of the moment, and wanting him to be impressed with my insightful skills, I looked him squarely in the eyes, smiled the good smile, and told him proudly how I knew this was a "friendship bracelet" and said, "I guess this means we are friends."

Without missing a beat, his big brown eyes looked me straight in the face, and he exclaimed, "We're more than friends... You're my dad!"

I don't even remember the rest of the game.

~Stanley R. Frager
Chicken Soup for the Father's Soul

Angel's Flight

"Fore!"

Instinctively I ducked, covering my head with my arms. A golf ball sizzled past me and landed no more than twenty feet from my quaking body. It careened off a hillock, rolled down a nearby cart path and, then, as if to punctuate its passing, neatly plopped into the water hazard beyond the green.

"What the?" I turned slowly, nostrils flaring, my eyes fixing upon the culprit. Marching up the fairway and smiling radiantly was a creature of such incredible beauty I have yet to recover. Her hair, blowing back from her temples, was fiery red. Her prancing gait ran a shock through my senses. It was the kind of shock any man would love to receive.

"Oh, I am sorry," she said, glancing at me and then peering beyond to the murky pond. Her enormous green eyes returned to me and she said, "Did I frighten you?"

I began to stammer my response. I was frightened, but more as a result of being intimidated by her ravishing beauty. She stood patiently, alternating her gaze between me and the pond. I finally emitted something audible.

"No, no, certainly it's a part of the game. Nothing special about having a ball fly by."

She looked again at the pond and then said, "Well, I must say, I never will trust the yardage on this scorecard. I was sure I had at least a hundred yards to the pin." She frowned and then again looked directly into my eyes.

"Ah, well, this is a short hole," I offered. "The seventh has something of a reputation for being deceptive that way."

"The seventh?! Oh, I feel so foolish." She paused, and then began fumbling through the pockets of her neatly tailored windbreaker. Then, after examining a wrinkled scorecard, she said, "I thought I was playing the sixth."

She smiled and looked at me sheepishly, perhaps expecting me to be amused by her mistake. But I stood silently, my face expressionless. Finally, after a moment, she extended her hand.

"I'm so sorry. I have neglected to introduce myself."

Her soft hand, warm for so brisk an autumn morning, fell across my palm as gently as a feather. Her voice betrayed a Southern gentility. This beauty had so soundly smitten me, I was nearly catatonic.

"I'm Clarice McGraw," she said.

Fumbling with my golf bag, and feeling as if my cardigan sweater was starting to unravel, I mimicked her polite gestures and sputtered, "Ah yes, ah well... I'm Jimmy Olden."

As I shook her hand and looked into her eyes, I imagined I saw a growing discernment of my condition. She must encounter fools like me often, I thought. But in a comfortable way she gave my hand one last shake, surprisingly firm for so soft a hand, and released it. Somehow, I felt assured that I would not be so quickly dismissed.

I gradually loosened up, and we had something of a conversation. Since we were both playing alone we finished the front nine together. She had an appointment, so I continued on alone, enjoying the back nine. But before we parted I did learn that she was new to the area, had opened up a ladies' dress shop along the boardwalk in town and liked to play golf in the early morning. I told her a little about myself and expressed the hope I would see her again soon. She smiled warmly.

That night I couldn't sleep, and it was still dark when I pulled my car into the club. As I rolled down the long sloping drive to the parking lot I could hear sprinklers clacking faintly somewhere in the distance. I parked and turned off my headlights. A lone light shone over the door of the golf shop.

I sat quietly, clutching a cup of decaffeinated coffee. As the rays of morning sun began to filter through the stand of eucalyptus at the edge of the course, I started wondering if I was doing the right thing. What if we did hit it off? What if my dreams came true? Could I take all the pressure of being at my best every moment of the day? How could I survive with this beauty?

The sunlight strengthened, and the warming glow of a new day filled my car. I stretched my arms out across the rim of the steering wheel, and cracked my neck with a sudden twist. After a while the assistant pro opened the shop and turned on the lights. Soon he would be brewing his own coffee, dark and strong, and setting up for the morning business. His name was Ted, and we called him "Go Ball." He was a young, strong man who could drive the ball prodigiously. When he really laid the wood on he'd shout out, "Go ball!" He had such exuberance — it was more natural than anything.

There it was. It struck me that I had the perfect medium through which I could speak to Clarice. It was the game of golf. There is nothing more natural or easy than the bond that grows between players enjoying a round. All I had to do was to play a round of golf with her. I thought of the many times I had teed off with three strangers who soon became three friends. In fact I had met many of my oldest and dearest friends playing golf.

Clarice drove her Volvo into the parking lot and pulled in right alongside my old Fiat Spider. I just happened to have arrived there a mere hour before, and so I casually dismounted my rusting steed.

"Oh, hello," I said in my best Gary Cooper voice.

"Oh, Jimmy, so nice to see you again."

"Are you about to go play?" she asked, looking at me with those beautiful eyes.

I was slightly dumbstruck but finally said, "Yeah sure, you bet. Would you like to join me?"

She smiled broadly and laughed. "I suppose you think it might be safer to play with me instead of ahead of me."

I had to laugh.

We teed off and walked down the fairway, speaking of the things golfers do.

By the time we had completed the front nine we knew each other well enough to say we were friends. We laughed and commiserated over errant shots and generously conceded putts. I was encouraged when she asked if I would play the back nine with her. By the time we came up the eighteenth fairway we each in our own way began to hatch plans. I asked if she would have dinner with me.

She feigned a moment of concentration, as if to envision her cluttered social calendar. Then, smiling impishly, she invited me to her house for meatloaf and mashed potatoes.

Our friendship was born, and we met regularly to play during the remaining fall days. We found new passion in the winter months as a snowy shroud covered the greens. She gave me a driver for Christmas. I gave her a putter. We became more than friends and traveled to a warmer climate to try them out. By spring, I had asked her for her hand.

We were married at the church on the road behind the tenth green, and as we walked out the front door a band of our golfing friends saluted us with golf clubs held high, splashing us with grass seed. At first, the game did all the talking, but soon our hearts were filled with love. It all was so natural and relaxed. And I grew to like being at my best all the time for Clarice.

In sharing our new life together we spent what time we could on the links. We vacationed by traveling across the country and playing all the finest courses.

One year I cheered as Clarice nearly won the ladies' championship at the club. I bought a bottle of champagne with which we celebrated her third-place finish and drowned her disappointment. Our heads clouded with the bubbles, I told her she had easily won the championship of my heart. She was my champion of all champions. She was the winner of the Angel's flight.

For twelve years the game gave us joy, and made it possible for us to see each other in ways that were otherwise probably impossible. Our lives together were filled with many rich experiences. The people and places and our love for the game that brought us together were all so interwoven. It was like a warm quilt, and my memories of it will never tarnish with time.

But one day my Clarice came home from a checkup with her doctor and told me that she had been diagnosed with breast cancer. We sat for an eternity, looking into each other's eyes, neither wanting to show weakness in the face of so daunting an ordeal. Her last days in the hospital came just after Christmas. At home for the last time, we had exchanged gifts beneath the tree. She gave me a new driver, one picked out by our head pro, Ted. I gave her a red sweater with a pattern of falling leaves. It reminded me of the day we met.

My Clarice passed away the first Tuesday of January.

I took a long trip, but I left my clubs at home. When I returned in early spring, my first impulse was to go out to the club. When I arrived I was greeted by all our dear friends. I decided to go to the range and see if I could loosen my spine. After a while I found I was hitting the ball pretty well. I decided to go out and play a few holes alone. As I set my bag down aside the first tee, I realized that this would be my first opportunity to see how my new driver felt. It was a beauty. I laced a good drive straight up the fairway. From the golf shop window I heard Ted yell out, "Go ball!" I smiled and waved to him.

Of course, my mind was on Clarice. The first buds of spring were just beginning to open and the grass was a deep lush green. We always reveled in the beauty of springtime. I was playing well for so long a layoff; I hit a nice shot toward the seventh green. My ball lay at the edge of the green, so I used my surefire 7-iron and chipped it to the very lip of the cup.

As I walked toward the hole a gentle breeze gave my ball just a nudge and in it went. A warmth filled my senses as I looked skyward and whispered, "Are you with me, my Angel?"

As I collected my ball from the cup, I heard a distant voice. It spoke to me with urgency, and sounded almost like...

"Fore!"

A golf ball landed with a thud no more than twenty feet away.

I raised one arm belatedly to protect my head. Then I turned and looked up the fairway. There, in half-gallop, was a young redheaded lad with a bag nearly equal his size draped over his back.

"Sorry, mister, I didn't think I could reach this green."

As he stood before me I smiled, thinking back to someone else who didn't think she could reach this green. I looked into this young boy's green eyes and said, "It's all right, boy. It's part of the game. Nothing special about having a ball fly by."

We walked in together and talked of the things golfers do.

That evening I sat near our fireplace in the company of a glass of red wine. As the embers cast an orange glow about the room, I looked back over the years and thought about how the game of golf had enriched my life. I thought of Clarice and how golf had introduced us, nurturing first our friendship and then our love. Somehow, I knew that every day I spent on the course Clarice would be with me, and perhaps occasionally, with the gentle breeze of her wing, would give my ball a nudge into the hole.

~J. G. Nursall
Chicken Soup for the Golfer's Soul

~Share with Us~
~More Chicken Soup~

Share with Us

We would like to know how these stories affected you and which ones were your favorites. Please e-mail us and let us know.

We also would like to share your stories with future readers. You may be able to help another reader, and become a published author at the same time. Please send us your own stories and poems for our future books. Some of our past contributors have launched writing and speaking careers from the publication of their stories in our books!

Your stories have the best chance of being used if you submit them through our web site, at:

www.chickensoup.com

If you do not have access to the Internet, you may submit your stories by mail or by facsimile. Please do not send us any book manuscripts, unless through a literary agent, as these will be automatically discarded.

Chicken Soup for the Soul
P.O. Box 700
Cos Cob, CT 06807-0700
Fax 203-861-7194

More Great books
for Sports Fans & Men
from the Chicken Soup Library...
for the Soul.

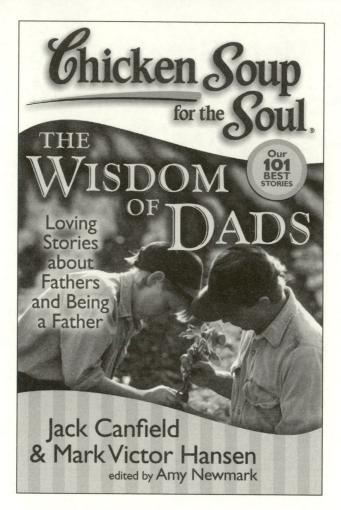

Children view their fathers with awe from the day they are born. Fathers are big and strong and seem to know everything, except for a few teenage years when fathers are perceived to know nothing! This book represents a new theme for Chicken Soup—101 stories selected from 35 past books, all stories focusing on the wisdom of dads. Stories are written by sons and daughters about their fathers, and by fathers relating stories about their children.

978-1-935096-18-4

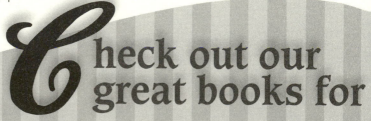

Check out our
great books for

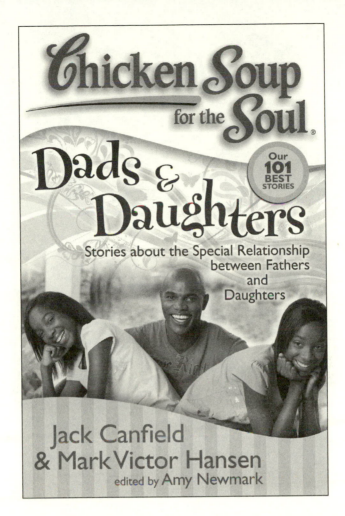

Whether she is ten years old or fifty — she will always be his little girl. And daughters take care of their dads too, whether it is a tea party for two at age five or loving care fifty years later. This wide-ranging exploration of the relationship between fathers and daughters contains selections from forty past Chicken Soup books. Stories were written by fathers about their daughters and by daughters about their fathers, celebrating the special bond between fathers and daughters.

978-1-935096-19-1

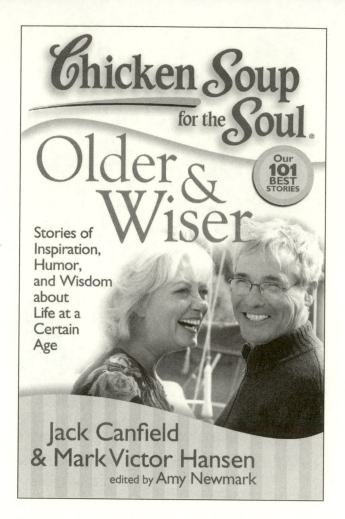

Chicken Soup for the Soul

Older & Wiser

Stories of Inspiration, Humor, and Wisdom about Life at a Certain Age

Our 101 BEST STORIES

Jack Canfield & Mark Victor Hansen
edited by Amy Newmark

We know how it is to cross the magic 60-year mark and feel young at heart despite a few new wrinkles. We wouldn't trade away a bit of our wisdom and experience to get rid of all those life markers. This is the first Chicken Soup book to focus on the wonders of getting older, with many stories focusing on dynamic older singles and couples finding new careers, new sports, new love, and new meaning to their lives. Includes the best 101 stories for today's young seniors from Chicken Soup's library.

978-1-935096-17-7

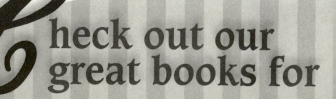

Check out our great books for

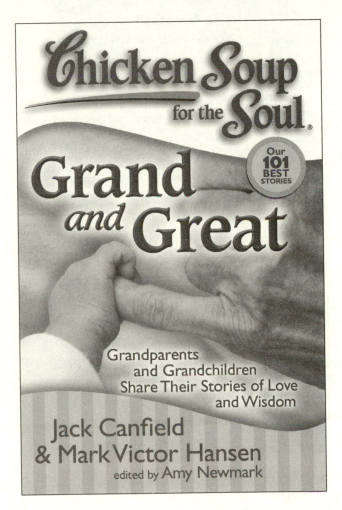

Chicken Soup for the Soul®

Our 101 BEST STORIES

Grand and Great

Grandparents
and Grandchildren
Share Their Stories of Love
and Wisdom

Jack Canfield
& Mark Victor Hansen

edited by Amy Newmark

A parent becomes a new person the day the first grandchild is born. Formerly serious adults become grandparents who dote on their grandchildren. This new book includes the best stories on being a grandparent from past Chicken soup books, representing a new reading experience for even the most devoted Chicken Soup fan. Everyone can understand the special ties between grandparents and grandchildren—the unlimited love, the mutual admiration and unqualified acceptance.

978-1-935096-09-2

SENIORS

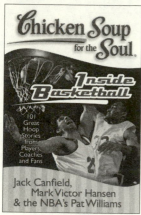

Inside Basketball

Chicken Soup has a slam dunk with its first sports book in years, and its first on basketball, with the Orlando Magic's very own Pat Williams, well-known author and motivational speaker. Pat has drawn on his basketball industry connections to compile great stories from on and off the court. Fans will be inspired, surprised, and amused by inside stories from well-known coaches and players, fascinating looks behind the scenes, and anecdotes from the fans.

Teens Talk Getting In... to College

These days, colleges are deluged with applications, and the application process has become something traumatic that students and parents experience together. This book isn't about how to get into college — it's about providing emotional support from kids who have been there. Story topics include parental and peer pressure, the stress of grades and standardized tests, applications and interviews, recruiting, disappointments, and successes.

The Golf Book

Chicken Soup and Golf Digest magazine's Max Adler and team have put together a great collection of personal stories that will inspire, amuse, and surprise golfers. Celebrity golfers, weekend golfers, beginners, and pros all share the best stories they've told at the 19th hole about good times on and off the course. Chicken Soup's golf books have always been very successful — with the addition of Golf Digest's industry connections, this book should hit a hole in one.

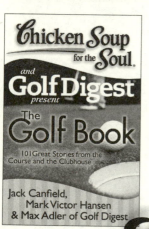

Check out our great books for

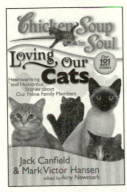

Loving Our Cats

Heartwarming and Humorous Stories about
Our Feline Family Members
978-1-935096-08-5
We are all crazy about our mysterious cats. Sometimes they are our best friends; sometimes they are aloof. They are fun to watch and often surprise us. These true stories, the best from Chicken Soup's library, will make readers appreciate their own cats and see them with a new eye. Readers will revel in the heartwarming, amusing, inspirational, and occasionally tearful stories about our best friends and faithful companions — our cats.

Loving Our Dogs

Heartwarming and Humorous Stories about
Our Companions and Best Friends
978-1-935096-05-4
We are all crazy about our dogs and can't read enough about them, whether they're misbehaving and giving us big, innocent looks, or loyally standing by us in times of need. This new book from Chicken Soup for the Soul contains the 101 best dog stories from the company's extensive library. Readers will revel in the heartwarming, amusing, inspirational, and occasionally tearful stories about our best friends and faithful companions — our dogs.

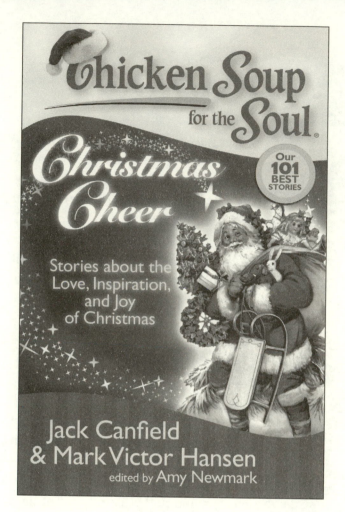

Everyone loves Christmas and the holiday season. We reunite scattered family members, watch the wonder in a child's eyes, and feel the joy of giving gifts. The rituals of the holiday season give a rhythm to the years and create a foundation for our lives, as we gather with family, with our communities at church, at school, and even at the mall, to share the special spirit of the season, brightening those long winter days.

978-1-935096-15-3

Check out our

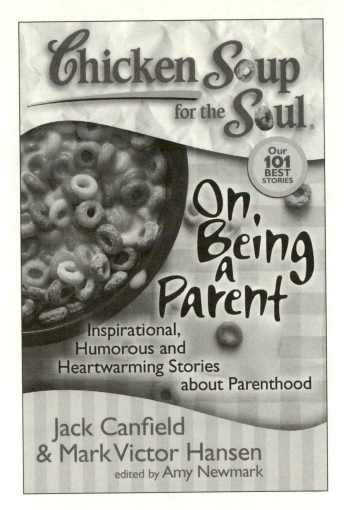

Chicken Soup for the Soul

On Being a Parent

Inspirational, Humorous and Heartwarming Stories about Parenthood

Jack Canfield & Mark Victor Hansen
edited by Amy Newmark

Our 101 BEST STORIES

Parenting is the hardest and most rewarding job in the world. This upbeat and compelling new book includes the best selections on parenting from Chicken Soup's rich history, with 101 stories carefully selected to appeal to both mothers and fathers. This is a great book for couples to share, whether they are just embarking on their new adventure as parents or reflecting on their lifetime experience.

978-1-935096-10-8

FAVORITES

~About the Authors~
~Acknowledgments~

Chicken Soup for the Soul

Who Is
Jack Canfield?

Jack Canfield is the co-creator and editor of the *Chicken Soup for the Soul* series, which *Time* magazine has called "the publishing phenomenon of the decade." Jack is also the co-author of eight other bestselling books including *The Success Principles™: How to Get from Where You Are to Where You Want to Be*, *Dare to Win*, *The Aladdin Factor*, *You've Got to Read This Book*, and *The Power of Focus: How to Hit Your Business and Personal and Financial Targets with Absolute Certainty*.

Jack has recently developed a telephone coaching program and an online coaching program based on his most recent book *The Success Principles*. He also offers a seven-day *Breakthrough to Success* seminar every summer, which attracts 400 people from fifteen countries around the world.

Jack is the CEO of the Canfield Training Group in Santa Barbara, California, and founder of the Foundation for Self-Esteem in Culver City, California. He has conducted intensive personal and professional development seminars on the principles of success for over a million people in twenty-three countries. Jack is a dynamic keynote speaker and he has spoken to hundreds of thousands of others at more than 1,000 corporations, universities, professional conferences and conventions, and has been seen by millions more on national television shows such as *The Today Show*, *Fox and Friends*, *Inside Edition*, *Hard Copy*, *CNN's Talk Back Live*, *20/20*, *Eye to Eye*, and the *NBC Nightly News* and the *CBS Evening News*.

Jack is the recipient of many awards and honors, including three honorary doctorates and a *Guinness World Records Certificate* for having seven books from the *Chicken Soup for the Soul* series appearing on the *New York Times* bestseller list on May 24, 1998.

To write to Jack or for inquiries about Jack as a speaker, his coaching programs, trainings or seminars, use the following contact information:

Jack Canfield
The Canfield Companies
P.O. Box 30880 • Santa Barbara, CA 93130
phone: 805-563-2935 • fax: 805-563-2945
E-mail: info@jackcanfield.com
www.jackcanfield.com

Who Is
Mark Victor Hansen?

Mark Victor Hansen is the co-founder of *Chicken Soup for the Soul*, along with Jack Canfield. He is also a sought-after keynote speaker, bestselling author, and marketing maven. For more than thirty years, Mark has focused solely on helping people from all walks of life reshape their personal vision of what's possible. His powerful messages of possibility, opportunity, and action have created powerful change in thousands of organizations and millions of individuals worldwide.

Mark's credentials include a lifetime of entrepreneurial success. He is a prolific writer with many bestselling books, such as *The One Minute Millionaire*, *Cracking the Millionaire Code*, *How to Make the Rest of Your Life the Best of Your Life*, *The Power of Focus*, *The Aladdin Factor*, and *Dare to Win*, in addition to the *Chicken Soup for the Soul* series. Mark has had a profound influence in the field of human potential through his library of audios, videos, and articles in the areas of big thinking, sales achievement, wealth building, publishing success, and personal and professional development.

Mark is the founder of the *MEGA Seminar Series*. *MEGA Book Marketing University* and *Building Your MEGA Speaking Empire* are annual conferences where Mark coaches and teaches new and aspiring authors, speakers, and experts on building lucrative publishing and speaking careers. Other MEGA events include *MEGA Info-Marketing* and *My MEGA Life*.

He has appeared on *Oprah*, *CNN*, and *The Today Show*. He has been quoted in *Time, U.S. News & World Report, USA Today, New York Times,* and *Entrepreneur* and has had countless radio interviews, assuring our planet's people that "You can easily create the life you deserve."

As a philanthropist and humanitarian, Mark works tirelessly for organizations such as Habitat for Humanity, American Red Cross, March of Dimes, Childhelp USA, and many others. He is the recipient of numerous awards that honor his entrepreneurial spirit, philanthropic heart, and business acumen. He is a lifetime member of the Horatio Alger Association of Distinguished Americans, an organization that honored Mark with the prestigious Horatio Alger Award for his extraordinary life achievements.

Mark Victor Hansen is an enthusiastic crusader of what's possible and is driven to make the world a better place.

Mark Victor Hansen & Associates, Inc.
P.O. Box 7665 • Newport Beach, CA 92658
phone: 949-764-2640 • fax: 949-722-6912
www.markvictorhansen.com

Who Is
Amy Newmark?

Amy Newmark was recently named publisher of Chicken Soup for the Soul, after a thirty-year career as a writer, speaker, financial analyst, and business executive in the worlds of finance and telecommunications.

Amy is a graduate of Harvard College, where she majored in Portuguese, minored in French, and traveled extensively. She is also the mother of two children in college and has two grown stepchildren.

After a long career writing books on telecommunications, voluminous financial reports, business plans, and corporate press releases, Chicken Soup for the Soul is a breath of fresh air for Amy. She has fallen in love with Chicken Soup for the Soul and its life-changing books, and found it a true pleasure to conceptualize, compile, and edit the "101 Best Stories" books for our readers.

The best way to contact Chicken Soup for the Soul is through our web site, at www.chickensoup.com. This will always get the fastest attention.

If you do not have access to the Internet, please contact us by mail or by facsimile.

Chicken Soup for the Soul
P.O. Box 700
Cos Cob, CT 06807-0700
Fax 203-861-7194

Thank You!

Our first thanks go to our loyal readers who have inspired the entire Chicken Soup team for the past fifteen years. Your appreciative letters and emails have reminded us why we work so hard on these books.

We owe huge thanks to all of our contributors as well. We know that you pour your hearts and souls into the stories and poems that you share with us, and ultimately with each other. We appreciate your willingness to open up your lives to other Chicken Soup readers.

We can only publish a small percentage of the stories that are submitted, but we read every single one and even the ones that do not appear in a book have an influence on us and on the final manuscripts.

As always, we would like to thank the entire staff of Chicken Soup for the Soul for their help on this project and the 101 Best series in general.

Among our California staff, we would especially like to single out the following people:

- D'ette Corona, our Assistant Publisher, who is the heart and soul of the Chicken Soup publishing operation, and who put together the first draft of this manuscript

- Barbara LoMonaco, our Webmaster and Chicken Soup for the Soul Editor, for invaluable assistance in obtaining the fabulous quotations that add depth and meaning to this book

- Patty Hansen for her extra special help with the permissions for these fabulous stories and for her amazing knowledge of the Chicken Soup library

- and Patti Clement for her help with permissions and other organizational matters.

In our Connecticut office, we would like to thank our able editor, Madeline Clapps.

We would also like to thank our Creative Director and book producer, Brian Taylor at Pneuma Books, for his brilliant vision for our covers and interiors.

Finally, none of this would be possible without the business and creative leadership of our CEO, Bill Rouhana, and our president, Bob Jacobs.